# TECHNOLOGICAL INNOVATION AND THE ECONOMY

# TECHNOLOGICAL INNOVATION AND THE ECONOMY

A Science of Science Foundation
Symposium on Technological Innovation
and the Growth of the Economy, held
at Churchill College, Cambridge,
England, April 11-13 1969

*Edited by*
**Maurice Goldsmith**

**WILEY-INTERSCIENCE**
a division of John Wiley & Sons Ltd.
London · New York · Sydney · Toronto

Library of Congress catalog card number 75 – 121901

ISBN 0 471 31180 4

PRINTED IN GREAT BRITAIN BY ROBERT MACLEHOSE AND CO. LTD
THE UNIVERSITY PRESS, GLASGOW

# PARTICIPANTS

**LORD JACKSON of Burnley (Chairman)**
*Pro-Rector, Imperial College, London, S.W. 7.*

**DR BRUCE ARCHER**
*Head of Industrial Design (Engineering) Research Unit, Royal College of Art, London, S.W.7.*

**H. AUJAC**
*Director, Bureau d'Informations et de Previsions Economique, Neuilly/ s/Seine, France*

**S. BODINGTON**
*Emcon, London, W.C.1.*

**LORD BOWDEN**
*Principal, University of Manchester Institute of Science and Technology*

**PROFESSOR ERIC BURKE**
*Faculty of Engineering, University of Waterloo, Ontario*

**PROFESSOR DUNCAN BURN**
*Visiting Professor of Economics, University of Manchester*

**LORD DELACOURT-SMITH**
*Minister of State, Ministry of Technology; formerly General Sectrary, Post Office Engineering Union*

**DR ROBERT A. CHARPIE**
*President, The Cabot Corporation; formerly President, Bell & Howell Co., U.S.A.*

**J. C. DUCKWORTH**
*Managing Director, National Research Development Corporation, London, S.W.1.*

**PROFESSOR SIR BRIAN FLOWERS, FRS**
*Chairman, Science Research Council, State House, London, W.C.1.*

**PROFESSOR C. FREEMAN**
*Director, Science Policy Research Unit, University of Sussex*

**DR GORDON FRYERS**
*Consultant; formerly Managing Director, The Bayer Products Company, England*

**DR A. J. GELLMAN**
*Vice-President – Planning, The Budd Company, Philadelphia, U.S.A.*

**DR J. E. GOLDMAN**
*Group Vice-President (R. and D.) Xerox Corporation, Rochester, NY, U.S.A.*

**MAURICE GOLDSMITH**
*Director, The Science of Science Foundation, London, W.C.2.*

**K. R. H. JOHNSTON, QC**
*Haslemere, Surrey*

**DR F. E. JONES, FRS**
*Managing Director, Mullard Limited, Mullard House, London, W.C.1.*

**DR A. KING**
*Director-General for Scientific Affairs, OECD, Paris XVI, France*

**DR ANTONIE T. KNOPPERS**
*Senior Vice-President, Merck & Co. Inc., Rahway, New Jersey, U.S.A.*

**I. MADDOCK, FRS**
*Controller (Industrial Technology) Ministry of Technology, London, S.W.1.*

**DR A. MENCHER**
*Scientific Attache, American Embassy, London, W.1.*

**DR.-ING. WINFRIED K. MUTTELSEE**
*Bundesministerium für Wirtschaft, 53 Bonn, German Federal Republic*

**PROFESSOR KEICHI OSHIMA**
*Department of Nuclear Engineering, Faculty of Engineering, University of Tokyo, Bunkyoku Tokyo, Japan*

**DR A. E. PANNENBORG**
*Director, N. V. Philips' Gloeilampenfabrieken, Philips' Industries, Netherlands*

**K. PAVITT**
*OECD, Paris XVI, France*

**DR A. PECCEI**
*Vice-President, Olivetti & Company, Rome, Italy; President, Italconsult, Rome; Head, Latin American Affairs Division, Fiat Company of Turin*

**M. SHANKS**
*Director of Marketing Services & Economic Planning, British Leyland Motor Corporation, London, W.1.*

**G. TEELING-SMITH**
*Director, Office of Health Economics, London, W.1.*

**ANDREW H. WILSON**
*Science Adviser, Science Council of Canada, Ottawa, Ontario*

**DR E. G. WOODROOFE**
*Chairman, formerly Vice-Chairman, Unilever, London, E.C.4.*

**HEINZ WOLFF**
*Director, Biomedical Engineering Division, Medical Research Council, London, N.W.3.*

**ADMINISTRATIVE STAFF:**
*Margaret Bourke (Mrs.)*
*Sara Gulland*
*Robert Jones*

# The Science of Science Foundation

The purpose of the Science of Science Foundation is to promote the scientific investigation of science itself as a social phenomenon. That is to say, it exists to advance the study of and research into the sociology and economics of science; the psychology of scientists and of scientific work; the principles and philosophy of planning research; the analysis of the flow of scientific communications; the role and evolution of science in diverse types of societies including our own; and the relationships between science and technology and society.

The activities of the Foundation, guided by its Advisory Council, include seminars on topics connected with the national and international management of science, management and productivity, research and national wealth, etc, attended by members of government agencies, industry and the universities; it arranges an annual lecture at the Royal Institution; it has established a library of books, periodicals and documents relating to science policy at the University of Sussex; it issues a bi-monthly, *Science Policy News*, in collaboration with OECD; and it organizes a lecture service for universities in the United Kingdom. The Foundation is planning, as finances permit, to initiate and support research on the science of science, and publishes reports and books in that field.

The Science of Science Foundation has no endowment and so must rely for it resources on the subscriptions of its members, donations and grants from industry, foundations and institutions, and gifts and bequests from individuals wishing to advance its objects. The Foundation is registered as a non-profit making company limited by guarantee with the name the Science of Science Foundation Limited, and is also registered as an educational charity under the Charities Act 1960.

The constitution of the Foundation is its Memorandum and Articles of Association. It is managed by a Committee of Management with an Advisory Council. There are various informal Specialist Committees which report to and assist the Committee of Management.

# Contents

# Introduction

When asked in which country he would like to be when the world was coming to an end, Heine, the German poet, is reported to have said: 'In England, of course'. 'But why?' he was asked. 'Because', he replied, 'England is always one hundred years behind the times'.

We are indebted to Sir Gordon Sutherland, F. R. S., the Master of Emmanuel College, Cambridge, for this pointed story. The occasion on which he told it was a dinner party in the Fellows' Dining Room at Churchill College, at the end of the first full day of our Symposium discussions on Technological Innovation (T.I.). As we savoured the food and drink, it was easier to accept why the 'educational Purists' of the past, in such a cloistered, cultivated atmosphere, had been able to contribute to Britain's slow decline in industrial efficiency by insisting on the separation between the university, technology and industry.

Those 19th century dons, maintainers of the Greek tradition that gentlemen did not work, had reason to be smug, for the products of their scholastic environment were responsible for some remarkable basic discoveries in science. And why should those academics have expressed concern when Britain, alone in Europe, without any system of industrial education for the masters of factories and workshops, was indisputably a first-class manufacturing and political power?

This attitude was existent still in the 1920s. Professor Lord Blackett recalls that, when he was a student at the Cavendish Laboratory in Cambridge, an industrial scientist asked Rutherford for help in finding an outstanding physicist for his industrial research department. Rutherford replied, 'If I had such a man, do you think I would even let you smell him?'.

Management in industry reinforced this attitude. When, in about 1904, the British Prime Minister, A. J. Balfour, a highly educated man, received a deputation concerned with the neglect of schools of science in the universities, he acknowledged that England was far behind Germany in the application of science in industry. But he said that there was little point in substantially increasing the number of students of science so long as industry preferred to employ practical men who had been brought up to business in the old way at an early stage.

Britain is now a second-class power, with a government seeking desperately to meet a chronic 'balance-of-payments crisis' by stressing the relationship between science and national wealth, and endeavouring to establish organizational forms to express this. There is no worry about fundamental science; it is good by any standards, and the atmosphere responsible for this is unlikely to change as it is part of the country's cultural heritage. What is urgent, and necessary, is to see T.I. as a broad spectrum of behaviour to which each separate band makes a necessary and important contribution. The different 'wavelengths' in the spectrum, making up a schematic chain of activities, are: pure science, applied science, development, design, production, marketing, sales and profits. Clearly, in a capitalist economy, only from profits is there money available to pay for the other activities.

A decade ago, T.I. was a comparatively unknown concept. Look at any book concerned with economic growth and the contribution of science published then, and it will be rare to find a reference to T.I. The change came in 1964 when the President of the U.S.A. directed the Department of Commerce to explore new ways for 'speeding the development and spread of new technology'. An ad hoc *Panel on Invention and Innovation* was set up to consider how the climate for technological change might be improved. The Panel report – *Technological Innovation: Its Environment and Management* – was a landmark in new thinking. (We are specially pleased, therefore, that the Chairman of the Panel, Dr. Robert A. Charpie, and one of its members, Dr. Aaron J. Gellman, were participants in our Symposium.)

Since the publication of the Charpie report in January, 1967, there have been similar reports in countries such as Canada and the U.K. All have leaned heavily on the American document. In Britain there has been a spate of conferences, discussion meetings, and so on, on 'aspects of technology. . . . '. We believed it was appropriate, therefore, for the Science of Science Foundation to bring together a number of key people – active in industry, the academic world and government – all involved with T.I. We were concerned that the discussions might provide some originality in a debate which because of its intensity had begun to become a repetitive statement of generalities.

Did we succeed? In part, yes – as this volume of the Proceedings demonstrates. Why only 'in part'? Because the process of T.I. is dynamic, multi-dimensional and, therefore, highly complex.

What we require is more specific understanding of the role of the various mechanisms, institutions and types of activity needed for T.I. We need to define more clearly what is the right place, the right time, and what are the right conditions for ensuring the appearance of the phenomenon we call T.I. In fact, we are concerned with a new field of social study in which there is a rich yield of phenomena awaiting discovery.

I make two comments arising from our discussions. First, success in innovation, and consequent economic growth, depend on developing appropriate attitudes in the community as a whole, and a commitment by the community (at all levels) to make the process work for it, economically and socially. We need to recognize that the pace of material change possible – and likely – is potentially disruptive. The concept of 'culturology', as expressed by the American anthropologist Leslie A. White, seems relevant. For him, 'all sociocultural systems are composed of technological, sociological and ideological parts. Of these, the technological component is the fundamental one because it is at this point that the life-sustaining adjustment with terrestrial habitat is effected; social systems and ideologies are functions of technological systems.' He asserts that we could predict the kind of social system and ideology of a culture that has a steam engine, or a nuclear reactor.

| United States 21,075 | United States 110.5 | United States 3.7 |
| United Kingdom 2,160 | United Kingdom 39.8 | United Kingdom 2.6 |
| Germany 1,436 | Germany 24.6 | Germany 1.6 |
| France 1,299 | France 27.1 | France 1.9 |
| Japan 892 | Japan 9.3 | Japan 1.5 |
| Total GERD Million U.S. $ | *Per capita* population Million U.S. $ | % compared with gross National Product |

Figure 1. Gross National Expenditure on Research and Development (GERD).[1] The figures quoted, taken from a 1967 DECD report, show the comparison between the five member countries with the highest GERD in 1963/64

Let us consider the possibility of doing the same for a technological innovative society. We, in Britain, do not lack technological knowledge: we do not know how to tackle the institutional barriers to the application of that knowledge. This is seen, for example, in the fact that our gross national expenditure on Research and Development (R and D) is high and the pay-off is low compared with other countries (see Figure 1).

Second, T.I. may be regarded as an expression of a new societal force based on those involved in science-based industry (and this includes mass communications). Those who work in the 'traditional' industries in 'traditional' ways – dockers, miners, railwaymen – by and large see in innovation an immediate and direct threat to established patterns of behaviour. They are the incipient Luddites. This is not true, on the whole, of those working in the automotive–electronic–chemical complex. For them, change is still of the essence of everyday behaviour: they are key elements within an up-to-date kind of reformism concerned with modifying rigid and obsolescent structures of society – the educational system, industrial relations, management and government.

T.I. implies revolt of a special kind. In Europe – and in Britain, in particular — we have need to understand this so that we can build the right organizational support for, and even encourage, revolt of this kind to contribute to change. Although the U.S.A. leads the world in T.I., I believe the revolt there is stmptomatic, a by-product of social crisis. The U.S.A. does not lead Europe in fundamental science, and once the cultural crisis is resolved she will cease to have an advantage over Europe in T.I.

The American skills lie in adapting and exploiting rather than in creating (see Figure 2). Already many American firms are coming to Europe for ideas and inventions. The following are some of the recent European developments which have had a major impact on American engineering techniques: the triple-deck railway wagon for transporting automobiles (German); the horizontal climbing crane (French); the flotation process for plate glass (British); the basic oxygen furnace (Austrian); electrochemical machines

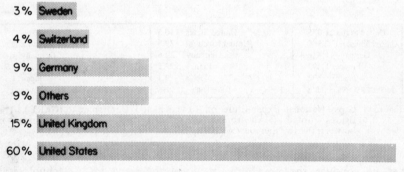

Figure 2. Performances in innovation

(Russian); the hovercraft (British patent); the fundamental digital computer (British).

Over the years, the list is more impressive: it includes, for example, television, Cellophane, penicillin, the motor car and electric light.

Similarly, Japan's astonishing contribution to T.I. is already beginning to show signs of lagging. To maintain and develop her innovative capacity, she will need to develop as basic an attitude to fundamental science as there is in Europe.

Lord Jackson of Burnley, F.R.S., insists that all advanced countries must consider the needs of the developing nations. We accept that, but deliberately did not invite representatives from such countries to the Symposium because we felt that their problems were different in quality from those of T.I. in the industrialized countries.

For those who would like to have a personal statement of the main points that arose in the Symposium, one of the participants, Dr. Gordon Fryers, has described these in some detail (see *Science Policy News*, 1, No. 1, June 1969).

It is a pleasure to record our thanks to Robert Jones, of the Innovating Industry Project, for his editorial assistance, particularly in his skilful treatment of the discussion sessions. We sought here to get away from the edited verbatim statement and to extract instead what we thought was significant and relevant from the many hours of animated talk. Without him this volume would have been much delayed. Naturally, I take full responsibility for its weight, balance and tone. Also, thanks to Sara Gulland (of the Office of Health Economics) and to my secretary, Margaret Bourke: their administrative efficiency ensured that all went well.

We are deeply indebted to Lord Jackson for his inspired chairmanship and guidance, which ensured that we kept to the main road, but we were allowed some pleasant sidepath meandering.

*London, June* 1969                    MAURICE GOLDSMITH

# Chapter 1

# Technological Innovation and the International Economy

*Robert A. Charpie*

In the first Science of Science Foundation Lecture, Professor Derek De Solla Price[1] summarized his statistical research into the growth of science and scientific manpower over the century. His several studies of the expanding quantities of scientific literature and manpower in the various countries of the world, based on library statistics covering journals and technical publications plus manpower reports from government agencies, all point to the same conclusion: that in first approximation science activity increases exponentially at a compound interest rate of roughly seven per cent. per annum. At this rate science, and science manpower, double in size every 10 to 15 years and have expanded by a factor of approximately one million in the three hundred years since the publication of the first scientific paper.

De Solla Price made two startling observations in his lecture, to which I would like to add a third point. First, when we look at the growth of international science without reference to field and to country, the growth rate has been remarkably constant, exponentiating at approximately seven per cent. per year for 25 or 30 doubling periods; second, he pointed out that the accumulation of scientific literature is growing at a much faster rate than either the population explosion or the world rate of industrialization, both of which are standing still by comparison.

## The Relationship Between Science and Economic Growth

My purpose in citing these statistics is not to rehash, in an amateurish way, De Solla Price's interesting analysis of the past and his extrapolations into the future, but rather to go to the heart of the problem we have been assembled here this weekend to discuss: namely, our knowledge of the innovation process. Each of us — average man, scientist, technologist or businessman — pays homage at the altar of science because of our belief that science, expressed in technology, is the handmaiden of industrialization; that as such, science is responsible for some fraction of human progress and economic growth.

I do not want to claim too much pragmatisim for scientists in terms of the motivations which drive a scientific man to success; nor do I wish to overstate the competence of the commercial world to make use of the scientists' discoveries. I find, however, that we are all confident that a direct relationship exists between scientific progress and economic well-being. It is this widely accepted causal relationship that has been responsible for the spectacular growth of large-scale science during the last three decades. The cause and effect theorem relating science and economic growth is dearly held by governments, and is deeply rooted in our general population.

Given this remarkable and widely accepted consensus, I find a most striking result when I attempt to apply De Solla Price's methodology to the technical literature describing the process of innovation. If we look back two, or at most three 'science doubling times' (say 20 years) in the technical literature, we find hardly any mention of the process of technological innovation. Yet we assembled in Cambridge this weekend in April, at an international meeting, world-famous scientists, political figures and business-men probing and prodding into the dynamics of the innovation process, stemming from our collective belief that successful technological innovation lies at the root of economic growth. When I estimate the doubling time for the growth of knowledge concerning technological innovation, I arrive at a figure of two to three years. And this is the remarkable third point I would like to add to De Solla Price's observations: namely, despite the widely held belief that economic growth and technological innovation are intimately related, and in the face of the fact that scientific effort has grown to flood-tide proportions, it is remarkable that academic interest in the innovation process is virtually limited to the last decade.

## Innovation and Economic Growth

I must pause here and define the terms 'invention' and 'innovation'. I shall use the word 'invention' in the sense of 'to discover' — to discover a phenomenon, to discover a fact, to discover or create an idea. This may be conception with paper and pencil; it may be observation of a physical or biological phenomenon; or it may be articulation of an idea in the form of a specific piece of hardware or a complete system of equipment.

By 'innovation' I mean the act or the process of *using* an idea or an invention and translating it into impact within the context of the economy. I deliberately couple 'innovation' with 'the economy' in order to underline the final commercial result which an innovation must have to be important.

We are currently riding the crest of a wave of enormous interest in technological innovation, both by the political power structures which guide the destinies of the nations of the world, and among the scientists, engineers and businessmen who have the ultimate responsibility for translating creative concepts and inventions into economic impact.

What convincing proof can we cite to show that technological innovation is an important force for economic growth? Most of the clearly quantitative studies available on the subject were made of specific segments of the U.S.A. economy. In recent years, however, the great interest in the relation between innovation and economic growth has bubbled over into extensive studies in Western Europe and in selected developing countries, notably Brazil, India and Taiwan.

The OECD has contributed enormously to our knowledge of the dynamics and flow of technological innovation, as have the systematic studies of the source of inventions by Jewkes[2] and others in the United Kingdom. *Every* such study[3] has shown that more than half of the over-all growth in national or international product, measured in constant money terms, can be attributed to technological innovation. These studies help us to classify innovations into (1) those which bring about productivity gains, (2) those which represent new contributions to existing products, processes or industries and (3) those which express themselves in the spectacular creation of completely new industries. The impact resulting from an innovation which causes productivity gains and one which results in the creation of a completely new industry is likely to be dramatically different in different economies. The more sophisticated an economy is, in the industrial and technological sense, the more likely it is to create a completely new industry based on technology, and in such a highly developed economy that class of innovation can have a profound impact on the national economy.

There remain within a highly developed economy, however, many opportunities for GNP growth terms from productivity gains which result from the application of technology. In the less industrialized economies the productivity gain type of economic growth, which usually entails a lower cost and produces a higher benefit-to-cost ratio, will probably be the dominant vehicle of economic growth.

In industrialized economies all of the studies show that 30–50 per cent. of long-term economic growth stems from innovation which improves productivity, and approximately the same amount from innovations which lead to new products, processes or completely new industries.

In this connection, one of the most common questions I am asked is to provide specific examples of new industries arising from technological innovation. The easiest ones to cite are those spectacular ones so omnipresent in our lives, specifically the television, jet travel and digital computer industries, none of which existed as commercial ventures in 1945, and which today add up to more than 10 billions of dollars of gross international product, and an estimated minimum of two million direct jobs throughout the world, plus uncounted indirect jobs.

At another level of innovative complexity we can easily find many examples of important technological innovations which served to restructure existing businesses rather than creating completely new industries. For example, dry copying via xerography, the transistor which replaced the vacuum tube and also led to the whole field of microelectronics, Dr. Land's successful instant photography and, in more prosaic and basic industries, the introduction of basic oxygen into steel making, or the rationalization of the glass making business by the introduction of the float glass process. We still have glass, we still have office copiers, we still take photographs, but the worldwide gross product has been increased because of these innovations.

## International Aspects of Innovation

My prime assignment tonight is to focus attention on those aspects of technological innovation which are important in international economics; to try to make clear the roles technological innovation plays in national and regional growth planning, and to highlight the opportunities which better management of technological innovation offers the nations of the world in their search for sustained economic growth.

It is tempting to take the simple view of technological innovation that the more innovation there is the better it is for everybody, on the grounds that once inventions have been made and consequent innovations have been introduced, then the benefits which flow from those successes will ultimately derive to everyone's advantage.

That's an appealing argument, but in the short run nothing could be farther from the truth. The simple facts are that large scale success in technological innovation has been limited to relatively few areas of the world, and rather than having the benefits flow equally to all inhabitants of the planet, the harsh fact is that the gap between the 'haves' and the 'have-nots' has broadened at an increasing rate in recent years because of the innovative performance of the wealthier nations.

Another distressing characteristic of technological innovation is that innovations which lead to productivity gains, and thereby tend to come earliest in emerging economies, frequently displace jobs, while those innovations which create new industries, and thereby new employment, tend to occur preferentially in the most industrialized areas. Thus, technological innovation selectively increases the unemployment gap in the short run, in the underemployed economies.

It is obvious that each country cannot separately, and simultaneously, have a favourable balance of trade. And yet we all know that the balance-of-payments figure is among the most important indices of national or regional economic well-being. In under-industrialized countries there is often a critical need to maintain a favourable balance of payments in order to provide the limited amounts of scarce, *hard* currencies required for scarce item purchases, which help to shorten the lead times in industrialization projects.

Technological change affects international trade in subtle ways. International payments for technology such as patent royalties, payments for technical know-how and so on, flow predominantly to the innovative nations. According to OECD figures, for example, the U.S.A. receives 10 times as much in technological payments from abroad as it makes in such payments to other nations.

I think we can all agree that this unbalanced flow of international payments for technical know-how and patent rights is likely to continue to favour the 'have' nations for a long time, thereby increasing the pressure for internal economic growth on the 'have-nots'.

A more subtle aspect of innovation is the second generation, or 'displacement', effects which again usually work to the disadvantage of the emerging nations. Perhaps an example is in order here. In 1956 the U.S.A. exported about $187 million worth of cotton and wool yarns and fabrics. In 1965 these exports had fallen to $125 million because of the huge flow of cotton and wool products from the industrializing nations, many of which had chosen to concentrate investment in the agricultural sector to exploit their available land and low labour costs by producing yarns and fabrics. We are all aware of the enormous success which Pakistan and India, as well as some of the African nations, have had using this strategy. As a consequence, the U.S.A. currently imports large quantities of cotton and wool yarns and fabrics from these nations.

Before drawing any conclusions about the impact on American trade of this strategy by the low labour cost agricultural countries, we must look at another market, namely, synthetic fibres and fabrics. In this area the U.S.A. exported in 1956 $158 million, whereas by 1965 exports of synthetics rose to $241 million. Thus, for the U.S.A., the low technology natural products which could be produced in other parts of the world at a lower cost than in the U.S.A. were more than replaced within the U.S.A. export mix by high technology synthetics. So the total export account in the yarns, fibres and fabrics field actually grew from $345 million in 1956 to $366 million in 1965, notwithstanding the enormous impact which low-cost cotton and wool from the emerging nations had on the world market. Here, again, we see that the possession of high technology innovative capacity has worked to the disadvantage of the international payments accounts of the less innovative nations.

A third factor of importance in the international economy is that those nations which have the highest demonstrated innovative performance and effort are most likely, by sheer weight of force, to come upon new innovative opportunities which further improve their technological position in the hierarchy of nations, *provided* they understand the innovative process, its management and environment, and *provided* they are able to create the requisite climate for innovative success.

When you get right down to the nub of the matter, this proviso is what the Cambridge meeting has been all about. We all came to Cambridge, convinced in advance that technological innovation is an important factor in economic growth and one which should be promoted at every level of an economy. Our primary concern is just how to achieve success in promoting technological innovation.

## The Anatomy of Invention and Innovation

Let us review together some important facets of innovation. We know that there are no simple predictive measures of innovative activity or propensity. Many people at one time believed that the pace of innovation could be quickened by massive national, or company, investments in basic R and D. The several studies of innovations of prime importance made in the first half of the twentieth century all point to the conclusions that most innovations of great economic impact are not causally related to sophisticated scientific discoveries.

While we have the counter example of the emergence of the micro-electronics industry as a multi-billion dollar international enterprise, following hard on the heels of the discovery of the transistor, most technological innovations are based on well-known, not too recent, scientific and engineering knowledge.

We have learned, also from systematic study, that at the company level a remarkable percentage of the important economic innovations made during this century were made by isolated individuals working alone, or within very small companies. In the U.S.A. over 80 per cent. of the R and D dollars are spent in two hundred large companies. Yet the separate studies made by Jewkes[4] in England, Hamburg[5] in Maryland, Peck[6] in Harvard, and Enos[7] in Massachusetts Institute of Technology all concluded that more than two-thirds of the basic discoveries which resulted in important innovations came from independent inventors or small firms. A short-list of some of the important contributions will drive this point home: consider the FM radio, the mercury dry cell, the dry electrostatic copier, penicillin, streptomycin and insulin, the modern rocket engine, the zipper, the self-winding wrist watch, instant photography, air conditioning and, in the heavy industries, the gas turbine, automatic transmission, catalytic cracking of petroleum, terylene fibres, and the vacuum tube. All of them came from individuals not working in large companies.

Just as it is impossible to establish a correlation between total size of effort and results, it is also impossible to establish any correlation between geography and inventive results. The basic inventions which have proven most important in this century have come from throughout the world. The innovations however, have been brought to full fruition in a relatively small number of countries. Europe is well represented in the important inventive contributions: the Geigy Company of Switzerland, DDT; Alexander Fleming in the U.K., penicillin; Dixon and Winfield, in the U.K., the discovery of terylene; Leo Esaki in Japan, the tunnel diode; the German and Austrian effort of Schwarz, Miles and Durrer in oxygen steelmaking; and Karl Schroeder's contribution to tungsten carbide; Kodachrome was the brainchild of Mannes and Godowsky, and float glass came from the British Pilkington group. Finally, there is the whole range of basic contributions to modern pharmacology which flowed from the German, Swiss and Austrian chemical institutions and universities.

One of the questions I have often asked myself is, given this *dilute base* for discovery, why is it that so few of the inventive contributions are articulated by the inventor, or even within the inventor's own company, and occasionally not even within his own country, to innovative success.

### The Environment for Innovation

I know this is treacherous ground, but I think it is important that we discuss openly and dispassionately the environmental requirements for successful innovation, for without the ability to understand and create the requisite environment I believe there is no possibility of organizing for success from technological innovation, equally for companies and for nations.

In order to discuss the environment it is first necessary that we talk about the innovator: who is he and what is he like? Our experience teaches us that he is often an anti-establishment type. Perhaps that is the reason that his important contributions are frequently made either as an individual or in the context of a small company which he can dominate or influence in a pivotal way. Ordinarily, he has a stronger technical background than he does an administrative or management background. He is better able to deal with things than with people. He is more fluent in discussing ideas than in processing formal organizations. He is more at home with technical products than with marketing problems, and he is often inclined to be disdainful of the professional judgements of others. He is usually a man committed completely to the innovative concept, or product notion, which drives him forward. He cannot be talked out of this basic idea, for it is as much a part of his fibre as is his family. We can cite instances with ease in which the would-be innovator has starved his own family because of his firm conviction that he was right and the rest of the world was wrong.

How does such a man ever provoke a success? We cannot answer that question completely, but do know that such successes occur. In a sense it is an altogether remarkable fact that *any* innovation ever becomes an economic success. Our entire social system at times seems to have been designed to keep innovations from happening. We are all more at home with the familiar than the unfamiliar. Almost to the man, we would rather suffer the pain of the known rather than cope with the risk of the unknown. And so the 'not invented here' syndrome, the 'it won't work' syndrome, the 'I know a better way' syndrome, the 'I'm not going to invest my money in a crazy idea like that' syndrome, whether expressed by individuals or companies or national governments, all serve as dissuasion for the would-be innovator.

And as if that weren't enough, the formal organization of government often makes his already difficult job harder in his search for success. In the U.S.A., for example, the structure of the tax system is stacked against the would-be innovator. He cannot enjoy the benefits of having the government share in his business expenses, for he has no profits from which to deduct them. The tax code which provides for loss carry-forwards from one year to the next against future profits is presently limited to five years, which is a short time in the life of a successful innovation. Often the basic successful business embryo will be in a loss position for periods longer than five years, so as to be unable to recoup all the tax losses which the law allows.

The impact of the antitrust laws in the U.S.A., and the emerging antitrust regulations within the Common Market, serve to make it more difficult to achieve innovative successes than would otherwise be the case. And, as if these legal impediments were not enough, the lack of organization of the venture capital sources required to provide the small quantities of high risk capital that are needed to be successful is a cause for discouragement to would-be entrepreneurs.

To take the positive view of matters for a moment, we may observe fairly that things are not as bad as they used to be for technological innovation, perhaps because of the conspicuous success of some of the innovators who have achieved enormous public respect and very considerable personal success as measured in terms of power or financial fulfilment. It was interesting to me to see, in a recent issue of *Fortune* which documented the wealthiest men of America, that fully half of the twenty wealthiest men in America have made their personal fortunes via the technological innovation route.

### Innovation in Europe and the American Challenge

Let me close by making some observations about technological innovation in the United Kingdom and North Europe. In anticipation of making this talk, I have questioned friends around the world in order to develop a similar list of dramatically successful technological entrepreneurs outside the U.S.A. I find that there are some, but the list is short. I'm certain this will change during the decade of the 1970s, for there is high interest indeed in technological innovation.

We have all heard the standard arguments as to why technological innovation should be more successful in the U.S.A. than anywhere else in the world, but I am persuaded that the 'easy explanations' of a large unified market, or large scale government support of R and D spending are only secondary forces which, by themselves, would lead to nothing. Other nations, notably in Europe, have tried to imitate these factors in the hope of producing explosive innovative economic growth, but without much success. It seems that there truly is more innovation success in America than anywhere else, and I urge us to look deeper into that environment than simply appealing to general prosperity, or to government expenditures in computers, military hardware or space programmes to find the seeds of success.

There are three specific suggestions about the U.S.A. environment that I believe may be worth emulating. Each of them reflects a characteristic way in which the U.S.A. differs significantly from most European countries. Taken together, I believe they are responsible for much of the differential in innovative performance between North America and Northern Europe. Because of my experience I must deal with these from the American point of view.

First, the same U.S.A. tax code which makes the operating problems of the entrepreneur in a company more difficult, provides an assured flow of high risk investment capital to those would-be innovators who are able to establish contact with adequate venture capital sources. The arbitrage of the capital gains provisions of the U.S.A. tax laws, as against paying ordinary income taxes, makes it advantageous for tax payers in high income brackets to assume substantial investment risks in anticipation of sharply reduced tax rates on high profits.

The second factor is that America has a tradition of publicly appreciating and recognizing success on the part of anti-establishment people. The relatively less structured American society, which is highly mobile, technologically sophisticated and receptive to new ideas and things, is conditioned to accord praise and prestige rather than to ignore a man of humble beginnings who chooses to fight the system and thereby achieves personal success. I recognize that the U.S.A. attributes of mobility, technical sophistication and acceptance of novelty are anathema to many who would prefer to hold on to older cultural values which have stood the test of time. My point in citing them as group characteristics is to identify the intimate relationship between the rate of change of the American social scene and the environment for acceptance of disruptive technological change.

The third, and in my view the most important, factor which operates uniquely in America is that the would-be entrepreneur is surrounded by evidences of the simple fact that there *are* successful entrepreneurs emerging every day in the U.S.A. Dick Morse says that entrepreneurship breeds entrepreneurship, and I guess I would have to say that that is the most important fact I have discovered about technological innovation.

We have written lengthy learned papers on the environment of techno-logical innovation and its management, on the anatomy of innovation and its causal relationship to invention; but the most important fact is that technological innovation can only happen if the would-be innovators are motivated to make it happen, and *that* motivation is best achieved, I believe, by the stimulation of successful, highly visible, technological entrepreneurs who have achieved personal and financial recognition and power because of their success.

In my view, it is only in this area of 'entrepreneurship breeding entrepreneurship' that the U.S.A. is decisively better endowed than the other nations of the world. I deeply believe that this entrepreneurship is the fundamental force which underlies *Le Défi Americain*, and not the art of organization or the talent for managing and conquering development, production and marketing problems on a systematic basis within the context of huge multi-national, multi-industry companies.

To those nations who aspire to the encouragement of the new breed of technological entrepreneurs I offer the suggestion that you give them financial reward and economic power, but most important of all, give them the opportunity to change your daily lives and then give them favourable public recognition. No other emolument can attract the would-be technical entrepreneur so successfully.

Note: This is the text of the Fifth Annual Lecture of the Science Foundation, delivered at the Royal Institution in London on April 14, 1969, before an invited audience which included members of the Symposium.

### References

1.  D. J. D. S. Price, *Nature, Lond.*, 206, 233 (1965)
2.  J. Jewkes, D. Sawers, and R. Stillerman, *Sources of Invention*, New York, 1958
3.  See, for examples, R. A. Charpie et al., *Technological Innovation: Its Environment and Management* U.S. Government Printing Office, January, 1967
4.  J. Jewkes et al., *op. cit.*
5.  D. Hamburg, 'Inventions in the Industrial Research Laboratory', *J. Pol. Econ.*, 96, April, 1963
6.  M. J. Peck, 'Inventions in the Post-War American Aluminum Industry', *The Rate and Direction of Inventive Activity: Economic and Social Factors* NBER, 279 ff., Princeton, 1962
7.  J. L. Enos, 'Invention and Innovation in the Petroleum Refining Industry', *The Rate and Direction of Economic Activity*, *op. cit.*, 299 ff.

# Setting the Scene

Chapter 2

# Setting the Scene
# One: the United States

*J. E. Goldman*

The starting point of my comments is the various fine reports and summaries on the subject of technical innovation that have appeared within the past few years. Noteworthy among these is the 'Charpie Report' on invention and innovation put out by U.S. Department of Commerce[1] and some of the recent OECD reports on the same subject.

I do not wish to belabour that which has already been said. Instead, let me take off from their conclusions and, by citing some case histories of recent innovations that have taken place in American industry, assess those common denominators which couple technical innovation to economic growth.

To begin, let me dispel two myths that seem to be rampant. First, the myth of spin-off. Much has been said about spin-off from defence to the commercial sector, and from one industry to another. In point of fact, the former is virtually non-existent and the latter very rare indeed. So-called spin-off from defence and space research and development efforts to the private sector is over-exaggerated. Certainly, there are a few examples that are beaten to death in the repetition to document the need for more research and more budgets; in fact, there has been little technical innovative spin-off. The spin-off has been really in the creation of organizational entities which started with the guaranteed markets of space and defence, thereby achieving organizational viability. Such organizations then were able to move into the private sector supported by a cushion of assured overhead funds. There is perhaps one outgrowth of large Government-supported R and D efforts that could be considered spin-off. I refer to the techniques of Systems Analysis that were developed and refined in the space and defence programmes and are now widely employed in the private sector. We might call this soft spin-off.

The second myth that I must dispel at the risk of repeating things that were said in the Charpie report is that of the team effort. Large technical systems programmes, such as the Apollo programme or the Polaris missile, are indeed team efforts. But, in nearly all those instances of innovation with which we are here concerned, namely those that have led to economic expansion, it is the single individual champion, the technical entrepreneur, who carries the ball as it were and pushes the technology ahead.

A study group of the Materials Advisory Board in the U.S.A. reported on an investigation of a series of ten innovations in the materials field and were able in every instance to identify a single champion who could claim responsibility and credit for seeing through the idea from germination to ultimate exploitation.

I propose now to examine the climate and environment conducive to practical innovation leading to economic expansion by reviewing a series of major innovations that have made an impact both on technology and in the marketplace in a revolutionary manner. My purpose is to seek common denominators characteristic of successful technical innovations. There will be others that do not necessarily fit the same pattern, but the exercise should prove useful.

In order not to go back too far in time, I propose that we begin in the decade before World War II and the invention of nylon. Most of you must be well aware of this chronology: DuPont brought Carothers down from Harvard and set him up in the laboratory with the freedom and the facilities to pursue that which he felt was his professional and personal goal — the chemistry of polyamides. Although this is not the first, it is certainly an early example of true basic research practised within the confines of a single industrial enterprise. As is so often the case in the history of discovery and invention, a series of laboratory accidents produced a discovery that might have been many years in coming had nature had to take its course. But in the environment in which Carothers was situated, i.e. the DuPont Company, he and his colleagues were motivated to seek full exploitation of the unusual properties that fortuitously revealed themselves. So, DuPont set to work running down all the unusual properties of this material, characterizing its chemistry, mechanics and physics, and ultimately evolving a magnificent new class of materials that were to reshape not so much the chemical as the textile industry.

A second celebrated example is the transistor. The history of this device is most intriguing, for it, in a sense, is an outgrowth of the type of systems analysis and technological forecasting done by the Bell Laboratories in the 1920s and 1930s, but was called neither and anticipated both. Bell had been known to take periodic long-range looks at the future and concluded that the communications needs of the marketplace in the 1950s and 1960s could not be assured if it were to be based on tube technology.

Bell set out to seek other pregnant areas that could hold some secret to unlocking the mystery of electron current control, without the barriers characteristic of modulation of electric currents in vacuum tubes, such as capacity effects and time-of-flight problems. It was clear that to supersede the radio tube it would be necessary to control electrons inside solids, and a management decision was made in the late 1930s to mount an extensive programme in solid-state physics. This was at a time when the science of solid-state was just getting off the ground and the only definitive texts in the field were your own Mott and Jones, and A. H. Wilson.[2,3] Bardeen, Brattain and Shockley, responsive to some rather anomalous results that were then being obtained in a number of laboratories, particularly at Purdue University, in a fit of innovative skill tried and succeeded in building what became the transistor. (They shared the 1956 Nobel prize in physics for their discovery of this.) Again, the major impact did not so immediately revolutionize the telephone industry as it did the fields of electronics, electronic communications and, of course, the computer industry.

Speaking of the computer, let us look at the case of the ferrites, another invention bred from science whose impact on computers has been indescribably great. Here is an exception, where a scientific discovery made at a university led directly to an innovation in an industrial laboratory, largely through the communications skills of individual researches or in continuous communication with the world of science. This story begins at Grenoble in France where the great French physicist, Louis Neel, proposed a new theory to explain the anomalous magnetic properties of the oxides of iron. He called this 'ferrimagnetism'. J. L. Snoek, at the Philips Laboratories in Holland, jumped on this suggestion and speculated what might happen if there were selective substitution of certain of the constituents of the oxides of iron by other elements. He and his colleagues were able to predict, and later verify experimentally, the creation of an entire series of new magnetic compounds with unusual properties, and these came to form the basis of ferrite core memories, ferrite antennae and coated magnetic tapes.

Synthetic diamonds from the General Electric Laboratories constitute another case in point where high-pressure research undertaken at the G.E. Laboratories led to synthesis of diamond from graphite, with important implications in the machine tool industry.

I will close this catalogue of innovation that spurred economic growth in the industrial sector of the U.S.A. economy with a few examples that have been close to my personal involvement, first at the Ford Laboratories and more recently at Xerox. The Ford sodium—sulfur battery, although not as yet a profit-making device, appears potentially to be the most important invention in the field of electro-chemical energy storage in 30 years. This story, too, starts with a scientific investigation: in this instance an exploratory programme seeking a relationship between electrical and mechanical properties of certain sodium-bearing glasses. It was observed that sodium ions are very mobile in certain glasses and lead to unusual electrical properties. It was proposed (on a golf course, in fact) that perhaps a battery could be made taking advantage of the high permeability of a glass to sodium ions by using a reaction in which molten sodium, after passing through a glass membrane, is oxidized by sulphur. The principle worked but the glass did not. The glass deteriorated rapidly and had too high an electrical resistivity to be practical from a power density standpoint.

However, with the materials and solid-state physics and chemistry capability resident in the Ford Scientific Laboratory, it was possible to synthesize a new proprietary material that had just the desired properties to form a useful solid electrolyte in such a cell. The result was a reversible battery, with approximately 15 times the energy density of a lead-acid battery. Whether or not an electric automobile will become practical as a result of this invention remains to be seen, but I have no doubt that a host of applications — running the gamut from small portable equipment, such as lawnmowers to tools, to standby and peak-power demands for central power stations — will emerge.

The same laboratory at Ford produced a new technique for polymerizing paints at room temperature in a matter of seconds based on electron radiation. As in so many instances, the initial profitable impact of this innovation is not on the automobile industry, where the innovative effect is peripheral, but rather on the wood industry, where the result is a qualitatively different product.

Finally, I must mention a most celebrated instance, now well known and recognized: namely, xerography. You must all be familiar with the legendary figure of Chester Carlson and his dogged determination to reproduce an image electrically using a photoconductive surface. The story that is not told often is the impracticality of the materials, from the electrical and mechanical standpoints. The fortuitous replacement of sulphur by selenium, and later fundamental efforts in scientific research on understanding of the photo-conductivity process in various materials, led to a series of new inventions that made much more practical the techniques for copying, whch helped this new industry to great economic growth and has been a great boon to many other industries. It is perhaps germane to point out that this represents an example where corporate growth based on a new technological innovation was largely facilitated by marketing innovations.

The list of such examples is endless and can be made to include not only revolutionary new devices and materials but also quantitative improvements in old ones, as well as innovations in processes and manufacturing methods which play their role in economic growth through innovation. These are discussed more fully in the recent volume *Applied Research and Techno-logical Progress* published by the U.S. National Academy of Sciences, a volume on a subject of great relevance to this conference that I highly recommend.

Let us now seek to establish some patterns common to the innovations cited in order to help define those characteristics of successful innovations that may serve as guidelines in catalyzing new ones.

First, we cannot help but note the confirmation of a construct made clear in the Charpie report: namely, that more often than not a great innovation benefits not necessarily the industry that spawned it but new industries that are sometimes lethargic in their own innovation. Sometimes, entirely new industries and new enterprises are created as a result of such innovations, in which the economic value cannot be measured in its effect on the microcosms of the organization that gave birth to the idea.

The second characteristic is that innovation tends to be promoted when the opportunity to create new science exists side by side with those who would exploit the science. Note that so many of these inventions emanated from great industrial laboratories many of them American, and at least one Dutch: of course, if we extended our catalogue we would find others. Also, in all the cases mentioned these were laboratories that had some commitment to the support of scientific as well as engineering research. Basic science introduces two very valuable ingredients, not often recognized by those who would seek to optimize the innovative 'instincts' of industrial organizations. It provides a communications link with the outside world and, in turn, keeps the inside world honest by setting standards derivable from the outside technical community. Many, indeed most, engineering organizations need this yardstick but lack it because they are totally inward facing, preoccupied with engineering proprietary or marketable items. A corollary to this is that the organization must have the ability to couple the science to technology and the technology to the marketplace.

Third is the interdisciplinary character of the technical organizations in which innovation thrives.

Fourth, and this is true in almost all instances cited, the personality of the entrepreneur, scientist or engineer emerges – the champion that I mentioned earlier. It is a characteristic of the innovative organization that it is people-oriented rather than product-oriented, and that the people around whom the organization is built enjoy the freedom to move about within their disciplines, from discipline to discipline, and from research to development to testing and engineering.

Fifth, I would venture that the truly innovative organization is systems-oriented rather than product-oriented. The latter organization, particularly if its product is somehow related to technology, is most readily rendered obsolete and is ultimately doomed to obsolesence unless it undertakes to render its own product obsolete. Simple probability dictates that a creative research and development enterprise is not likely to be bound in its innovative 'instincts' to the narrow field delimited by the marketplace of the existing product. To maintain a force of creative people their horizons must be broadened; to continue to motivate them requires that the organization prepare itself to exploit the output, even when such output is tangential to the product-line of the company. Some companies do this through separate new ventures groups, others by joint ventures, and still others through licensing. But it must be done somehow if research and innovation are to thrive.

Finally, I must mention the often neglected role of geography. Environment is perhaps the most important ingredient that promotes good research and successful innovation. The technologist, be he scientist or engineer, depends upon outside influences — contact with his professional peers. It is not purely fortuitous that the first innovative regions in the U.S.A., Palo Alto and Route 128 near Boston, are in close proximity to centres of scholarship. But that is not all. These particular centres of scholarship — Stamford and M.I.T. — have taken a particularly benign view of the involvements of their faculty in the commercial exploitation of technical innovation. I daresay the most salutary impact on the economic growth of these two regions has been the sympathetic influence of the universities. It has given tone and substance to the entrepreneurial 'instincts' of generations of highly skilled technical innovators.

### References

1. *Technological Innovation: Its Environment and Management* U.S. Department of Commerce, 1967
2. Nevill F. Mott and H. Jones, *Theory of the Properties of Metals and Alloys*. Dover Press 1936
3. A. H. Wilson, *Theory of Metals*. Cambridge University Press, 1936

# Chapter 3

# Setting the Scene
# Two: Italy

*A. Peccei*

## The Changing Images

Sweeping changes and striking contrasts have been the hallmark of Italian development in the 1950s and through the 1960s. The peasant society in the south has been shattered, uprooting masses of people in a wave of internal migration to the prosperous north. It was an event unknown in the history of the country, and unforeseen, in its suddenness and dimension, by those in responsible State positions. In the industrial triangle in the booming north, glimpses of the next century have already been making their impact felt with new problems and new opportunities.

But Italian structures and institutions are slow to adjust and seem unable, thus far, to channel the dynamics of Italian society. The State apparatus is obsolete; so is the main body of laws. Urgent basic reforms, for example in the civil service, the universities, fiscal and corporate law, social security, the judiciary, municipalities, and family status, in many cases are still on the drawing board.

But the 'Italian miracle' goes on. Italian household appliances have been sweeping European export markets; FIAT is surpassing Volkswagen as the first European company in the motor sector; Olivetti is in the front of the world's giants in the advanced industry of information. Italian businessmen and investors are at work in four continents; Italian technicians and workers help build industrial plants in the Soviet Union, refineries, dams, electric power plants, roads, and bridges in Africa, Asia and Latin America. Twenty years after the ravages of World War II Italy has improved its backward agriculture, developed an efficient industrial system, created one of the best tourist industries and possesses a strong currency.

But prosperity is still a privilege of too few, and a decent living still an expectation of too many. Professional manpower supply remains scarce, and capital flow to entrepreneurial activities continues to be unsatisfactory. This dichotomy in the changing of the Italian society, this rather schizophrenic development, should be borne in mind if we want to assess the past and look to the future.

### Statistical Evidence 1951–1967

The Gross National Product (GNP) increased in Italy in the period 1951–1967 at an average rate of 5.4 per cent. per year in real terms; private consumption increased in the same period at a rate of 5.05 per cent. and total consumption at 4.4 per cent.; gross investments increased at a rate of 6.99 per cent.; exports 13.5 per cent.; imports 11.6 per cent. This means that the global consumption income more than doubled in Italy in 16 years, and that investment increased threefold.

The national balance of payments has registered a large surplus for the last four years, and in 1968, for the first time ever, the trade balance for goods and services broke even. Italian exports represent roughly 4.7 per cent. of total world exports. The lira is one of the strongest world currencies, and Italy is a full member of the Club of Ten; she ranks amongst the 10 leading industrial countries and is the sixth largest exporter in the world.

Looked at in detail, the gross product of the industrial sector increased in the period 1951–1967 at a yearly rate of 7.5 per cent. It was 34.9 per cent. of the total gross product of the private sector in 1951 – agriculture being 24.4 per cent. and services 40.7 per cent. – but in 1967 it increased to 47.1 per cent., with agriculture down to 14.9 per cent. and services to 37.9 per cent. The percentage of the working population employed in agriculture went down from 42.6 per cent. in 1951 to 23.9 per cent. in 1967. In industry, on the contrary, the percentage of the working population increased from 32 per cent. to 40.4 per cent in the same years. This is a trend typical of an economy moving into a higher stage of development.

Furthermore, if we consider the dynamics of productivity in the economy, we find that the net product per unit of labour employed in the private sector doubled in 15 years (+ 104 per cent.); this occurred by means of an exceptional increase in the industrial sector (+ 128 per cent.). If we disaggregate this increase in productivity and eliminate the increase due to a larger use of capital, we reach the conclusion that the improvement of the 'global productivity' of the industrial system, in the period 1951–1966, was truly exceptional: + 99 per cent. By 'global productivity', we refer to that increment in production not due to a larger use of capital and labour, and therefore considered as 'residual' and conventionally attributed by econometricians to 'technical progress'.

According to statistical evidence and econometric considerations, therefore, the preliminary conclusion that could be drawn is that Italian economic development in the 1950s and most of the 1960s was due mainly to the development of the system of industrial production, and that within this system, over 88 per cent. of this development is attributable to 'technical progress'.

These aggregated data lead us to the basic question of this paper, namely: what are in fact the various factors responsible for this rather exceptional growth of the Italian economy, and in particular of the Italian industrial system? What is really meant by saying, as suggested by econometrists, that such growth is due to a large extent to a factor conventionally denominated as 'technical progress'?

## Technical Progress and Technological Innovation

We know that with reference to technical progress and technological innovation, many conceptual issues are still not fully clarified and their respective weight and interaction are still subject to debate.

Technical progress is a loose term: in its widest sense it covers all the changes, due to advances in knowledge, which promote economic growth. It embraces all factors other than capital and labour. In all economies, the rates of growth can be explained only partly by inputs of capital and labour, the rest being due to a rise in labour and capital productivity; that is, to all the determinants of growth other than the volume of the capital and labour inputs. These heterogeneous factors are embodied in the concept of technical progress. One of its main determinants is technological innovation, but technical progress includes other determinants such as quality of labour and managerial skill, economies of scale and external economies, structural changes in production and employment and the degree of capacity utilization.

Technological innovation per se has been defined as all cost-reducing technological improvements, based on new inventions or introduced by imitation, applied in the production process. Technological innovation is usually the final product of long research processes, starting with basic break-through discoveries, followed by practical inventions, and leading towards innovations in production processes. (Economic Commission for Europe, *Policy for Technical Progress*, October 1967.)

This is a somewhat narrow, and to me rather uncomfortable definition of technological innovation, worth using purely in an economic analysis, such as the one we are making in this paper. We must be aware, however, of the broad social context to which technology and innovation apply and of the many facets and implications their meaning holds in society.

We can now take our discussion a step further and better define the question which we raised earlier, namely: how much of technical progress, which according to econometrists is responsible for global productivity, can be attributed to technological innovation? In simpler terms, what was the role, if any, of technological innovation in Italian economic development in the past, and what will be its role in the future?

## Anatomy of Italian Economic Development

It can be argued that in the rather unique and unrepeatable blend which engineered and sustained Italian economic development in the 1950s and early 1960s, technological innovation as an original and creative process was largely absent.

It is a widely shared opinion that in the period 1951–1963 the motor of the Italian economic system was ignited by what we could call paradoxically the advantages of disadvantages. The first of them was *backwardness*. Obsolete plant and equipment had to be rebuilt and substituted in the process of post-war reconstruction, allowing for higher standards of organization and utilization. Technological progress was thus achieved, although in relative terms, largely by applying the available technology. This was a process of adjustment rather than innovation.

The second advantage was *unemployment*, which provided a large supply of manpower at low cost both in relative and absolute terms. A third advantage derived from what we might call candidly, *poverty*. This meant that when demand rose the home market was in need of practically everything. It should be noted in passing that the mix of domestic demand was shifting at the time, as a consequence of new patterns of consumption, from sectors structurally characterized by low productivity, such as bicycles and textiles, to high productivity sectors, such as motor-cars and household appliances.

Thus, economic growth can be explained by the shifting of productive factors from low to higher productivity sectors; by the territorial shifting of resources from backward to higher developed areas; by continuous improvement in manpower qualification; by the increasing domestic demand; and by the opening up of foreign markets through the liberalization of trade (this factor being pivotal).

This process of development, however, has been accompanied by disequilibria in various economic sectors, in terms of production, productivity, competition, export drive and so on. The modification of the productive structure has witnessed processes of concentration among major industries, the multiplication of new enterprises to respond to new demands and new opportunities, and a relative stagnation in traditional industries.

Therefore, the trend has been towards a cumulative process of technical progress in certain sectors and stagnation and backwardness in others. This, in turn, has given rise to and maintained large 'gaps' between the Italian industrial system and those of more advanced western countries.

Today, at the end of the 1960s, most of 'the advantages of disadvantages' outlined have disappeared. Qualitative problems have replaced quantitative ones. The experience of the 1964–1965 economic recession showed the insufficiency and fragility of an industrial system such as ours, based mainly on investments extensive in character. The challenge of international competition has made the Italian aware of the impact of technological innovation in industrial and economic development, raising serious fears and doubts as to the adequacy of the present pattern to ensure that such innovation will be brought about eventually.

Also, it so happens that Italian society is setting itself high social and economic goals to overcome the no longer acceptable social contrasts, economic discrepancies and obsolete institutions. This calls for a sustained process of growth, unattainable by the simple and impossible repetition of the 1951–1963 pattern. As we have seen, technological innovation played a very limited role, if any at all, in economic development of the 1950s and early 1960s. This was consistent with the nature and level of the economy at the time. It seems, however, that in these coming years, under the pressure of international competition and the spur of the overall goals of development, Italy should proceed on a pattern more and more focused on innovation. The model of development rightly proposed is one whose 'originator' must be found in the growing wealth offered by the available advance in knowledge and its tremendous opportunities to innovate.

### State of Scientific and Technological Research

Total expenditure in 1968 for scientific and technological research in Italy by both the public and private sectors has been evaluated at 414 billion lire; the public sector totalled 201 billion (48.5 per cent.) and the private sector 213 billion (51.5 per cent.), of which state enterprises accounted for 44 billion (10.5 per cent. of total expenditure). In 1963, the first year for which official data are available (ISTAT survey), total expenditure was 182 billion lire. The public sector spent 37.4 per cent. of this sum, state enterprises 8.6 per cent., and the remaining 54 per cent. was spent by private business. With regard to the type of research carried out, a tentative breakdown indicates that 18.6 per cent. of total expenditure was spent on basic research, 40 per cent. on applied research, and 41.5 per cent. on development.

Data for the years 1965–1967 show total expenditure increasing from 261 billion in 1965 to 307 in 1966 and 375 in 1967; the percentage distribution between the public and private sectors remaining steady around the 50–50 level (see Table 1). Most of the spending in the public sector is on basic research. In 1968 major increases were registered in public expenditure on technological and engineering research (+ 45 per cent.), biology and medical sciences (+ 13 per cent.), agriculture (+ 47 per cent.). According to a recent survey by the Italian National Association of Manufacturers — Confindustria — in the private sector (excluding state enterprises) the industries that proved

Table 1. Global Data for Scientific and Technological Research Expenditure
in Italy from 1965 to 1968
(Millions of Lire)

|  |  | At current prices | | | |
| --- | --- | --- | --- | --- | --- |
| Sectors | | 1965 | 1966 | 1967 | 1968 |
| *Public* | | | | | |
| In Italy | | 94,883 | 105,784 | 144,344 | 164,095 |
| Participation by international organizations | | 22,250 | 33,666 | 37,273 | 37,284 |
| Total | | 117,083 | 139,450 | 181,617 | 201,379 |
| *Private* | | | | | |
| Enterprises with State participation | | 20,630 | 25,583 | 36,337 | 44,215 |
| Private enterprises | | 124,480 | 142,862 | 157,774 | 168,000 |
| **Total** | | **145,110** | **168,445** | **194,111** | **212,215** |
| **General total** | | **262,193** | **307,895** | **375,728** | **413,594** |

Source: *Relazione Generale sullo Stato della Ricerca Scientifica e Tecnologica in
Italia, 1968.* Atti Parlamentari.

**Table 2. Expenditures for Scientific Research by Private Industries According to Size**

| Size | Absolute values (millions of lire) | | | Percentages | | | Index numbers base 1965 = 100 | |
| --- | --- | --- | --- | --- | --- | --- | --- | --- |
|  | 1965 | 1966 | 1967 | 1965 | 1966 | 1967 | 1966 | 1967 |
| Large firms | 121,991 | 139,847 | 154,257 | 98.00 | 97.89 | 97.77 | 114.6 | 126.4 |
| Small firms | 2,489 | 3,015 | 3,517 | 2.00 | 2.11 | 2.23 | 121.1 | 141.3 |
| **Total** | **124,480** | **142,862** | **157,774** | **100.00** | **100.00** | **100.00** | **114.8** | **126.9** |

Source: *La Spesa per la Ricerca Scientifica nelle Imprese Industriali Private
1965-1967,* Confederazione Generale dell'Industria Italiana, collana di studi
e documentazioni No. 17, Roma 1968.

most active in the period 1965–1968 were chemicals, pharmaceuticals, machine tools, precision engineering, electrical machinery, telecommunications, electronic apparatus and a few others.

The findings of this survey show that research in the private sector is still highly concentrated in a limited number of large industries. In 1965, 73 per

Table 3. Breakdown of Scientific and Technological Research Expenditure by Private Industries

| Companies with research expenditure | 1965 | | 1967 | |
|---|---|---|---|---|
| | Companies | Total expenditure (millions of lire) | Companies | Total expenditure (millions of lire) |
| Over 1 billion | 21 | 90,859 | 26 | 120,423 |
| From 501 million to 1 billion | 18 | 13,231 | 21 | 14,561 |
| From 100 to 500 million | 80 | 18,558 | 87 | 20,009 |
| Less than 100 million | 214 | 1,832 | 199 | 2,781 |
| **Total** | **333** | **124,480** | **333** | **157,774** |

Source: *La Spesa per la Ricerca Scientifica nelle Imprese Industriali Private 1965-1967*, Confederazione Generale dell'Industria Italiana, collana di studi e documentazioni No. 17, Roma 1968.

Table 4. Percentage of Firm's Turnover Used for Scientific Research by Private Industries, According to Size

| Size | 1965 | 1966 |
|---|---|---|
| Large firms | 2.34 | 2.56 |
| Small firms | 4.00 | 4.55 |
| **Total** | **2.36** | **2.58** |

Source: *La Spesa per la Ricerca Scientifica nelle Imprese Industriali Private 1965-1967*, Confederazione Generale dell'Industria Italiana, collana di studi e documentazioni No. 17, Roma 1968.

cent. of the total research expenditures by the private sector was made by 21 companies out of a total of 333 surveyed. In 1967 (latest available data), this percentage remained practically unchanged. An element of confidence, however, is the comforting trend which indicates that smaller firms are becoming increasingly active in research. More is being invested by a number

Table 5. Scientific and Technological Research Expenditure
Per Capita and as a Percentage of GNP
(Dollars)

| Countries | Year | Research expenditure | Research expenditure per capita | % GNP | Researchers and technicians Total | Researchers and technicians Per 10,000 inhabitants |
|---|---|---|---|---|---|---|
| Belgium | 1965 | 222,340,000 | 23.5 | 1.3 | 15,598 | 16 |
| France | 1965 | 1,857,403,000 | 37.9 | 1.9 | 85,207 (1963) | 17 |
| Germany | 1964 | 1,346,275,000 | 24.6 | 1.4 | 89,868 | 15 |
| Japan | 1966 | 1,352,721,600 | 13.6 | 1.7 | 187,083 (1963) | 19 |
| Great Britain | 1964-65 | 2,159,884,000 | 39.8 | 2.3 | 161,763 | 29 |
| Netherlands | 1964 | 330,585,000 | 27.2 | 1.9 | 43,140 | 35 |
| Sweden | 1964 | 253,760,000 | 33.1 | 1.5 | 26,690 | 32 |
|  | 1966 | 421,562,000 | 7.9 | 0.7 | 31,783 (1965) | 6 |
| Italy | 1967 | 520,312,000 | 9.7 | 0.8 | 35,221 | 6 |
|  | 1968 | 614,497,600 | 11.4 | 0.9 | 41.412 | 7 |

Source: *OCSE - CNR - ISTAT.*

of small companies, and many companies are moving from the low to a higher expenditure bracket (see Tables 2 and 3). In relative terms, the rate of increase of research expenditure by smaller firms was greater than that of large firms. This is also confirmed by the percentage of funds spent on research in relation to the companies' turnover (see Table 4).

Does all this mean that Italy is aligning herself with the advanced industrial societies? Or could it be taken as a sign that technological innovation has become a driving element in development? We believe that we are still far from this and that there is still a long way to go until Italy adopts, as she should, technological innovation as a national aim.

International comparison proves our contention. Although the Italian effort in scientific and technological research is increasing progressively, from 0.7 per cent. of the 1966 GNP to 0.9 per cent. in 1968, it is still far behind that of other European countries which averaged between 1.3 (Belgium) and 2.3 (United Kingdom) in 1965-1966. The number of research personnel is inadequate, and very much lower in total and relative terms than that of other countries (see Table 5). The Italian technological balance of payments showed larger increasing deficits from 1956 to 1965 (see Table 6). According

Table 6. Italian Balance of Technological Payments
(Million US Dollars)

| Year | Receipts | Payments | Balance |
|------|----------|----------|---------|
| 1956 | 5.1 | 16.1 | −11.0 |
| 1957 | 9.3 | 23.0 | −13.7 |
| 1958 | 11.3 | 29.9 | −18.6 |
| 1959 | 19.3 | 37.8 | −18.5 |
| 1960 | 20.6 | 48.1 | −27.5 |
| 1961 | 27.5 | 82.5 | −55.0 |
| 1962 | 26.3 | 114.8 | −88.5 |
| 1963 | 32.8 | 139.1 | −106.3 |
| 1964 | 39.3 | 158.6 | −119.3 |
| 1965 | 43.4 | 155.5 | −112.1 |
| 1966 | 49.4 | 182.0 | −132.6 |

Source: *Relazione Generale sulla Situazione Economica del Paese*
Years 1956–1966. Atti Parlamentari.

to an OECD study, out of 139 important innovations brought about since 1945, 92 of them originated in the U.S.A., 21 in the United Kingdom, 12 in Germany and only 3 in Italy.

The reason for this rather backward state of research effort is to be found mainly in the obsolescence of the educational system, in the complacent attitude of industry, which had things rather easy in the 1950s and 1960s, and in the lack of a consistent official science policy.

It is a crisis situation which the educational system is facing today. Universities are out of tune with modern times both in terms of what they teach and of how they teach. Worse still is the fact that even today they cater for a minority of people, when in fact making education available to the broadest cross-section of the population was one of the principal factors of development in countries such as the U.S.A. and Japan.

Italian industry at large has followed the pattern of acquiring existing technology available on the market instead of directly investing in research. The importance of this drawback should not be overemphasized, at least for the period 1951–1963. By acquiring technology on the market, Italian industries in those years saved resources much needed for reconstruction and avoided the high risks involved in an R and D effort. However, industry seldom innovated with such an acquired technological background, failing to invest in development and application engineering, and above all in management and marketing techniques.

Italy was able to develop an attitude of 'creative imitation'. As has been pointed out, Japanese patents carry already developed products and processes one or two steps further, improving quality, cost-effectiveness of production and marketability.

Finally, no science policy has been developed by the authorities. As has been made abundantly clear by OECD, Italy lacked almost completely any definition of scientific and technical goals, related priorities, coordination of researches and their interaction with the production and diffusion of scientific and technical information. Italy is beginning just now to cope seriously with these bottlenecks: time is running short.

## The Choice Ahead

What could be an advisable course of action to ensure an adequate growth of the economy in the future? What policies could best induce the level of development which is needed to solve many, if not most, of the souring problems of the still unbalanced Italian society? What might, or should, be the role of technological innovation in this context? What choices lie ahead to implement our decisions?

As we have seen, the growth of the economy in the period 1951–1967 was due to a number of factors that to some extent are grouped under the general heading of 'technical progress'. We have argued, therefore, that technological innovation, either by autonomous research or by 'creative imitation', was largely absent. We pointed out, however, that the availability of the above-mentioned factors has been rapidly coming to an end, and we suggested that Italy must proceed on a pattern more and more focused on innovation.

The first order of business must be to devise ways and means to spread and diffuse the existing or potentially available body of technology at large (in the sense described above), as including not only what is usually understood as technology, namely the technology of design and production, but also, and more so, those of management, organization, marketing and so on. This process of diffusion creates substantial opportunities to innovate, and the benefits accruing thereby may be greater for the economy as a whole than those of uncoordinated and secluded, although successful, effort in research. The wealth of advanced knowledge is abundant in the world today, and we are tempted to say that there is even a surplus of it, as compared with the capacities for actual applications. The issue, then, is to spur managers and entrepreneurs to tap this reservoir and choose in it the best and most viable opportunities.

Second, a policy of innovative developments must be devised. Its aim should be not just to cope with the insufficiences of the system of production as a whole, but to focus industrial development on a few sectors and fields, highly qualified and specialized, which will be able to anticipate both private and public demand within Italian society and foreign competition on world markets.

A policy, such as the one outlined, should not be conceived as a policy of simple prestige, nor should it be in contrast with the social goals set for the development of Italian society. It implies, however, a departure from the Italian and partly European tradition of considering development policies as constrained by the necessity of safeguarding obsolete but socially exposed industries (aid to weaker industries, less developed areas, etc.). A forward-looking concept of development policy should be targeted on growth industries (help the strong ones, so that they can help the whole economy).

The great, basic problems of the country could be solved — if not by virtue of, certainly with the help of advanced industries — by the application of advanced managerial methods in private and public enterprises and agencies. It is my contention that in Italy we should not conceive of an abstract strategy for the balanced application of innovative processes; on the contrary, we should devise a strategy of breakthroughs and high plateaux, hence of disequilibria. Therefore, a fundamental condition for future Italian economic development, I trust, will be the creation of new dynamic factors, capable of promoting and supporting growth industries. In the economic and social environment, they will play the role which has been traditionally performed by, for example, the 'trinomial' of defence, space and nuclear energy in the U.S.A. The pressure and the attraction exerted by these industries will propagate technical progress at large to other sectors, with a certain multiplier effect. Their action, however, must be supported by public projects intended to give modern solutions to long-standing problems, such as education, transport, communications, natural resources and health and welfare. To illustrate my contention, let us assume that the structure of industrial production varies with the level of per capita income (see Tables 7, 8 and 9). Therefore, it could be anticipated that when the average Italian income reaches the $1,300–$1,500 bracket it is not only the demand for consumer goods which will increase but also that for investment goods, with the corollary demand for automation. This implies development of what are

*A. Peccei*

called 'mature products': that is, those derived mainly from the most productive use and diffusion of available technologies. But when the threshold of $1,500 is reached and passed, then a large demand will develop

Table 7. Structure of Employment and GNP Per Capita - 1965

| Countries | Break-down of employment | | | Total population (in thousand inhabitants) | GNP at market prices (million dollars 1965) | GNP per capita (dollars) |
|---|---|---|---|---|---|---|
| | Agriculture (%) | Industry (%) | Services (%) | | | |
| Belgium | 5 | 42 | 53 | 9,464 | 16,822 | 1,777 |
| France | 17.3 | 39.9 | 42.8 | 48,920 | 94,002 | 1,922 |
| Federal Germany | 10.9 | 48.7 | 40.4 | 59.012 | 112,915 | 1,913 |
| C.E.E. | | | | | | |
| Luxemburg | 13 | 46 | 41 | 331 | 554 (1963) | 1,674 |
| Italy | 25.9 | 40.2 | 33.9 | 51,119 | 56,587 | 1,107 |
| Netherlands | 10 | 42 | 48 | 12,292 | 18,889 | 1,537 |
| C.E.E. | 18 | 44 | 38 | 181,138 | 299,769 | 1,655 |
| Canada | 10.1 | 33.7 | 56.2 | 19,604 | 49,011 | 2,500 |
| Japan | 25.5 | 32.2 | 42.3 | 98,030 | 84,833 | 865 |
| Great Britain | 3.5 | 47.5 | 49 | 54,595 | 98,386 | 1,802 |
| Portugal | (41.6) | (31.5) | (26.9) | 9,167 | 3,729 | 407 |
| Spain | 35.1 | 34.4 | 30.5 | 31,604 | 21,475 | 679 |
| Sweden | 11.5 | 42.6 | 45.9 | 7,734 | 19,684 | 2,545 |
| Switzerland | 9.2 | 51.6 | 39.2 | 5,945 | 13,686 | 2,302 |
| U.S.A. | 6.4 | 32.7 | 60.9 | 194,572 | 691,337 | 3,553 |

Source: CEE-OECD *La Relazione Generale sullo Stato della Ricerca Scientifica e Tecnologica in Italia*. Atti Parlamentari.

Table 8. Structure of Industrial Production

Structure of industrial production at factors cost in 1965 - % value

| Sectors | Italy | Germany | France | Netherlands | Belgium | U.K. | U.S.A. |
|---|---|---|---|---|---|---|---|
| Food | 12.2 | 11.6 | 14.6 | 15.6 | 18.2 | 10.5 | 9.5 |
| Textiles, clothing, shoes | 15.4 | 10.6 | 11.7 | 11.6 | 12.9 | 10.3 | 7.1 |
| Chemicals | 14.4 | 10.6 | 14.5 | 14.4 | 8.5 | 13.0 | 11.4 |
| Metalworking | 39.4 | 51.6 | 42.0 | 38.1 | 41.4 | 51.5 | 51.5 |
| Other | 18.6 | 15.6 | 17.2 | 20.3 | 12.0 | 14.7 | 20.5 |
| Total | 100 | 100 | 100 | 100 | 100 | 100 | 100 |

Source: *CEE - OCSE - ONU*.

for 'growth and new products' of which electronics is a case in point, and which require a policy of innorative developments.

These broad lines of policy for the private and the public sectors must be framed within the context of a plan, whose guidelines will serve as terms of reference for the sectoral options of industries. Industries, for their part, must plan far in advance their diversification and innovation in production. Innovation, in operational terms, is the result of three conditions: namely, the capacity to secure wider technological knowledge, to apply this knowledge to the production of new products, and finally to market these. There must be timing and balance among the three; a simple approach to innovation by R and D only may be totally ineffective. To ensure that these three conditions be implemented, a high level of managerial capacity is demanded. In Italy, management is still too much based on ingenuity and flair, and too little on

Table 9. GNP Per Capita — Projections by Regions
(US Dollars 1965)

| Description | 1965 | | 1975 | 1985 |
|---|---|---|---|---|
| OECD | 1,966 | | 2,808 | 4,039 |
| EFTA | 1,736 | | 2,474 | 3,571 |
| CEE | 1,687 | | 2,388 | 3,503 |
| European members OECD | 1,504 | | 2,156 | 3,129 |
| COMECON | 1,230 | | 1,800 | 2,656 |
| | | 4.5% | 1,710 | 2,656 |
| Italy | 1,101 | 5.0% | 1,794 | 2,921 |
| | | 5.5% | 1,881 | 3,213 |

Source: Kahn and Wiener, *The Year 2000*, Consiglio Nazionale delle Ricerche.

schooling and training. Therefore, managerial capacity is still in very scarce supply and represents a perilous bottleneck for any process of selection and application of innovation.

A short-term solution to this problem can be mobility, both professional and geographical. A far greater mobility of the scarce professional skills could increase the spread of advanced knowledge and the diffusion of innovative capacities at a faster pace than the establishment of five or ten more research centres. Skills, managerial as well as scientific, must be considered as a currency whose value depends on its quantity as well as its velocity; the lesser its quantity, the greater must be its velocity.

In the medium and long-term period, better and broader education, training and recycling must be the solution. The quality of man is pivotal in the control and exploitation of advanced knowledge and modern technologies, and in their use and direction for the improvement of society. It is a tall order for Italy, such as to raise a sort of dilemma. The prospects are that Italy cannot possibly organize and support all these efforts alone; but is this really necessary? Could she not take advantage of international cooperation, and if so, in which way?

### Role and Importance of External Factors

I submit that Italian technical, economic and social progress will depend increasingly on external factors, such as rapid and effective economic integration in Europe; the possible definition of European or, better, Atlantic policies on science; joint programmes for research, study centres and education; Italy's capacity to attract technology-intensive foreign investments; the emergence of truly international corporations. In an ever more interdependent world, no country can proceed, or face alone, the complex problems of what has been called the 'technetronic' age. (The word 'technetronic' is taken from a text by Professor Zbigiew Brzezinski in *Encounter*, January 1968, and combines 'technological' and 'electronic'.) This is particularly true of Italy, with her burden of unresolved problems, and yet with her well deserved status of an industrial country and the responsibilities implied by that.

European integration – and in this regard *when* outweighs *how* – not only supplies outlets but eventually will compel Italy to align her outmoded laws and her obsolete structures with those of more advanced countries. However, we have to set our sights higher, above the parochialism typical of certain European approaches to problems. We must conceive of wider initiatives in the context of the western industrialized countries and of the world as a whole. I am thinking, for example, of the fascinating prospects which will be brought about by the emergence and development of truly international corporations. Italian participation in them will be decisive in helping to solve, for example, the problem of the transfer of technology from advanced countries. It will be instrumental in achieving the higher level of research effort which will be needed in the future. At the same time, Italy must provide a proper framework to attract technology-intensive international investments.

I have indicated some external factors which I consider of importance for the progress of Italy. I conclude by mentioning two international initiatives which deal with the problem of education and management qualification. I refer to the Institute of Systems Methodology and to the International Institute of Technology, both recent offsprings of international cooperation. The Institute of Systems Methodology will be devoted to research in, and development of, new methods of systems analysis, operational research and cybernetics. The complex problems which characterize activities such as urban development, communications and higher education are common problems of modern societies, and as such are faced by many nations. There is no reason for going it alone, and least of all for Italy. Those who wrestle with those problems in different countries, although at different levels, have much to learn from each other.

The International Institute of Technology originates from the problem of adapting advanced knowledge to modern economies. This is a vital problem in the transfer of science and its application to industry; we know that management capacity is a strategic element in this process. Modern management calls for considerable efforts in continued professional training and research. The implementation of such programmes demands close co-operation among the industrial sector, universities and governments. The overall objective of the Institute, therefore, will be the training of leaders for the management of technological research and development and innovation.

In conclusion, we have seen that Italian economic development in the 1950s and through the 1960s has benefitted from the ingenuity and the capacity to improvise typical of our national character. To continue, or to try to repeat, this pattern in the 1970s will be a perilous and self-defeating illusion. The structure of the economy remains fragile in spite of its successes. It must be strengthened by making the right choices and by applying proper methods and modern organizational systems. It is a positive coincidence that the world itself is just beginning to shape up to a new phase of development. Italy must take advantage of this notable concurrence of events and gear her economy to what is becoming a new international division of production. Technological innovation is one of the motors, if not the motor, of this change. But Italian society demands overdue attention and care for its pressing needs and no longer acceptable imbalances. In the future, an ever larger share of the Italian capacity to innovate will be absorbed by domestic reforms. Therefore, external factors will play an increasing role in our economic development. Italy is bound to benefit greatly from the international exchange and cross-fertilization of ideas, efforts and initiatives.

## Works Consulted

*General Report on the State of Scientific and Technological Research in Italy, 1968,* Parliamentary Proceedings, Chamber of Deputies, Doc. XIII, No. 1 (b)

OCSE. Report on the State of Scientific Research in Italy, 1967, Institute for International Affairs Series on *Problems of the Economy and its Development*, No. 11

*The Cost of Scientific Research in Private Industrial Undertakings (1965–1967)*, Trades Union Congress, Collection of Studies and Documentation, No. 17, Rome, 1968

*Policy for Technical Progress*, Economic Commission for Europe, October, 1967

Giorgio Ruffolo, *Scientific Research and Economic Programming* , Centre for Economic Studies and Plans, 1967

'Industrial Research for the Italy of Tomorrow', *Proceedings of the FAST Congress, Milan, June, 1967*, Il Saggiatore, Mondadori, 1968

# Chapter 4

# Setting the Scene
# Three: Japan

*Keichi Oshima*

The Japanese economy grew at a remarkable rate after World War II. The GNP increased 3.7 times in 10 years, from 11,206,000 million yen ($30,800 million) in 1957 to 41,913,000 million yen ($151,000 million) in 1967. This was an average annual growth of 11 per cent., and this high rate was achieved not by a simple expansion of the economy but by a vigorous transformation of the industrial structure.

When Japan started the reconstruction of her industry, which was destroyed almost completely by the War, and with the entire loss of her territories abroad, emphasis was laid on strengthening her competitive capability in international trade and on transformation of the industrial structure towards a more advanced type, namely heavy and chemical industries. This necessitated promotion of industries requiring high technological capacities, which needed to be supported by substantial technological innovation.

It is well known that in Japan technological innovation in these industries has been based mainly on imported technologies. However, due to a high domestic technical standard and a hard competitive climate among private companies, these foreign technologies were not simply introduced but in most cases were digested and improved through further developments by Japanese industries.

**Transformation of Industrial Structure**

The transformation of the industrial structure can be seen in the figures showing the relative percentage of heavy and chemical industries, namely the percentage of products of machinery (including electric), metals, and chemical industries within the total of all industries. The figure was about 50 per cent. in 1950, 52 per cent. in 1955 and reached 64 per cent. in 1960, which is almost equivalent to industrialized countries in Europe and the U.S.A.

In the period just after the War, the growth of the economy was supported by demand in the domestic market. The products of heavy and chemical industries were supplied to the market as substitutes for imported products, or to meet with a potential demand of products already produced abroad. At this stage, most of the industries did not have a competitive capability high enough to enable them to export their products. However, by the time the

Table 1. Contribution of Imported Technology to Sales

| Industries | Sales related to imported technology in the total (%) | R and D expenditure related to imported technology in the total (%) |
|---|---|---|
| Food | 7 | 1 |
| Fibre | 13 | 47 |
| Wood products | 12 | 29 |
| Pulp and paper | 10 | 8 |
| Chemicals | 49 | 33 |
| Synthetic fibre | 69 | 72 |
| Fat and paint | 7 | 5 |
| Medicals | 13 | 7 |
| Petroleum, coal | 28 | 15 |
| Rubber products | 81 | 69 |
| Glass | 16 | 15 |
| Ceramics | 19 | 7 |
| Iron and steel | 20 | 18 |
| Non-ferrous metals | 20 | 16 |
| Metal products | 16 | 15 |
| Machinery | 18 | 17 |
| Electric machinery | 34 | 21 |
| Electronics | 42 | 41 |
| Automobile | 9 | 15 |
| Shipbuilding | 3 | 4 |
| Vehicle | 32 | 16 |
| Precision machinery | 5 | 7 |
| Average | 28 | 28 |

domestic market started 'to saturate' they acquired, in most cases, capability to compete with foreign products in the international market and could continue to expand their sales by export.

It has to be emphasized that the transformation of the industrial structure corresponded well with the change of demand in international trade; the international demand for heavy and chemical industries, such as machinery, vehicles and chemicals, has largely increased in these 20 years, while that for raw materials, food and natural fibres was declining.

The relative percentage of heavy and chemical industries in Japanese exports was 38 per cent. in 1955, 43 per cent. in 1960 and 62 per cent. in 1965. This transformation of export structure has contributed a great deal to expand Japanese export, and followed within a few years of the transformation of industrial structure.

Heavy and chemical industries are research-intensive, and their R and D expenditure covers the major part of the total expenditure of all private companies. For example, in 1964, 72 per cent. of all R and D expenditures by private companies was spent by eight industrial sectors – machinery, automobile, iron and steel, medicals' chemicals, synthetic fibres, electronics, and electric machinery. These are the main 'heavy and chemical industries', with the highest R and D expenditure spent by electronics at 17 per cent., followed by chemicals with 12 per cent.

This means that the transformation of the industrial structure to heavy and chemical industries required high technological innovation. The innovations were supplied chiefly by imported foreign technologies. A study of the Ministry of International Trade Industry, given in Table 1, shows that sales of products based on imported technologies constituted a very high percentage of the total sales of such technology-intensive industries. This is especially true in chemicals with 50 per cent.; synthetic fibres, 20 per cent.; electronics, 45 per cent.; and machinery, 30 per cent.

This fact can have two interpretations: one is that imported technologies have improved the quality of products to increase their sales, and the other is that these technologies were introduced for products which already had large potential markets. In any case, it indicates that the technological innovations for these industries were supported, to a large extent, by technologies imported.

Furthermore, the ratio of amount of payment for imported technology to that of export of industrial products remains almost constant at 0.2 per cent. This shows a close connection between the export capacity of industry and imported technology.

### R and D in Industry

The total national R and D expenditure of Japan is about 1.3 per cent. of GNP, and amounted to 606,000 million yen ($1,680 million) in 1967, lower than U.S.A. and European countries. Moreover, partially due to little military research, the contribution of the Government is only about 30 per cent. of the total: the expenditure of industry was 62.5 per cent.

A special feature of Japan is that a high proportion of R and D expenditure is spent for economic purposes. This reflects the fact that although the total amount of R and D expenditure was not very large, it had a rather clear economic objective, especially in industry, and the monies were utilized very effectively.

In most industries there is a good correlation between expenditure for import of technologies and that for their own R and D. For Japanese industries, then, import of foreign technologies was a part of the programme of technological innovation, and was well co-ordinated with their own R and D. This can be seen from the fact that industries with a larger expenditure of

Table 2. Improvement of Imported Technology and R & D Expenditures

| Industries | Imported technology improved (%) | R and D expenditure related to imported technology in the total (%) |
|---|---|---|
| Petroleum, coal | 1 | 15 |
| Fibre | 13 | 47 |
| Medicals | 29 | 7 |
| Vehicle | 37 | 16 |
| Non-ferrous metals | 51 | 16 |
| Machinery | 61 | 17 |
| Chemicals | 63 | 33 |
| Iron and steel | 65 | 12 |
| Automobile | 71 | 15 |
| Electric machinery | 72 | 21 |
| Rubber products | 80 | 69 |
| Electronics | 82 | 41 |
| Synthetic fibre | 96 | 72 |

R and D had a higher rate in further improvement and development of imported technology, as shown in Table 2.

On the other hand, a study of the development of new processes and products in Japan shows that among 3,000 innovations after 1957, about 20 per cent. were based on imported technologies and 60 per cent. on original developments made inside enterprises. This figure is almost the same for most technology-intensive industries, with a few exceptions such as oil refineries. It indicates that although imported technologies have played a major role in innovation for Japanese industry, they were supported fully by domestic technologies and developments. In other words, Japanese industries took full advantage of imported technologies, and in some cases they were successful even in commercializing new technologies before the foreign companies from which they were imported: for example, 30 per cent. of the imported technologies for the synthetic fibre industry in 1962 to 1964 were commercialized first in Japan.

## Basic Research and Manpower

It is quite evident that technological developments and innovation in industry should have a close relation with the national effort in basic research. In spite of some occasional complaints of insufficient support for basic research, the Japanese expenditure on basic research is even higher than that of European countries. In 1965 it amounted to 132,500 million yen ($367 million), equal to 31 per cent. of the total R and D expenditure. This percentage is the highest in the world, and the actual amount is second to the U.S.A. Most basic research is carried out in universities, but what is classified as basic research in industry is also pretty high compared with other countries: 16 per cent. in the chemical, and about 10 per cent. in other industries.

These figures seem to be in some contradiction to the generally low national R and D expenditure, and especially to the lower contribution of the Government. This can be explained by the small effort in large national or military projects, which was only 4.4 per cent. of the total R and D expenditure of the Government in 1964. Most basic research in universities and public institutions had little direct link with technological innovations in industry, and its contribution was to supply the general scientific and technological background for them.

Another important factor for rapid technological innovation is an ample supply of high-quality manpower. In Japan, the percentage of attendance at primary schools is 99.9 per cent., the highest in the world; the period of compulsory education is 9 years, second to the United Kingdom; attendance at high school is 70 per cent., and college and university attendance is 20 per cent., second in the world only to the U.S.A.

The percentage of students of natural science and engineering in higher education is about 20 per cent., much lower than European countries, but the proportion of engineering students among this group is extremely high, more than 70 per cent. This trend indicates that the education policy of the Government is influenced by the demand of industry for high-quality technical manpower. The number of researchers is also very high, 157,500 in 1967, second only to the U.S.A. About 52 per cent. of this total work in industry.

We can see from these figures that even though most fundamental technological innovations were supplied by foreign technologies, there exists scientific and technological soil of very broad and high standard to cultivate and to enable development into an original and integrated industrial technological system.

### Economic Incentives

Japanese industries were highly efficient and successful in combining foreign technologies and domestic technological potentiality. The economic circumstances and Government policy have been strongly influential in promoting this behaviour in industry.

After the War, there were many opportunities for new enterprises to enter into a rapidly developing market with the recovery of the economy. This resulted in very hard competition between companies, although the expansion of the economy was extremely fast. On the other hand, due to a shortage of foreign currency, the Government imposed strict regulation on imports, including foreign technology, and made use of this regulation to influence private enterprises to implement Government policy by establishing technology-intensive industries competitive with those abroad.

The basic aim was to transform the industrial structure to technology-intensive heavy and chemical industries, even though the import of advanced technology was encouraged in general. The Government secured the autonomy and initiative of Japanese enterprises by checking the condition of contracts for the import of technology. This was accomplished by giving approval to applications.

Enterprises were asked also to submit their programme, sales plan and proposed production capacity. This information was used to balance and to control, at least through unofficial guidance, the enterprises in each area. On the one hand, the newcomers were limited to avoid too much competition between domestic enterprises until the earlier ones had reached a minimum economic scale and had established their technology to some extent. On the other hand, approval for the import of competitive technology had to be permitted to several enterprises so as to avoid technological monopoly by a few. In fact, the competition was extremely hard. Once production was begun, the import of foreign products was severely restricted, and the existing and potential domestic market was given to Japanese industry. As a result, an enterprise which introduced superior foreign technology at an earlier stage could obtain a dominant economic position.

Under these circumstances, enterprises were obliged to have great interest in foreign technology to be able to evaluate it, and a sufficient technological level to be successful in its early introduction. In connection, one important factor was that owing to the break-up of large concerns after the War, the executive was separated from the capitalist in most first-class enterprises, and new investment was supplied by public capital through banks and security corporations. This enabled enterprises to take a progressive attitude in investment for new technology with the support of the Government which also had a strong influence on the policy of financial circles.

Promoted with such economic incentives and competition, Japanese industries have made a great effort to utilize fully ample high-quality technical manpower and domestic technological activities together with the introduction of highly advanced foreign technology; this turned out to be the most efficient strategy to realize technological innovations for economic growth.

## Social Background

Some mention of the social background is necessary to understand the rapid transformation we have described.

After the War, the primary objective was to reconstruct the economy and reach the level of western industrial countries. The first priority was economic growth, and this contributed a great deal to the success of industry.

Another point to be taken into account is the dominant influence of innovation in the U.S.A. In addition to the traditional relationship and geographical position, the occupation by the U.S.A. strengthened the economic tie between the two countries. For example, payment for technology to the U.S.A. in 1963 was $84.7 million, the highest of all countries according to OECD statistics; even higher than the United Kingdom. This means that Japanese industry had good access to advanced technology and management.

As regards cultural attitudes, the Japanese feel that industrial products and technology are essentially occidental, and have little to do with traditional Japanese culture. They take them as a means for economic growth and for reaching a better standard of living. Thus, there exists less psychological resistance than in Europe to the introduction of new technology and management into economic life. Also, new industrial products are accepted much more easily into the market, as can be seen with cameras, television, transistor radios and so on.

The mobility of technical manpower between companies although small is on the increase, but inside individual enterprises it is rather large. Seniority is a major factor for payment and position. Nonetheless, it is also essential for an individual to show outstanding ability to be promoted and stay as a top executive, a position which is open in principle to all senior employees of most enterprises. Furthermore, because of rapid expansion, comparatively large power is given to younger people. In fact, due to speedily changing technology, senior executives have to rely to a great extent on the advice and judgement of able young people to make proper decisions.

Therefore, despite the apparent rather rigid seniority system, there does exist in practice an atmosphere to stimulate creative activities by talented technical personnel.

### Future Policies

Japan's successful progress was due to an efficient combination of foreign technology and domestic technological capability under the protective measures of the Government. Now with liberalization of trade and capital the economic circumstances have changed greatly, and industries and the Government are obliged to take a new look at their R and D policies.

Future technological innovation will be exposed to international competition without any protection, even for domestic markets. The technology has to be of high originality and superiority, and the enterprise must have an economic capability strong enough to meet competition until the technology is established and the products gain a large enough market for commercial operation.

To help industry, the Government introduced several measures to encourage their efforts. Among them, two rather unique measures.

One is 'the national R and D programmes' of the Ministry of International Trade and Industry. This is designed to strengthen the competitive power of industries by starting national projects in leading technological fields, where the technical and economic risk is too large for private enterprise to take. It started in 1966, and the Government spent 3,900 million yen ($10.8 million) in 1968 for four projects: MHD power generation, high-speed computer, desulphurization processes, and new process for olefine from heavy oil. In 1969, water desalination will be added. The total budget for these projects has increased to 4,700 million yen ($13 million).

A special feature is that the Government is operating the projects as contract research, not as subsidy, to private companies, even though most projects have an entirely economic goal aimed at the development of industrial technology.

The other measure is a generous tax repayment system for enterprises which increase their expenditures for R and D. Although the plan is only temporary (three years), up to 50 per cent. of the increased amount in excess of a standard will be tax-exempt. As a counterpart to the national projects, this is a kind of subsidy to induce industries to spend their money for R and D in their own technology.

In the end, however, the most important point as regards the present policy is that despite such notable success in economic growth with technological innovation, there are doubts whether first priority should still be given to economic growth in policies aimed at better living for people. R and D investments for studies of the living environment and public sectors are much in delay. Some people are starting to think seriously about what is real happiness and the best way of living, and claim that much effort should be made in R and D for social problems rather than for the simple growth of the economy. The setting of a goal is the most important procedure for R and D policy, and it is anticipated that the Government will have to increase emphasis on social sectors in its R and D policy.

## Summary

The Japanese economy has made a remarkable growth since World War II. This growth was achieved not by a simple expansion of economy, but by transformation of the industrial structure towards advanced heavy and chemical industries.

The technological innovations in these industries were supported chiefly by foreign technologies imported. However, because of a high domestic technical standard and hard competitive climate among companies, these foreign technologies were digested and improved, in most cases, afterwards by industries in Japan.

Economic circumstances and policy of the Government were strongly influential in promoting such behaviour of industries. Through regulation of importation of foreign technology and products, the Government stimulated competition among Japanese enterprises while they were protected from foreign competitors until new developments reached a competitive commercial scale.

Social background in Japan has also contributed a great deal to the success of industry. For example, national consensus of giving first priority to policy of economic growth, less psychological resistance to the introduction of new innovations in economic life, and so on.

Now, with liberalization of trade and capital, the economic circumstances have changed. On the other hand, with increase of concerns on living environment and social problems, there started a reflection on a goal of simple growth of the economy.

These factors are starting to influence future policy of technological innovations in Japan.

## References

1.  *Report of Survey on Industrial Technology (1964)*, Ministry of International Trade and Industry. Jitsugyokohosha Ltd.
2.  *White Paper of Science and Technology* (published yearly), Science and Technology Agency. Government Publication
3.  *Economic Survey of Japan* (published yearly), Economic Planning Agency. Government Publication
4.  T. Ishiwatari, *Research-intensive Industries* (1969), Maruzen Co.
5.  A. Tatemoto, T. Watanabe, A. Tachibana, *Japan's Strength of International Competitiveness* (1966), Kodansha Ltd.

Chapter 5

# Setting the Scene
# Four: Federal Republic
# of Germany

*W. K. Muttelsee*

There has been for a long time an awareness in the Federal Republic of the necessity of technological progress. A Member of Parliament, Geiser, in a parliamentary debate on the occasion of the foundation of an important research institute, said, 'Modern technology, which is so closely connected to the enormous development of our gainful activity and which cannot be prevented from spreading further, requires for its development the assistance of all scientific sectors and fields of research'. This was on the occasion of the foundation of the Physikalisch-Technische Reichsanstalt, and the debate took place in 1887.[1]

German industry participated in the investigations made by OECD with respect to technological gaps on the occasion of the Third Ministerial Meeting on Science in 1968. Actually, it was a comparison of innovations. In many important sectors the products of the OECD-Member countries were compared. The result was that the technological gap is not at all as one-sided as Servan-Schreiber claims, particularly if the comparison includes wide sectors of technology. This result reflects the fact that no big nation could be industrialized without a well-functioning innovation system.

I should like to add some information on patents and licences. There has been a remarkable development in the application for patents and licences in the Federal Republic. In 1952, 48,830 patents were applied for from within the country and 10,180 from abroad. This was about 83 per cent. of domestic applications and 17 per cent. of applications from abroad. In 1967 37,102 inland patents were applied for and 30,393 from abroad: approximately 55 per cent. of domestic applications and 45 per cent. of applications from abroad.[2] The figures have been approaching each other steadily over the years.

Caution might be advised in assessing the significance of these figures. We cannot examine here whether the smaller number of applications for patents goes hand in hand with a positive or negative change of quality. Furthermore, the changes in patent legislation in recent years can have an influence on the figures. I believe, however, that we can draw the conclusion that patent protection in the Federal Republic has gained increasing attraction for foreign applicants, whether for new processes to be introduced or for new products to be produced there.

Payments for patents and licences present a comparable picture. It is known that patents and licensing agreements between firms in different countries can be implemented completely without cash settlement. That means that the volume of the exchange of patents and licences is unknown. Certainly it is larger than the volume shown by direct payments, of which a record is kept by the Deutsche Bundesbank. This is of importance when comparing receipts and payments.

Payments for patents and licences present the following picture.[3] In 1960, expenditure on patents and licences of DM 510 million compared with the receipts of DM 158 million, i.e. 31 per cent. as compared with expenditure. In 1963, expenditure of DM 637 million compared with receipts of DM 217 million, i.e. 34 per cent. In 1967, the figures were DM 888 million and DM 380 million, i.e. 43 per cent. as compared with expenditure. So the percentage is steadily increasing, although expenditure has risen from DM 510 million to DM 888 million since 1960.

The licence balances of some leading firms are in equilibrium. The Deutsche Bundesbank indicates that enterprises without foreign capital participation in the chemical industry, in the metal-working industries and in the electrical industry have favourable licence balances. Just 38 enterprises with foreign capital participation account for 40 per cent. of all expenditure on licences and patents. It is difficult to evaluate these facts. For one thing, what can be called an optimal licence balance is open to discussion. Secondly, the assessment cannot be made without knowing the business policy of foreign enterprises. However, I believe that these data reflect a continuous improvement of the technological situation.

A great need to study innovation processes emerges from labour market policy. Technological change is a major determinant in the labour market. The institute for Labour Market and Occupational Research at Erlangen and of the Federal Institution for Labour Placement and Unemployment Insurance have published two remarkable studies[4] on the question of the change of the rate of innovation. According to these studies the frequently expressed view about the acceleration of innovation calls for correction. As we start from today's point of observation, it is quite natural that we consider only those innovation processes that have already been completed. Of developments started a year ago, only those innovations are included that will be completed within a year. Similarly, of innovations started two years ago only those are included that have been successful in the course of two years. Confining the observations to the success of the innovation, therefore, results in a kind of fictitious reduction of innovation time for the most recent past. This conceals the reduction which may exist in the long term. In fact, there are today examples of long-term innovation processes that are not yet completed: for example, controlled nuclear fusion or the MHD–generator.

The evaluation of innovation processes on the basis of the history of inventions should be examined most carefully. In particular, we need information on earlier innovation processes which did not necessarily take a long time, and which naturally are easily forgotten.

The paper by Dinter shows that neither do structural changes in the economic sector suggest any clear trend towards acceleration. Rather that changes take place at a lower rate than in earlier decades.

To arrive at optimal innovation, optimal conditions for innovation must be created. I now go on to deal with some prerequisites of innovation.

### Expenditure on Research and Development

The Federal Government hopes that government and industry will be able by 1970 to increase the expenditure on science to about 3 per cent. of the Gross National Product. The second Report of the Federal Government on Research 1967 regards this aim as attainable. Expenditure on science includes expenditure on research, development, university teaching and some special sectors.

Expenditure of the Federal Government on science in 1966 amounted to about DM 2.7 billion.[5] The Laender spent DM 4.099 billion on science in 1966. Only 1965 data are available for the expenditure by industry, and this was about DM 4 billion. The estimated 1966 expenditure was 2.4 per cent. of the GNP, and expenditure on R and D amounted to 1.8 per cent. The difference between the two figures results from high building and maintenance costs of universities and colleges.

The rates of increase of expenditure on science in all three sectors are higher than the rate of growth of the GNP. In trade and industry, the rate of increase in 1964–1965, for example, amounted to 24 per cent., and expenditure of the Laender in 1965–1966 increased by 8.2 per cent. The Federal Government in 1967 spent DM 3.451 billion (estimate), that is 28.1 per cent. more on research than in 1966.

In the fiscal plan of the Federal Government until 1972 promotion of science and research is given a prominent position. Forward-looking research and technological development based on it are regarded as prerequisites for economic growth. Expenditure on research and development is expected to increase until 1972 by an average annual rate of 20 per cent. The budget of the Federal Ministry for Scientific Research will be raised to DM 4 billion by 1972.[6]

Statistics on the expenditure of trade and industry on research are gathered by the Stifterverband fur die deutsche Wissenschaft (Donors' Association for German Science) through voluntary reply to inquiries. The results are used officially. In 1965,[7] industry spent about DM 4.4 billion on R and D. The share paid from our own funds amounts to about 4 billion. Approximately three-quarters of this is accounted for by the following sectors: chemical industry, 28 per cent.; electrical industry, 26 per cent.; steel construction, mechanical engineering and vehicle construction, 24 per cent.

Research is implemented to an overwhelming extent in private industry. Joint research, which in all sectors is of particular significance to small and medium-sized enterprises, in some sectors, however, accounts for a remarkable share in total expenditure of this particular sector, e.g. 'stones, earths and glass' and 'food, tobacco and beverages'.

Statistics on the research intensity of the different sectors are available only for 1964.[8] The chemical industry and the mineral oil processing industry spent 4.2 per cent., as compared with total turnover, on R and D. The electrical industry, and the optical and precision instruments industry, 3.4 per cent.; steel construction, mechanical engineering and vehicle construction, 1.4 per cent. As there is no uniformity in the allocation of design costs in the Federal Republic, the last figure in particular is likely to be too low.

The concentration of expenditure on R and D in a few enterprises is a fact. In 1965, four enterprises together provided about 30 per cent. of this expenditure in industry; eight enterprises a total of 43.4 per cent.; 40 enterprises, 74.7 per cent.; and 100 enterprises, 86.3 per cent. To encourage the wider extension of R and D, the Federal Government introduced 'in March 1969 a Bill by which enterprises will receive a 10 per cent. investment grant for R and D.[9] This is to facilitate more comprehensive technological activity in industry.

### Availability of Scientific and Technical Personnel

The availability of scientific and technical personnel must be seen in the light of the total educational system. I comment first on the participation rate of young people in education. There are data available on the relative attendance within the educational system in 1965, based on all juveniles of the same age group.[10] As regards the younger male juveniles in the age group 16/17, 96 per cent. attended schools; in the age group 17/18, 78.8 per cent.; in the age group 18/19, 49.1 per cent.; in the age group 19/20, 29.2 per cent.; in the age group 20/21, 19.4 per cent.; in the age group 21/22, 16.4 per cent.; in the age group 22/23, 16.1 per cent.; in the age group 23/24, 13.9 per cent.; and in the age group 24/25, 11.3 per cent. The percentages are somewhat lower in the case of girls.

In recent years, more young people are attending schools leading to university or other forms of higher education. The percentages of school attendances in the higher age groups will therefore probably increase. In the early 1950s, about 30 per cent. of the 11-year-olds attended secondary schools leading to higher education. In 1968, the figure was about 50 per cent. and more in the majority of the Laender. The number of students at the universities increased from 140,000 in 1952 to 280,000 today. At the advanced technical schools ('Imgenieurschulen') there are about 90,000 students.[11]

The distribution of first enrolments at universities over the various disciplines reveals the following development. Between 1955-1956 and 1966-1967 the number of first enrolments in liberal arts rose from 5,900 to 14,000; in law, from 4,700 to 6,000; and in economics and social science from 4,700 to 8,000.[12] The number of first enrolments to mathematics and science rose from 4,800 to 13,000; in electrical engineering, from 1,000 to 1,700; and civil engineering from 900 to 1,100; but in mechanical engineering dropped from 1,800 to 1,500.

The relative proportion of all first enrolments rose from 16.1 per cent. to 24.4 per cent. in the case of mathematicians and scientists, it dropped from 3 per cent. to 2 per cent. for civil engineers, from 3.5 per cent. to 3.1 per cent. for electrical engineers, and from 6.2 per cent. to 2.8 per cent. for mechanical engineers.

Adding up these disciplines, the percentage of mathematics, natural science and engineering was 34.8 in 1955 and 35.0 in 1966. What do we know about demand for trained and qualified people? At present, there seems to be a lack of teachers in natural science and of experts in data processing. To give a view of the over-all situation, I quote two findings from a study undertaken by Hajo Riese on the demand for university graduates.[13] The problems of assessing any future demand are well known. Nevertheless, I would like to give some of his results.

According to the 1961 census of population and occupations, only 20 per cent. of the university graduates were employed in the manufacturing sectors of the èconomy. Almost 80 per cent. were in the sector of services. About 20 per cent. were engineers or scientists. Of the engineers and scientists 46.1 per cent. were employed in manufacturing industries. Of the university graduates employed in manufacturing, 32.5 per cent. had studied liberal arts and social science, 63.8 per cent. were scientists and engineers. It follows that the question of shortage, or of excessive supply, of university graduates is rather one of political decision than of technological development or innovation. The study, moreover, leads to the view that, according to the forecast, the demand for scientists and engineers might be met.

The distribution of highly qualified personnel among the various engineering activities is important for innovation. The results of the 1961 census on the employment of engineers in mechanical engineering[14] showed the following. By size of firms, the number of engineers as a percentage of the employed was 6.8 per cent. in firms with a staff of up to 49, 4 per cent. in firms with a staff of 50 to 99, and 4.3 per cent. with a staff of 100 to 299. In bigger firms, the percentage fluctuates between 4 and 4.5. Of the 43,600 engineers, 11.3 per cent. were employed in planning, 43.2 per cent. in design, 16.9 per cent. in operation, 5.7 per cent. in experiment and testing, 15.2 per cent. in administration and distribution, and 7.7 per cent. were unaccounted for. The R and D activities are not mentioned. This shows how much the comparability of data is suffering from differences in definition. No doubt, R and D are included in planning and design. It will be interesting to compare this distribution with that of other countries.

## Attitude of Society Towards Science and Technology

There are still two important conditions of innovation which I should like at least to touch upon.

One is the attitude of the employers' representatives and of the trade unions to technical progress. It is indicative of the positive attitude in the Federal Republic that since 1968 there exists a working party on automation made up of independent experts, representatives of employers and of the trade unions, of the Federal Ministry of Labour and the Social Structure, and of the Federal Ministry of Economics. Its task is to clarify economic and social questions arising from technical progress.[15] It has started by making an inventory of the analyses and statistics already available on this topic, and by conducting studies of its own to close the gaps in knowledge and to assist in finding new solutions. It expects to have research expenditures of about DM 5 million.

The second important condition is the positive approach of society towards natural science and technology. This approach certainly influences the possibilities and rate of innovative changes.

In the Federal Republic, we have no public debate which would be comparable with that in the United Kingdom on C.P. Snow; however, we have a similar situation. I need only mention the names F. Dessauer[16] or K. Steinbuch.[17]

A sociological study on the social standing of natural science, technology and engineering in contemporary society was carried out by R. Konig and H. Schmelzer on the initiative of the Verein Deutscher Ingenieure (Association of German Engineers).[18] In Germany, natural science and technology are still seen in the traditional pattern of the relationship between culture and civilization. Natural science and technology are mostly judged favourably by persons whose value-consciousness is clearly based on civilization. The approach is mostly a negative one by persons whose value-consciousness is symbol-oriented. The latter group is more strongly represented in publications than is the first. In society, too, such negative approaches exist in some circles. Society as a whole has a more positive approach towards natural science and technology than journalists have. The study concludes that the social conditions for optimum technical progress have not yet been provided. My personal impression is that in recent years natural science and technology have been gaining more ground in publications and are regarded in a more positive manner. But traditional ideas are powerful, and certainly will not be quickly displaced.

## Conclusion

It is impossible to express in one formula such a complex process as innovation presents in the economy of a country.

The studies which have been carried out together with the OECD, and the applications for patents as well as royalties, however, indicate that there is an awareness of the need for greater efforts in the field of innovation.

Important conditions of innovation are being improved, such as the amount of expenditures on research and development and the participation in the educational system.

The fact that representatives of employers and of the trade unions co-operate with the Government in the working party on automation reflects a positive basic attitude towards questions of technical progress.

I still feel, however, that in the Federal Republic of Germany as perhaps in some other countries the process of innovation, its conditions and its obstacles have to be more intensely studied before the optimization of innovation can be contemplated.

### References

1. *Protokol du 16, Sitzung des Deutschen Reichstages (Protocol of the 16th Meeting of the German Reichstag)*, 8th January 1887.
2. *Blatt fur Patent-, Muster- und Zeichenwesen (Register of Patents, Samples, and Trademarks)*, March 1968, p.88.
3. *Monatsberichte der Deutsche Bundesbank (Monthly Report of the Deutsche Bundesbank)*, June 1968.
4. M. Lahner, C. Ulrich, 'Analyse von Entwicklungsphasen technischer Neuerungen' ('Analysis of Phases of Development of Technical Inovations'); H. J. Dinter, 'Zum Tempo van Strukturwandlungen' ('The Tempo of Structural Change'). Both published by the Institut fur Arbeitsmarkt- und Berufsforschung, Erlangen, February 1969.
5. *Bundesbericht Forschung II der Bundesrgierung (Second Research Report of the State Government)*, 1967.
6. 'Die Finanzplanung des Bundes 1968 bis 1972 (State Finance Plan 1968-1972)', published by the State Finance Minister.

7.  Echterhoff-Severitt, 'Wissenschaftsaufwendungen in der Bundesrepublik Deutschland' ('Application of Science in the German Budesrepublic'), *Wirstchaft und Wissenschaft* (*Economics and Science*), No. 1/1969.

8.  'Wissenschaftsausgaben der Wirtschaft' ('Contribution of Economics to Science'), published by the Stifterverband fur die Deutsche Wissenschaft.

9.  *Tagesnachrichten des Bundesministers fur Wirtschaft* (*Daily Reports of the State Economics Minister*), 20th March 1969.

10. Bericht der Bundesregierung über den Stand der Massnahmen auf dem Gebiet der Bildungsplanung (Government Report on State of Measures in the Field of Building Planning): *Bundestagsdrucksache* V/2166 dated 13th October 1967.

11. *Pressedienst*, Bundesminister fur wissenschaftliche Forschung (*Press release*, Minister for Economic Research), 5th March 1969.

12. Empfehlungen des Wissenschaftsrates zum Ausbau der wissenschaftlichen Hochschulen bis 1970 (Recommendations of the Scientific Council for the Development of Scientific High Schools up to 1970).

13. Hajo Riese, 'Die Entwicklung des Bedarfs an Hochschulabsolventen in der Bundesrepublik Deutschland' ('Development of the Need for People with High School Education in the German Bundesrepublic'), Wiesbaden 1967.

14. Verein Deutscher Maschinenbau-Anstalten, 'Statistisches Handbuch' (Association of German Engineering Companies, Statistical Handbook), 1968.

15. *Tagesnachrichten des Bundesministers fur Wirtschaft* (*Daily Report of the State Economics Minister*, 14th February 1969.

16. Friedrich Dessauer, 'Streif um die Technik' ('Conflict about Technology'), Frankfurt 1958.

17. Karl Steinbuch, 'Falsch programmiert' ('False Programming'), Stuttgart 1968.

18. *VDI-Information* (*Association of German Engineers Report*), No. 17, March 1968.

## Discussion

Lord Jackson queried Dr. Goldman's use of the term 'spin-off'. Was he not being inconsistent in his claim that spin-off was a myth, yet referring later to inventions of one industry being developed and marketed by another? Further, although Dr. Goldman had emphasized the importance of the individual in innovation most of his examples related to projects where the essence surely was team work.

Dr. Goldman warned that questions of spin-off depended largely on definitions. In the sense of the spill-over of more widely applicable technology from big science, for example the U.S.A. space programme, he doubted that spin-off was significant. But there was another definition which he wished to include. One sometimes came across 'the assumption that industry just can jump in and take over a discovery that a scientist (in government or university) makes'. This concept, too, he rejected. A firm, or industry, must already have within its ranks active scientific ability before it could attempt to develop technical products discovered elsewhere. On Lord Jackson's second point, he agreed that many innovations were clearly the result of a team effort. But, he emphasized, generally there was a leader, a guiding light or 'champion': 'in most innovating activities you can identify a champion, an individual'.

Taking up the discussion of spin-off, Mr. Wolff asked whether the psychological impact of the space programme was not a spin-off, one which in terms of its effects on technological culture, or attitudes to technology, might be very much more profitable than direct technical spin-off, which he agreed was almost negligible. This Dr. Goldman accepted, and mentioned the current debate in the U.S.A. as to whether such psychological advantages were worth the expenditures compared with, for example, the urban problem which also needed solving. He re-emphasised that one type of spin-off which he did think was real and useful comprised the 'soft techniques' of systems analysis.

Dr. Mencher felt that the importance of spin-off was being somewhat underestimated: several developments might prove very important. In addition to the systems techniques cited by Dr. Goldman, there were fuel cells and the highly significant growth of satellite communications. We were certainly aware of the full social and political implications of the latter.

Dr. Fryers asked how the Japanese banks and finance houses selected potentially successful businesses to support, and how it was that the Japanese government had been able to encourage these institutions to enter into such progressive fields of financing. Professor Oshima pointed out that most new enterprises were successful since they were protected in their early stages. This reduced the risk of total loss. The government gave informal guidance to the banks as to which industries might most appropriately be financed, and the central banks supported this by providing risk coverage.

Dr. Knoppers said this relationship in Japan between industry and government was built upon practices of communication and cooperative relationships which were very different from anything in the western world. Much innovation in Japan tended to be what he called 'creative imitation'. He drew a distinction between 'core inventions', which occur rarely, and 'peripheral or marginal innovations, or creative imitation', which 'occur on the shock waves of core inventions'. Not infrequently peripheral innovations could prove to be economically far more worthwhile than their predecessor core inventions. Dr. Gellman agreed with this distinction. He pointed out, however, that if every industrial country had followed the Japanese policy we would have suffered a very serious reduction in international flow of technology. It could be said that Japan had succeeded because the rest of the world had let her operate in a different way.

Mr. Freeman turned to the question of relative contributions of large and small firms to innovation. The argument between opposing views was, he said, largely sterile. But he did note that all of Dr. Goldman's examples had concerned large corporations. Was there any significance in this? Dr. Goldman said not, but pointed out that a large organization was far more likely to have at its disposal all the facilities necessary for innovation. Whether or not it went on to be successful depended upon its management. But the very importance of management meant that innovation was not impossible in small firms. Dr. Gellman suggested that the question of size was rather more important than the discussion was assuming. Size was often a condition of environment. By creating the small-company environment in a large company it was possible to gain 'the small-company advantages in innovation'.

Lord Jackson asked if the inability to innovate successfully might reflect an inability to recruit the right type of people. This was only one, and perhaps not the most important, factor, said Dr. Goldman. It had been observed that low-innovative industries were often fragmented (e.g. construction), and this question of structure, for example, was more fundamental.

What was the relationship between innovation and economic growth? The U.S.A. was 'innovating and inventing like fury' commented Mr. Maddock, but its economy was not growing fast. Why was this? Mr. Freeman suggested that the closer an economy came to being the world's technological and economic leader, the more difficult it was to advance as rapidly as less developed economies. And Professor Burn pointed out that in any case a continuous high economic growth rate was not necessarily socially desirable. It could create an enormous social disturbance, which economic forecasting certainly could not predict. The rate that the U.S.A. had achieved over the last 50 years was, he suggested, about as much as could have been absorbed socially.

Chapter 6

# Setting the Scene
# Five: the United Kingdom

*Michael Shanks*

This symposium is about the relationship between the rate of technological innovation and the growth of GNP. In the U.K. in recent years not
much correlation between the two has been evident. The proportion of
national expenditure devoted to research and development has been ahead of
all other major powers, except the U.S.A. and U.S.S.R. (the proportion is
around 3 per cent.). Our overseas income from patents, licences and
technological know-how is second only to the U.S.A. — though the gap is a
very wide one. Yet in the rate of growth of GNP Britain has regularly lagged
behind all other advanced industrial countries. Moreover, the absolute level of
productivity in the average British business is now below that of West
Germany, possibly below France — and in some industries below Japan,
though none of these countries has reached our level of expertise in advanced
technology.

How is this apparent paradox to be explained? There are three possible
areas of explanation. One would be that non-technological factors of an
adverse nature have prevented us from reaping the proper benefit from our
investment in R and D. Another would be that managerial weaknesses have
prevented our industry from fully exploiting the advanced technology
available. And a third would be that the organization of our national
technological effort has been defective, and has produced misallocation of
resources.

I believe the answer lies in a combination of these factors.

First, of course, technological innovation is only one factor influencing the
rate of economic growth, and if it is offset by a combination of adverse
factors in the economy's environment or over-all direction it would be
unrealistic to expect it to offset them all. This has been our case. The adverse
factors in the British environment have been many — some external, some
due to internal mismanagement. Let me list a few:

(1) Since World War II, the U.K. has devoted regularly a greater proportion

of its income to overseas defence expenditure than any of its major competitors other than the U.S.A. This has imposed a unique strain on the balance of payments.

(2) Sterling's position as a reserve currency, with liabilities far in excess of its quick assets, and backed by a quite inadequate industrial structure, has led to periodic bursts of speculation such as no other major currency has had to endure over such a prolonged period, and these have intensified balance of payments problems.

(3) The traditional export markets of the U.K. have largely been in the Commonwealth (which immediately after the war was taking two-thirds of our exports). For a variety of reasons, the Commonwealth has been a relatively stagnant market in the last two decades, and the U.K. has had to switch the emphasis of its exports to Western Europe and North America, which today take more than half our exports. But exploitation of the biggest of these new markets is limited by Britain's exclusion from the European Economic Community.

(4) One result of these external constraints has been the phenomenon of 'stop—go' — the tendency for successive governments to cut back on domestic expansion in order to meet balance-of-payments crises, with the result that industry has found it peculiarly difficult to plan ahead, capital investment has lagged (investment has taken a smaller proportion of GNP than in other major industrial nations), and existing capacity has been under-utilized for substantial periods.

(5) In addition, it can be argued that the management of demand by successive governments has been unskilful, exaggerating rather than limiting fluctuations of demand, and leading to a bad distribution of resources — too big a proportion going to public and consumer spending, too little to exports and investment. At the same time, high rates of personal taxation have reduced the incentive to risk-taking.

In addition to these adverse factors in the macro-economic environment, there is a good deal of evidence that British management has been slow to exploit and develop the products of British pure research and invention. Too many British ideas have been developed overseas, and when industry has tried to exploit native inventions the lead-time has often been unacceptably long, particularly by comparison with the U.S.A.

The reasons for this are complex. In part it reflects the institutional rigidity which has tended to be a feature of the U.K. — as it has of some other countries, in perhaps different ways. We have suffered from a peculiarly ossified trade union structure, which has retarded efforts to achieve a better utilization of the labour force. British democracy places a very great — I am inclined to think excessive — store on the rights of the individual as against the demands of the community, with the result that the forces of resistance to change can be exceptionally strong. This is reflected also in the methods and attitudes of the Whitehall bureaucracy, which though thorough and well-meaning can be unduly ponderous. In view of these factors, and the discouraging economic background referred to above, it is not surprising, therefore, that industrial management has not always seized the opportunities presented by technology with the alacrity and enthusiasm that it should.

I do not want to suggest, however, that management itself has been blameless. The British market, in addition to being rather slow-growing, has also until recently been a fairly well-protected one. The seller's market for much of British industry lasted ten years longer after the war than in the U.S.A. for example. Thus, management has been deprived of the stick along with the carrot. Until recently, it was a fair criticism of much of British management that its technical proficiency was on a lower level than our leading competitors, and that the amount of feed-back between industry and the universities and research institutions was inadequate. Furthermore, the structure of many of our industries was defective from the point of view of successful innovation, in that in several key sectors the average size of firm was such that it could not sustain a worthwhile programme of R and D and new product development.

If one examines those firms, in all countries, which have been successful innovators, there would seem to me to be three characteristics which distinguish them from the unsuccessful: (a) luck; (b) entrepreneurial flair, which fortunately appears to exist in all advanced countries – indeed, I know of no evidence to suggest that its distribution varies significantly from country to country; and (c) the managerial ability to ensure coordination between the difficult aspects of the business – between R and D, design, engineering, production, finance, marketing and personnel. In this respect, there seems little doubt that by and large the U.K. and other European countries are still behind the standards being set by U.S.A. – and increasingly Japanese – business. A significant part of the 'management gap' between the two sides of the Atlantic is our relative lack of experience in the successful running of very large businesses.

The British innovator, then, has been working in a peculiarly difficult climate in the postwar era. However, recently there have been some very important changes for the better. In the macro-economic field, recent cutbacks in overseas defence and other public spending, the devaluation of sterling, and the slow but vital reform of the international monetary system, are improving the underpinning of the economy. There are signs, tentative but I believe unmistakable, that the intractable obstacles to change in the social environment and infrastructure are in process of erosion. Industrial structure is changing rapidly, partly as a result of a more competitive climate aided by the efforts of the Government-appointed Industrial Reorganization

Corporation. Perhaps most important of all, the standards of management itself are rising very sharply; Britain now leads most of Europe in the standards of its professional managers, in the extent of business education and the use of consultants. Over the last few years a whole generation of business managers has been replaced by younger, better-qualified men used to a tougher, more professional, more competitive climate.

These changes will take time, of course, to show their full effects — particularly as the trade unions and the Government machine have not yet fully experienced the winds of change. In the meantime, however, the Government itself has gone further than perhaps any other western country in trying to establish a policy for technological advance. I want now to assess the effectiveness of this policy, and to suggest where it could be improved.

The British authorities have long been aware of the gap between research and commercial development, and the National Research Development Corporation (NRDC) which exists to bridge this gap has had its scope and resources progressively expanded. Though the NRDC inevitably has its critics, my judgement would be that on the whole it has performed well.

Before the 1964 election the Labour Party, and Mr. Harold Wilson in particular, devoted much thought and energy to ways of improving technological performance in the U.K., and securing a quicker and more systematic exploitation of scientific discoveries. A new category of industries described as 'science-based' began to appear in election manifestoes, and it was assumed that these were the industries of the future.

After the 1964 election, a new Ministry of Technology was set up to carry the 'white-hot technological revolution' to which Mr. Wilson had referred in pre-election speeches. Initially, the Ministry was a bit of a hodge-podge. On the one hand, it marshalled under single over-all control the Government research stations, the Atomic Energy Authority, and responsibility for the NRDC and for the industrial research associations, financed 50 per cent. by the Government and 50 per cent. by private industry. This involved a very considerable concentration of scientific resources, which was to be still further extended by the subsequent take-over of the Ministry of Aviation. (The implications of all this will be discussed below.)

On the other hand, the Ministry had sponsorship responsibilities for a very limited range of 'science-based' industries — computers, electronics, machine tools, and telecommunications. As time went on, this was extended to include engineering, shipbuilding and aircraft, with the result that the Ministry effectively ceased to be a Ministry of Technology and became increasingly an all-embracing Ministry of Industry. It has always seemed to me a mistake to give to a Ministry charged with evolving and implementing a comprehensive strategy for technological advance sponsorship functions for individual industries. In the event, the technological function seems to have played second fiddle to the (very important – I do not wish to decry it, and the Ministry has done it rather well) function of industrial sponsorship.

It seems to me that the Government's technological strategy of the last few years has suffered from a number of defects, which I list as follows.

(1) In common with the U.S.A. and U.S.S.R., an excessive proportion of our national R and D effort has gone to the defence and aerospace industries. While we have avoided a major national space programme, in the non-defence field we have invested very heavily indeed in advanced civil aircraft projects – most notably, of course, the *Concorde*. This concentration of R and D effort on basically non-commercial projects was one of the things which the establishment of the Ministry of Technology was supposed to rectify, but there is not much evidence that it has done so.

(2) No kind of systematic cost-benefit exercise has been carried out – or if it has, it remains a Whitehall secret – to analyse how the nation's limited R and D resources could best be deployed. It is arguable, for example, that national needs would be better met by a modest R and D programme in the prosaic sectors of engineering on which the bulk of our exports still depend, than by concentrating on the more glamorous high-technology industries where the technology input–output ratio may be much less favourable.

(3) I think the Labour Party and Government have to some extent been mesmerized by the unreal, subjective distinction between 'science-based' and other industries. A computer obviously embodies more 'science' than a hydraulic pump. It does not follow that there is no scope for technological innovation in hydraulic pumps. Indeed, who knows? Tomorrow the hydraulic pump business may itself become 'science-based' as a result of the injection of R and D. To describe some industries as by nature 'science-based' and others not is to take a very static view of science and technology. And there are other, more difficult cases which are harder to fit into the schema. Are chemicals and chemical engineering, for example, more or less 'science-based' than electronics?

(4) Similarly, I believe the Wilson government has been profoundly mistaken in seeking, as it were, to hive off technological policy as a self-contained entity from the broad corpus of economic–industrial–social policy. A 'policy for technology' considered in isolation is, I think, a somewhat meaningless exercise.

(5) Finally, there has been what I would regard as an excessive concentration of R and D resources in the public sector. It would be unfair to blame the Ministry of Technology exclusively for this misallocation of resources, which has been an endemic feature of the British scientific scene. Compared with the U.S.A., for example, we do proportionately less R and D on an 'in-firm' or contract research basis, while the U.S.A. has virtually no equivalent to the industry-wide research association which works on projects

of interest to the sector of industry as a whole rather to any individual firm. This means that research in the U.S.A. tends to have a more immediate commercial orientation than in the U.K., which no doubt helps to explain why we have shone at pure research but have been much less good at its application.

This problem has been rendered somewhat more acute by the fact that the pay and conditions of the scientists employed in Government research establishments — and the Ministry of Technology is now almost certainly the biggest single employer of qualified scientists and engineers in the world — are highly competitive with private industry, while security is of course greater. The Ministry, I think, is aware of the need to spread its talent wider — but also it is aware of the danger that a run-down of public sector research establishments might lead, not to the strengthening of private industry but to an acceleration of the 'brain drain'. The answer may be to compel the research stations to earn an increasing part of their income by undertaking contract research for private industry (compared with the U.S.A. there are very few contract research firms in the U.K.).

One can sum up these criticisms of the Ministry of Technology by saying that it has not succeeded in articulating a comprehensive strategy for innovation. If this is a harsh criticism, let me make it clear that I know of no evidence that any other country has done so either — least of all the Soviet Union, where the failings to which I have drawn attention in this country are to be found on a much greater and more pronounced scale. The U.K., in my opinion, is not behind other countries in its technological policies; if anything, it is ahead. But, in view of the special weight of adverse factors mentioned at the beginning of this paper, it needs to be further ahead than it is if we are to be fully competitive.

Of what should a strategy for innovation consist? It would need to start with a comprehensive technological, market and manpower forecast. It would then need to assess the inputs available, in terms of capital, R and D establishments, qualified scientific manpower, information systems (data transmission and retrieval), and infrastructure investment (on which, for example, centres of excellence on the Boston Novosibirsk pattern could be based).

From this exercise it would appear rapidly that the resources available to an individual nation were not likely to be adequate to exploit all possible opportunities. So the next step would need to be the definition of priorities: the allocation of effort between the public and private sector, between commercial and non-commercial projects (with an objective assessment of possible 'spin-off' rather than the hopeful guesstimates which have been the norm hitherto on both sides of the Atlantic). It would be necessary, also, to decide the respective fields for a purely national effort, for supra-national co-operation, and for buying in technology on the open market through foreign investment and the purchase of patents and know-how.

The next stage would be to assess the implications for policy, and this would have to embrace all major aspects of industrial legislation, policy on inward investment, public purchasing, fiscal and monetary policy, policies for R and D, national economic planning, regional policies, social and manpower policies and so on. All of these must be relevant to an over-all innovation strategy.

And yet these are not the most important aspects. Of even greater importance are the status of entrepreneurship in the society and the incentives it can command, the degree of corporate creativity which is a function of managerial competence, the extent of social and institutional conservatism, and — above all — the willingness of the society to accept and embrace change. Ultimately, the ability of technology to promote economic growth must depend on the willingness of society to allow it to do so — bearing in mind that there is no such thing as painless innovation. It is perhaps, above all, because the forces working for change in postwar Britain have been rather weak in relation to those resisting change that the pay-off from our very heavy investment in R and D has been relatively so disappointing.

But the lessons of this go beyond the U.K., for, in the sense that I have described it above, no country, so far as I am aware, has devised and operated a consistent, comprehensive policy for innovation. I hope the proceedings of this Symposium will help to create a climate in which such policies will be possible.

Chapter 7

# Science Research Council, Support of Technology

*Sir Brian Flowers*

### General Remarks

The Science Research Council (SRC) has rather broad powers to support science and technology, under the terms of its Royal Charter, and as its range of interest is not so explicitly defined as those of the other four Research Councils it covers many disciplines. But the SRC is a part of the educational system for most of its activities, and it has a definite responsibility for fundamental scientific research as the principal agency in this country for supporting such research. Three of the Council's six establishments, including the two largest, were explicitly provided to assist and collaborate in research by universities and similar bodies. The incalculable long-term significance of fundamental research to our material future, as well as our culture, makes this a very important responsibility for the SRC.

In contrast, the SRC's support of technology is very small, in financial terms, compared with the total national expenditure of £770 million on R and D during 1967. Moreover, the universities are self-governing bodies, and no Research Council would wish to dictate to them what they should do, even if it were permitted to do so. Nevertheless, the SRC need not, and does not, fulfil a purely passive function. To the extent that it can influence the training of postgraduate students and the research topics pursued by university staff, its ultimate effect on technology in Britain can be vastly greater than its annual expenditure on the activities might suggest, particularly as it is in universities, where motivation by short-term profitability is least acute, that the longer range and more speculative ventures should find their most natural home. The support of technological research in universities and technical colleges, and of research students, is the greater part of the SRC's direct support of technology, and we have been deliberately increasing the proportion of our funds and effort devoted to it, notwithstanding our special responsibiltiy for fundamental research.

**Postgraduate Studentships**

Responsibility for making grants to students for postgraduate instruction in science and technology was given to the Department of Scientific and Industrial Research (DSIR) in its early days. For many years only research studentships were given, but since 1957 advanced course studentships have been awarded also. Research studentships are normally held for three years, and lead primarily to Ph.D. degrees, whereas advanced course studentships are usually for one year. The SRC, like the DSIR before it, supports rather more than a half of the postgraduate students in its field, and by selective allocation exerts a strong influence, which has been increasingly used, to guide university postgraduate education in directions considered to be of the greatest relevance to the needs of industry. This has to be done delicately because the factors affecting the training and the supply and demand of scientists and technologists are complex and are not fully understood. The Council keeps its policy under continuous review and development; for example, in 1966 it set up a Working Party on Postgraduate Training Awards Policy, under the Chairmanship of Lord Halsbury, and it played a full part in the work of the Swann Working Party on Manpower for Scientific Growth. Several new schemes have been introduced, and others are being considered.

In some industries (for example, some branches of the chemical industry) the traditional university research training leading to a Ph.D. is the most highly regarded; in some others it is not greatly favoured. But the Ph.D. training also provides the university teachers and research workers upon whom the future of higher education depends. The majority of SRC awards are still given for research students, but an increasing proportion of awards is being given to carefully selected advanced courses judged to be relevant to industry — and an increasing proportion of the research studentships is being allocated to applied science and engineering. The figures on page 65 illustrate these trends.

Thus, the overall proportion of advanced course awards has doubled in 10 years to 38 per cent. and this has been accompanied by a very critical selection, by SRC committees, of the courses for which most of the awards are held. Within the last few years several new schemes have been introduced, designed to meet the needs of industry:

**Awards for Science in Industry and Schoolteaching**

New graduates can have promises of SRC studentships to be taken up after 1 to 5 years spent in industry or schoolteaching: 25 were promised in 1966, and 201 in 1968. Of the 34 so far taken up, 17 students are doing postgraduate work, partly supported by their employers.

## Awards in Pure Science Departments

*(excluding geology)*

| Year | Research | Advanced course |
|------|----------|-----------------|
| 1958 | 587 (65%) | 97 (11%) |
| 1964 | 1274 (55%) | 442 (19%) |
| 1968 | 1462 (45%) | 723(22%) |

## Awards in Engineering and Technology Departments

| Year | Research | Advanced course |
|------|----------|-----------------|
| 1958 | 141 (16%) | 70  (8%) |
| 1964 | 353 (15%) | 230 (10%) |
| 1968 | 537 (17%) | 519 (16%) |

*Industrial Students*

SRC students who have industrial experience get higher awards, but employers can retain them and top-up an SRC award to the man's normal pay. There are 149 at present.

*Co-operative Awards in Pure Science*

The greater number, and on the whole highest quality, of students are in the pure science departments, where most of them get little contact with problems of science in industry. So the SRC now offers pure science departments more studentships on condition that the extra students work on topics in collaboration with industry: 128 of these Co-operative Awards in Pure Science were made in 1968 (from 200 suitable applications); 180 are proposed for 1969.

### 'Broader' Postgraduate Training

There are now studentships for the broader type of training, of the intellectual calibre of the Ph.D, but oriented to the requirements of industry, as recommended by the Swann Report. The SRC and the Social Science Research Council have set up a joint committee to support such developments, and the SRC has earmarked a number of awards to be allocated by this committee. Several universities are working out schemes.

### Courses for Pure Scientists

The SRC has selected some 60 of the one-year advanced courses which seem especially suited to preparing graduates in pure science for a career in industry, and 30 per cent. of the advanced course studentships are given to students on these particular courses.

### Short Vocation Courses

For the past two years, the SRC has commissioned the Careers Advisory Research Centre to organize four short courses at which second-year Ph.D. students meet young Ph.D.'s from industry for lectures on industrial science, technological case studies, business games, etc. Some 370 research students have attended these courses, which aroused a great deal of interest and enthusiasm.

In all these ways the SRC is seeking to improve the flow of good scientists and technologists into industry. Progress has not been as rapid as we would have liked, but is encouraging. We try as hard as we can to help universities to maintain the standards of the courses we select, to make way for new courses by pruning out the less successful ones, and to encourage more of the brighter science graduates to take up careers in technology instead of pure research.

### Research Grants

The SRC's other important direct support for technology is by making grants for technological research in universities and technical colleges. The projects are selected, from detailed applications made by the research workers, by committees composed of specialists in the particular disciplines concerned and an increasing number of interdisciplinary panels (e.g. on control engineering). Committee members are drawn increasingly from industry, as well as from universities, and there is frequent rotation of memberships. This practice of judgement by the applicant's professional peers was established by DSIR and has worked well. Under the SRC, with the guidance of the three Boards and of the Council itself, we are developing the use of these committees to further the SRC's policies with regard to manpower, selectivity by topics and places, and priorities between disciplines and interdisciplinary activities. The committees are well able to judge the quality of projects put forward in their fields, and their 'timeliness and promise', but are also aware of the Council's policies and, in general, the facts of life so far as finance and research manpower are concerned.

Figures for support of technological research depend on the definition of what constitutes technology; there is, of course, no sharp dividing line between pure science and technology. The following definitions are used in SRC figures quoted for science and technology:

## Pure Science
Astronomy, biology, chemistry, computing science, mathematics, nuclear physics, neutron beam research, other physics, radio, space research.

## Technology
Metallurgy and materials, aeronautical, civil, mechanical and production engineering, chemical engineering and technology, electrical and systems engineering.

On these definitions, support for technological research has increased from £40,000 in 1956–1957 to £2.6 million in 1967–1968. During the same period pure science grants have increased from £800,000 to £8.8 million; the proportion on technology items increased from about 5 per cent. in 1956–1957 to about 23 per cent. in 1967–1968. As already mentioned, the value of the work is out of proportion to the sums involved, when carefully selected and conducted at the best university departments. Samples of work recently supported are given in the SRC's Annual Report for 1966–1967, which contains a special review of the SRC's support of research in engineering and technology.

However, in spite of our best efforts to favour technology, the *proportion* of our funds devoted to it have hovered around the 23–35 per cent. mark since 1963, with no discernible upward trend (the absolute *amounts* have of course risen by more than a factor of 2). The SRC is determined to set high standards, for both pure research and technology, and will not lower these standards for technology to produce a more favourable image. The aim now is to improve the quality, and the policies on studentships already summarized are part of this. But we are also trying to place still more emphasis on industrial relevance in determining our criteria for accepting or rejecting applications; it may be that in some cases the committees are being over-influenced by factors more appropriate to pure science projects than to those with potential industrial application. Similarly, there is evidence that some university engineers like to work on problems best fitted for, and therefore best left to, pure science departments; these, when they appear, naturally invite treatment according to the pure science criteria. The SRC's attempts to deal with this problem, as in other matters, are of two kinds: to strengthen the committees with carefully selected industrial scientists and engineers, and to adopt when possible a less passive role than in the past, i.e. to prompt selected departments to work in particular fields or even on particular projects, rather than simply to say yes or no to the proposals which happen to come in.

## Exploitation of the Results of Research

A third type of direct sponsorship of technology by the SRC is the deliberate exploitation of techniques or devices developed at the SRC establishments, or in universities, in the course of research. In this case, much of the research is in pure science. We have arrangements with the National Research Development Corporation, and in the case of the nuclear physics laboratories with the United Kingdom Atomic Energy Authority, which enable these possibilities to be followed up. As always in these matters, of the many promising ideas promoted only a few achieve commerical success, but we regard this as an important activity and do not neglect it. A current example is the Galaxy measuring machine, developed for automatic astronomical measurements, which has potential applications for automatic counting of dispersed small objects or images for many purposes. Similarly, the more sophisticated measuring engines for elementary particle tracks could be applied to cartography. We keep in contact with the Ministry of Technology in matters of this kind.

## Indirect Support

This comes as an incidental, but necessary, by-product of something supported for its scientific merit, either in an SRC establishment or in a university with a research grant. For example, the nuclear physics laboratories require a great deal of advanced equipment which, whenever possible, is ordered from British industry. This has enabled firms to acquire expertise in advanced technology and, in some cases, to sell the same equipment in export markets. A film measuring machine developed in a collaboration between CERN (European Organisation for Nuclear Research) and the SRC's Rutherford Laboratory, and with its optical and mechanical components made in Britain, has become standard, and about 20 have been supplied to many Western European countries and to the U.S.S.R. SRC staff were helpful in securing a second order from the U.S.S.R. by helping the Russian scientists to commission their first machine. A special power supply requirement by the Rutherford Laboratory enabled the SRC to place the first order for a new type of homopolar generator in Britain. Collaboration between Rutherford

Laboratory staff and industry, on high-energy physics requirements, has speeded the development in Britain of superconductors for large high-field magnets.

# Chapter 8

# Setting the Scene
# Six: Canada

*A. H. Wilson*

## Introduction

In Canada, as in other industrialized countries, interest in the processes through which technology-based innovations may be coupled into an economic system has increased markedly in the last decade. This interest has been fostered in a number of ways. For example, the Economic Council of Canada in its First Annual Review in 1964[1] noted that scientific progress and technological change are themselves complex processes with powerful implications for the pace of economic growth. The more recently established Science Council of Canada said in its First Annual Report in 1967[2] that its two main purposes are to ensure that Canada has a strong, competent, alert and growing scientific community, and to advise the Government on how best to use science and technology in the solution of the country's economic and social problems. In addition, it has become clear that the Special Committee on Science Policy of the Senate of Canada, which has been sitting since March 1968, is paying particular attention at its hearings to the effectiveness of the co-ordination and follow-up relating to scientific and technical activities of all kinds, and to R and D activities in particular.

It has been generally understood, however, that the economy is only one area in which technological innovation may take place and in which entrepreneurial initiatives may be exercised. Science, technology and enterprise must also be harnessed to make contributions to the achievement of society's objectives, hopes and aspirations. At the same time, it is clear that a high rate of growth is only one of a number of desirable economic goals, which it may not be possible to achieve simultaneously.

In Canada, our work in this whole area has only just begun. We still lack much hard information about the mechanisms through which technological innovation 'works' in the socio-economic context. We do not yet know how to optimize expenditure on all our scientific and technical activities, or even on R and D activities by themselves. Our governments have tried in a number of ways to stimulate discovery, invention, innovation and economic growth, but the measures introduced so far have not been uniformly successful. We have given a great deal of credit for the technological advance of the past and present to transfers of technology from other countries. Indeed, we would be far behind today — both technologically and economically — if these transfers, and transfers of human and material capital, had not taken place at all.

This paper will attempt to highlight some of the factors which have influenced both technological innovation and economic growth in Canada. It will also discuss several of the problems which are preoccupying us today and will have something to say about the future. The total Canadian environment, like that of any other country, is unique. Nevertheless, a number of the elements that are indispensable to the understanding of the coupling between innovation and economic growth may emerge from our experience.

### Brief Techno-Economic History

The original inhabitants of Canada — the Eskimos and the North American Indians — had developed effective tools and skills for gathering food, for self-protection, for transportation and for communications long before the first Europeans discovered the country in the sixteenth century. These Europeans restricted their activities to eastern coastal waters, until the incentive to explore the inland forests and plains became sufficiently strong and until they had learned to survive in the rigorous climate. They supplemented their own tools, techniques and skills with those they learned from the indigenous people. But, with time and experience, the needs of the explorers changed. The problems and the opportunities which challenged them also changed. Both European and indigenous technologies had to be adapted accordingly.

The fur and forest resources of Eastern Canada, and the markets of Europe, sustained the economy of the country until well into the nineteenth century. Small-scale and primitive agricultural developments helped the slowly growing population. The rivers became the first main highways of the country. The *canot du maître*, the *canot du nord*, the York boat and the Durham boat were developed to carry goods and people across long distances and to establish and maintain communications and trade. The development of the St. Lawrence and Ottawa River routes opened up the way for the settlement of Central Canada and for the subsequent export of its produce, and explorations that began on the shores of Hudson's Bay led adventurers to the Prairie Provinces for the first time.

The development and construction of railways in Canada were considerably behind development and construction in Britain and in the U.S.A. In part, this was due to shortages of domestic and foreign capital and, in part, to the decision to go ahead with the completion of the system of canals in the Great Lakes Basin for which capital was also short. By 1850, for example, there were some 9,000 miles of track in the U.S.A. but fewer than 100 miles in the whole of Canada. Two of the particular advantages which the railway eventually had over water-borne forms of tranportation were that it did not freeze up in winter and could penetrate into areas that lacked the natural channels which canals could follow.

When the first trans-continental railway system was finally in place in Canada towards the end of the nineteenth century, it gave the country as a whole a new political life and a new economic potential. For example, it helped to draw British Columbia into the Canadian Confederation. It brought Far East markets closer to the products of Eastern and Central Canada. It gave the country its first heavy industry in the form of the foundries, engineering plants, and maintenance operations associated with rolling stock and other railway equipment. It also made feasible the settlement of the Prairie Provinces and, in this connection, the research done to develop varieties of wheat suitable for this region gave rise, in time, to economic benefits for Canada in the markets of the world.

The economic, political and technological growth and development of Canada also lagged well behind the corresponding growth and development in the U.S.A. during the nineteenth century. Canada remained the country of the few primary staple products, the country that was weak in secondary processing and manufacturing and was diversifying very slowly. Canada was therefore vulnerable to changes in European marketing and other external conditions over which Canadian suppliers had little control. The economic system in the U.S.A., however, acquired much more quickly a greater diversity of production, higher levels of internal trading activity, and a much more active class of entrepreneurs.

The interest of government in scientific and technical activities began effectively with the Union of Upper and Lower Canada. The Geological Survey of Canada, for example, was established shortly afterwards in 1842. The early members of the Survey were not only explorers and geologists, they were concerned also with locating mineral, forest, water and biological resources. Another agency, the Bureau of Agriculture, was established in 1852, and after Confederation in 1867, it became the Department of Agriculture. By 1884 it had become clear that the industry of agriculture was going to play an important role in the growth and prosperity of the country. But it was equally clear that the primitive agricultural methods and poor education of the farming communities had to be improved. To help remedy this situation, the Dominion Experimental Farms System was inaugurated in 1886.

One of the most significant technological developments which accelerated

Canadian economic growth took place around the turn of the present century. This was the harnessing of hydro-electric power at Niagara Falls and at several other locations. The availability of cheap power in large quantities made possible the establishment of large-scale chemical processing plants and the support of large centres of secondary manufacturing and of population. Living and working conditions were improved. These developments gave Canadian scientists and engineers opportunities to contribute to technical initiatives in Canada in a much wider variety of fields than had hitherto been possible.

The first dozen years of the twentieth century were eventful for Canada, both technically and economically. These were, for example, the years of the Aerial Experimental Association to which Alexander Graham Bell belonged. The Association built the aircraft in which J. A. D. McCurdy made the first powered flight in Canada. These were also the years during which Ernest Rutherford was professor of physics at McGill University. At the University of Toronto, the first doctorate degree in science was awarded. In industry, at Oshawa, Ontario, R. S. McLaughlin founded the automobile company which later became the nucleus of General Motors of Canada. And at Hamilton, the Steel Company of Canada established what was probably the first industrial research laboratory in the country.

World War I provided the opportunity for even more rapid growth and diversification of industrial capacity. The wartime demand for shells, for example, led to a significant increase in steel production. An aircraft industry began in Canada in 1917 and produced several thousand aircraft before the end of hostilities. Oil refineries increased their capacities significantly and catalytic cracking of crude oils was introduced for the first time. The manufacture of pharmaceuticals and fine chemicals reached substantial volumes after importation from Europe had been sharply reduced. Reductions in the availability of other manufactured goods stimulated the acquisition of many new Canadian technical skills.

Canada was affected no less than many other countries in the years of economic and political uncertainty between the world wars. Technological developments with implications for the economy did, however, continue. The aeroplane, for example, began to play a significant role in the exploration of remote natural resources and in the communications field. It was during this period that development began of the vast ore basin around Sudbury, in Northern Ontario; insulin was discovered at the University of Toronto and methods were developed for its extraction and purification. There were rapid developments in the pulp and paper, automobile, mineral and chemical industries.

World War II did more than the first to develop and diversify the Canadian economy and to broaden its technological base. Many of the changes were concerned with goods and services required for the war effort. Among the new products were synthetic rubber, nylon, magnesium and high octane fuels. Canadians also took part with French and British scientists in work in atomic and nuclear physics and, by so doing, were favourably placed to extend this work into the nuclear power field when the war was over.

In the postwar period, the processes of scientific and technical advance and change have continued. The product mix of the manufacturing industries has continued to broaden, although the primary staples and semi-processed and processed raw materials are still particularly important in export markets. A number of factors have influenced the patterns of expansion of particular industry groups during the period. These have included: increased demand for consumer goods resulting from a rising standard of living and rapid population growth; shifts in international trading patterns; certain pervasive technological innovations, such as the development of synthetic materials; the opening up of new mineral resources; the decline of certain existing mineral resources; and unique events such as the Korean War. Table 1[3] shows the percentage growth in annual aggregate production of each of the principal industrial groups in the 1946–1966 period:

| Industry | Percentage |
|---|---|
| Agriculture | 1.7 |
| Forestry, fishing, trapping | 1.8 |
| Mining | 8.9 |
| Manufacturing | 4.9 |
| Construction | 5.1 |
| Electric power and gas utilities | 9.6 |
| Transportation, storage and communications | 4.8 |
| Trade | 4.1 |
| Finance, insurance and real estate | 4.9 |
| Public administration and defence | 3.8 |
| Community, recreation, business and personal service | 3.7 |
| GROSS DOMESTIC PRODUCT (GDP) | 4.5 |

At the present time, the service industries together account for about 54 per cent. of the GDP and for about 56 per cent. of employment. The manufacturing industries account for 26 per cent. of the GDP and 25 per cent. of employment, agriculture and the other primary industries for about 11 per cent. of both the GDP and employment, and construction and utilities for the balance of 9 per cent. of GDP and 8 per cent. of employment. During the period from 1946 to 1966, the service and non-service industry groups maintained approximately the same percentage shares in the GDP. With regard to employment, however, the relative shares of the two groups were reversed between the beginning and the end of the period.

The following are a few additional statistics which will help 'set the scene' for Canada: early in 1969, the population may have passed the 21 million mark; the total labour force is now approximately 8 million; during the current academic year (1968–1969), the total enrolment in all university faculties has been in the neighbourhood of 300,000 undergraduate and 30,000 graduate students, and, of these, approximately 100,000 and 13,000 were undergraduate and graduate students in departments of natural science and engineering; in 1966, the most recent year for which firm estimates are available, aggregate expenditures on R and D activities were $770 million, and equivalent to 1.3 per cent. of the GNP; if recent rates of expansion in R and D expenditures have been maintained since 1966, the aggregate R and D figure for 1968 would be in the neighbourhood of $1 billion; the per capita GNP is approximately 75 per cent. of the corresponding level in the U.S.A.; the GNP for 1968 has been estimated at $67 billion, an increase of about 8 per cent. over 1967.

## Assessment of the Present

People in Canada, generally, have been enjoying one of the highest standards of living in the world since the end of World War II. Their geographical location next to the U.S.A., the natural resources of the country, and the fact that Canada has been able to attract investment and intellectual capital from abroad for a long period explain, in a large measure, why the standard is now at such a high level. On the other hand, Canada's rates of economic growth and productivity improvement have not been as high or as consistent as the corresponding rates in many of the other industrialized countries of the world. There are several other paradoxes that may be applied to Canada. For example, her aggregate expenditures on R and D activities, expressed as a percentage of the GNP, have been significantly below those of almost all other industrialized countries, yet Canadian processing and manufacturing industries have the high level of technical competence that may be expected in countries of this kind. Also, Canada has been able to attract many well-educated and highly skilled immigrants from abroad, but has lost some of the best-trained Canadian-born people to the U.S.A. and other countries.

The view has often been expressed that there are technological, managerial, and entrepreneurial 'gaps' existing between Canada and the U.S.A., and between Canada and the high-growth, high-productivity countries in the rest of the world. Economic, education, and R and D statistics have been cited in support of this view, as have the small domestic market, the predominance of the primary industry products in the export mix, and the extensive foreign ownership of Canadian production facilities in the resource and the technology-intensive manufacturing industries. A recent study by the Economic Council of Canada,[4] for example, has underscored the lag in productivity improvement in the postwar period between Canada and the countries of Northwest Europe, and has postulated that these countries may soon reach Canadian levels of output per worker, if they have not already done so.

The lag in productivity improvement between Canada and the U.S.A. has not been quite so marked. However, in both these countries, the relatively low-growth service industries account for about 60 per cent. of all employment. In several respects, Canada and the U.S.A. are also remarkably similar. For example, the tastes of Canadian and American consumers reflect, among other things, exposure to much of the same commercial advertising material. But there are many differences between the countries, some subtle, some much more obvious. Both countries have federal political structures, but the relationships between the federal and state or provincial governments are not the same. Canadians and Americans both play the same kind of football, but their rule books are not interchangeable. A Texan may spend as much in one year to air-condition his home as an Ontarian spends to heat his. Canadians, as people, are usually more relaxed than Americans. Canadians have tended to be the followers rather than the leaders.

The apparent proclivity of Canadian companies and of Canadians, generally, to avoid taking innovative initiatives has been discussed at some length in recent years by government and industry spokesmen and by individual commentators. One of these commentators, Dr. J. J. Brown,[5] has said that 'the story of Canadian invention and technology can be seen as a melancholy procession of golden opportunities which we have let slip through our fingers'. In his book, Brown has cited the variable-pitch propeller developed by W. R. Turnbull which was later manufactured by Curtiss-Wright in the U.S.A.; the electronic organ developed by Morse Robb; E. W. Leaver's original system for the automatic control of machine tools; and the more recent Heluva plotter, as examples of missed opportunities. Brown has, of course, acknowledged the importance for the Canadian economy of home-grown developments, such as bush aircraft and snow-moving equipment. Since the failures seem to have outnumbered the successes, and since this imbalance appears to be continuing, it has been all too easy for Brown and other commentators to dismiss Canada as an imitative rather than innovative country. Unfortunately, the problem of linking scientific discoveries with technological innovations and the marketplace in the context of the Canadian economic and social environment is most complex, and has not yet been adequately studied. While certain companies have made strenuous efforts in recent years to lessen Canadian dependence on the U.S.A. for innovative initiatives, perhaps the most serious problem is related to the lack of a coherent set of objectives for the Canadian economy and for Canadian scientific and technical activities.

The lack of study, or of objectives, has not discouraged the governments in Canada — both federal and provincial — from enacting measures and establishing programmes to encourage research, development and invention, to provide loan capital and to stimulate trade and regional development. Some of these measures and programmes — such as the National Research Council's Industrial Research Assistance Programme — have been fairly successful in achieving their objectives. Others have lacked flexibility, simplicity of administration or imagination. The lack of study and objectives has not discouraged the formulation of interim conclusions and prescriptions with regard to the state of innovation in Canada. For example, in its Fifth Review in 1968,[6] the Economic Council said that, if innovative activities are to be stimulated and encouraged, both public and private efforts must be directed to the full range of activities associated with innovation, and the capacity of business to understand and manage successfully the process must be strengthened. Both the Economic and Science Councils have said that there are gaps in the supply of new information on science, technology and innovation from abroad and from Canadian sources, and that Canada's indigenous scientific and technical efforts must be strengthened, particularly in industry.

In Canada, as in other industrialized countries, companies seem to prefer to give most of their support to research, development and inventive activities that can be performed under their own supervision, or under the supervision of companies with which they are closely associated. Relatively few companies support university research or award R and D contracts to a Research Association, a Research Council or another company. As a general rule, therefore, work on future product and process developments remains 'in-house' or 'in the family', and the reasons for this policy are not hard to find in the highly competitive business situation and in the desire of a growing number of companies to improve their 'know-how' bargaining positions. But, to an increasing extent, this general rule is being strengthened through the increasing awareness by companies that the technical competence related to processes, products and services has to reside 'in-house', regardless of whether or not it is available in affiliated companies, in the universities, government agencies or anywhere else.

In Canada, as in other countries, the innovative activities of companies and production units are strongly related to the markets they serve. Projects involving potential innovations are usually initiated on the basis of the best available information about these markets and about competitors' current and possible future activities in them. Market research and forecasting play at least as significant a part in a company's operations as do other kinds of research and forecasting. But in Canada, as opposed to most other countries, foreign ownership and control of production resources is often substantial. In some cases, the Canadian operation may represent only a small part of the total operations of an international corporation. It is not surprising, therefore, that the policies of these corporations can play the dominant role in the assignment of markets to their Canadian subsidiaries and can exert a strong influence on the inventive and innovative activities of these subsidiaries. Nevertheless, Canadian initiatives *can* be exercised within an international corporation, as recent innovations of Canadian origin in the aircraft, scientific instrument and communications industries have shown.

The majority of the foreign-controlled companies in Canada were established originally to provide supplies of basic resource materials, or as sales offices to cover the Canadian market. As the market grew, and in response to the Canadian tariff policy, the subsidiary began manufacturing on its own. Its products would often be similar in number, specification and design to those of the parent company, but would usually have a higher unit cost. Production processes might have to be scaled-down versions of the longer-run American or other foreign processes, but might require further development before they could be operated or before the Canadian raw materials could be incorporated. With time, domestic production and markets might expand further, but markets abroad might not. Nevertheless, the advantages that a subsidiary company might enjoy over a resident-owned one could be formidable: for example, access to the technical 'know-how' of its parent and other affiliated companies; access to trademarks and brand names; and access to venture capital, management talent and entrepreneurial initiative.

Several enquiries into the nature and implications of foreign ownership and control have been undertaken in recent years. The federal government, for example, set up a task force of economists under Professor M. H. Watkins to study foreign ownership in relation to the structure of Canadian industry. The following factual information has been taken from the report of this task force:[7]

Between 1945 and 1964, foreign direct investments in Canada rose from $2.7 billion, or about 40 per cent. of foreign long-term investments, to $15.9 billion, or about 60 per cent. of these investments, and $12.9 billion of the 1964 total came from the United States;

Foreign ownership and control of corporations located in Canada is concentrated in manufacturing (1963: ownership – 54 per cent., control 60 per cent.), petroleum and natural gas (1963: ownership – 64 per cent., control 74 per cent.), and mining and smelting

(1963: ownership – 62 per cent., control 59 per cent.);

Within the manufacturing sector, there are certain industries where foreign control is very high and, in all cases, ownership is predominantly by U.S. residents (for example: in 1963, foreigners controlled 97 per cent. of the capital employed in the manufacture of automobiles and parts, 97 per cent. in rubber, 78 per cent. in chemicals, and 77 per cent. in electrical apparatus);

Not only is foreign equity capital concentrated in certain industries, but it is also concentrated in large corporations;

Foreign ownership, however, is to be found across the broad spectrum of Canadian production, from highly efficient to highly inefficient industries, as measured by labour productivity relative to the United States;

There is evidence which suggests that foreign-owned firms do relatively more research in Canada than resident-owned firms, even when allowance is made for the tendency for foreign firms to be concentrated in research-oriented industries.

There can be no doubt that foreign-owned and foreign-controlled companies, whether they are part of North American or world-wide corporations, have stimulated economic growth and technological innovation in Canada. From the Canadian point of view, subsidiary companies have not always been good citizens, but the blame for their behaviour should not be placed on their shoulders entirely. In some ways the Canadian environment – including government policies, the size of the market, the nature of competition, the abundance of natural resources and other factors – has not always encouraged good behaviour or good economic performance. It has, for example, been relatively easy to import new skills rather than to train them at home, although in recent years the education systems in the country as a whole have been strengthened and managements have become more expert. It has also been relatively easy to look to the U.S.A. for risk capital, although in the government and in the private sector there has recently been a somewhat greater willingness to encourage Canadian initiatives and take commercial risks. Even so, many a small, science-based, resident-owned Canadian company has still to look over the border for help. And, with regard to the Canadian patent system, its effectiveness in the encouragement of 'native' inventions and subsequent innovations appears to have been considerably less than have the British and American systems on which the Canadian system was based.

In recent years, the governments in Canada have striven to encourage increased efficiency and specialization in production and increased competitiveness in domestic and foreign markets in both subsidiary and resident-owned companies. Steps have also been taken to redress some of the imbalances in the economic development of the various regions of the country. The majority of the provincial governments, for example, operate development loan funds to provide for the establishment of new industries or for the expansion of existing ones. In some cases, those programmes also provide for managerial, technical and other advisory services. At the federal level, the government has recently carried through the establishment of a Department of Consumer and Corporate Affairs and a Department of Regional Economic Expansion, and has merged the former Departments of Industry and Trade and Commerce. The effectiveness of the federal R and D incentive programmes also is under study. In the international sphere, the federal government has participated through the Kennedy Round Agreements in the general reduction of tariff levels. But many problems remain. In the domestic market, for example, there is the matter of federal-provincial jurisdiction, and the problem of assessing when there is too much, as well as too little, competition in a particular section of industry. In foreign markets there are problems relating to market access and involving non-tariff barriers, patent protection, tendering regulations, import restrictions and so on.

Up to the present time, Canadian companies of both resident and foreign ownership may have been extremely astute in their search for new and useful technical information with which to achieve their business goals. On a dollar-for-dollar basis, some of these companies may have performed more effective invention and innovation than the 'equivalent' companies in the U.S.A., in Europe, or even in Japan. So much is speculation, but it is clear that expensive innovative activities will not be performed in any company unless it has the need and the opportunity to perform them, and the resources to exploit them fully in the marketplace.

## Some Considerations for the Future

In its First Annual Review, the Economic Council noted that if Canada is to realize the high rate of growth needed for a very rapidly expanding labour force and is to achieve the betterment in productivity required for competitiveness and for continued improvement in standards of living, there will be all the more reason for calling upon the resources of science and technology. Canadians will continue to draw heavily on foreign sources for technology which, in many cases, will be the only source and, in others, will be the cheapest and quickest way to get the 'know-how'. However, this will not be enough. Canada will also need substantially to expand its own efforts in the use of Canadian resources, and will have to participate adequately in the fastest growing technologies and industries.

In its recently published policy report,[8] the Science Council attempted to lay down broad guidelines for the future use and development of science and technology in Canada. The Council identified a set of six goals which, while not comprehensive, appeared to contain the main aspirations of most Canadians. These goals were: national prosperity; physical and mental health and high life expectancy; a high and rising standard of education, readily available to all; personal freedom, justice and security for all in a united Canada; increasing availability of leisure and enhancement of the opportunities for personal development; and world peace, based on a fair distribution of the world's existing and potential wealth.

Of these six goals, the first deserves some further discussion in the context of the subject matter of this paper. Among the contributions that science and technology might make to the achievement of this goal, the Council identified the following: increased industrial productivity; innovation in selected manufacturing and specialized service industries that have inherent comparative advantages in a Canadian setting to improve their competitive position in international trade; improvement of the efficiencies of the service industries, particularly in distribution systems; reduction of costs of many basic elements such as energy, housing, transportation, communications; and the development and application of new technology, as a contribution to the reduction of regional disparities in productivity and income levels.

Canada is likely to remain a large exporter of food and raw and semi-processed materials. But part of the promise of the future will lie in the further development of the processing and refinement of these materials. Other parts will lie in the manufacture of technically sophisticated products and in the provision of more efficient services. And Canada still has a relatively unexplored frontier to the North. However, as in any resident-owned company or international corporation, Canadians will have to decide for themselves what business they wish to be in and explore its future potential before determining the appropriate places in which to expend their available resources.

## Summary

In the 400 years since the first European peoples began to explore and develop the vast continental land mass that is now Canada and the waters that surround it, technological advances, changes and innovations have played a number of special roles in support of Canadian economic activities. These special roles have been related to: human survival in the environments of Canada; the transportation of people and goods over difficult terrain and long distances; inter-personal communications over long distances; the discovery and exploitation of remote natural resources; and the provision of plentiful, but inexpensive, sources of electrical energy.

The past 60 years have seen the broadening and expansion of the Canadian economy. The influence of the U.S.A. has become generally stronger and more pervasive in Canada as a whole than the influence of either of the two founding countries. Canadians have become competent technically.

There have been problems, some associated with the growth of the economy and the requirements and opportunities for technological innovation, and others associated with the foreign ownership and control of resources and production facilities, with multiple jurisdictions, management, education and competitiveness in domestic and foreign markets.

As has been stated elsewhere,[9] discussions of the ways in which the effectiveness of future Canadian scientific, technical and innovative activities may be increased are predicated on the acceptance of two broad premises. The first is that the social and economic growth and development of Canada, and the prosperity and well-being of Canadians generally, will become increasingly dependent upon rising levels of scientific and technical competence and entrepreneurial ability. The second is that Canadian institutions and individuals will become increasingly skilled in the management and administration of their scientific, technical and innovative activities and in the conception and prosecution of forward-looking and anticipatory studies in these fields. But in the last analysis, future growth and well-being will be dependent upon the degrees of encouragement and support given to the most talented and creative Canadians.

### References

1. Economic Council of Canada (1964). *Economic Goals for Canada to 1970*, First Annual Review, Ottawa: Queen's Printer
2. Science Council of Canada (1967). *First Annual Report*, Ottawa: Queen's Printer
3. Canada Year Book (1968). *Trends in Economic Aggregates*, Dominion Bureau of Statistics, Ottawa: Queen's Printer
4. Walters, Dorothy (1968). *Canadian Income Levels and Growth: An International Perspective*, Staff Study No. 23, Economic Council of Canada, Ottawa: Queen's Printer
5. J. J. Brown, (1967). *Ideas in Exile*, Montreal: McClelland and Stewart
6. Economic Council of Canada (1968). *The Challenge of Growth and Change.* Fifth Annual Review, Ottawa: Queen's Printer
7. M. H. Watkins et al. (1968). *Foreign Ownership and the Structure of Canadian Industry*, Report of the Task Force on the Structure of Canadian Industry, Ottawa: Queen's Printer
8. Science Council of Canada (1968). *Towards a National Science Policy for Canada*, Report No. 4, Ottawa: Queen's Printer
9. Andrew H. Wilson, (1968). *Science, Technology and Innovation*, Special Study No. 8, Economic Council of Canada, Ottawa: Queen's Printer

Chapter 9

# Setting the Scene
# Seven: the Netherlands

*A. E. Pannenborg*

If we look at the Netherlands with the aim of detecting phenomena pertinent to the central theme of this Symposium, one major event ranges above all others: the rapid and unexpectedly successful evolution from a largely agricultural and trading nation to a largely industrial and trading nation during the first 15 years after the end of World War II. It is worthwhile listing a number of the initial conditions which probably had a beneficial influence on this process of transformation. Subsequently we will try to describe the contribution of R and D in this process. It will be understood that successful industrialization was instrumental in allowing the Netherlands to keep up with the growth of the economies of other Western nations.

Probably the most important single element supporting economic growth in the Netherlands is one provided by nature: the geographical location across the delta of the river Rhine (together with the Meuse and the Scheldt). The impact is best illustrated by the fact that for a few years now Rotterdam is the largest port in the world. Through this, and many other interactions, the Dutch economy is closely coupled to the German hinterland.

This location across the river delta on the North Sea coast has bred a deeply seated outward look in the national character. The consequences in education and in the attitude of the individual are manifold. In secondary education, English, French and German are compulsory subjects for all pupils, with a corresponding lack of emphasis on the native language as compared with neighbouring countries. Aided by a tradition over many centuries, in foreign trade, and by the fact that a large number of ancestors of the present generation sought their career in the Dutch East Indies, the Dutchman today is quite willing to go and live abroad. This, in turn, has a profound influence on the ease of decision for an industrial firm based in the Netherlands to expand abroad.

The same attitude can be found in government policy. Not only has this country a notable record of tolerance and acceptance towards the political refugee, but also an equally liberal frame of mind with regard to the foreign product. The Netherlands rely, as a matter of principle, on *international* competition to safeguard the population against unwanted monopolies and to keep industry in a healthy state. This explains the absence of legislation similar to a Monopolies Act or Anti-Trust Laws.

Another aspect of the national character conducive to growth of industry is the high degree of social stability. Few countries can boast a better record of absence of strikes during the postwar period. We can speculate about the underlying causes for this happy situation. The virtual disappearance of the nobility as a social class some few hundred years ago and an absence of landlordism are likely to be relevant in this context. Possibly even more fundamental is the never abating threat of the sea, the foe common to everybody. We can go back a thousand years and find legislation which subordinates the interests of the individual or the group to the overriding principle of safety for the community. We will come back to another important consequence of the relentless battle against the water.

At this point, it is important to note that organized labour has the form of industry unions as distinct from craft unions. This has led to the recognition that long term objectives of labour and management can only be reached under the same conditions, that is in a healthy, competitive industry. The unions accordingly have shown, generally, a clear sense of responsibility in the national context.

Turning now to competence in science and technology as an important input parameter for industrial activity, we can observe again that historical tradition is helpful in the Netherlands. Throughout the nineteenth century, in many respects a period of mental and economic stagnancy, the awareness of the 'Golden Age' (the seventeenth century) was kept alive. The prosperity and political power of the Dutch republic in the seventeenth century has a solid foundation on, for those days, a very advanced technology. The nation was leading then, for example, ship-construction, primary power (windmills), and civil (polders) and military engineering. This established at an early moment the professional engineer as a respected member of the community.

In parallel to the above, throughout the ages there have been Dutch mathematicians and scientists of world level, as shown, for example, by a number of Nobel prizes during the first quarter of this century. The respect for the scientific and technical profession on the one hand, and the mildness of social stratification on the other, assisted in bringing the talent hidden in the lower strata to the surface. Given the availability of talent it is, of course, important that the means to develop it are forthcoming. Here it was the need of the Ministry of Public Works, responsible for the eternal defence of the country against the sea, that led to the establishment of the polytechnical school towards the middle of last century, which developed later into the

Technical University of Delft.

As an illustration of the fact that a fruitful co-operation between science and technology has existed almost always, we point out that the great theoretical physicist, H. A. Lorentz, made important contributions in the preparatory study of the closing of the Zuiderzee during the first quarter of this century.

So much for the historical background. If we survey the present we observe a fairly large volume of industrial R and D, carried out in private industry and in some (semi-) government institutions, the largest of which is TNO.

The large company plays a prominent role in industry in the Netherlands, a situation which generally is conducive to R and D. This is combined with apparently a fairly open mind for the long-term benefits to be derived from industrial R and D on the part of top management. Another important aspect for the rapid postwar growth of industrial R and D is the fact that its usefulness was proven and generally recognized before World War II. This is illustrated also by the establishment of TNO by law as early as 1930. This organization was assisted unintentionally in its growth by the German occupation of the Netherlands, because many capable young scientists succeeded in avoiding co-operation in the German war effort by joining TNO temporarily, and stayed on after the war.

The absence of 'a mentality gap' between academic and industrial research is important for the proper distribution of the national talent between basic and applied research, between universities and industrial laboratories. Though the radicals among the present student generation denounce vehemently the supposedly large influence of big business on the academic world, the present situation can be described as complete autonomy of university science within a network of many personal relations, brought about not in the least by the former employment in industry of many science and technical professors.

The above indicates the plausible assumption that a sizeable effort in R and D has been a *sine qua non* for the impressive postwar expansion of industry in the Netherlands. I should like to point to another element which, in my opinion, has had at least as important an effect. It is generally conceded that the German 'Wirtschaftswunder' (economic miracle) was supported to a great extent by the massive influx of additional manpower which flowed each year out of the Russian occupation zone, until this was stopped effectively by the Berlin Wall. A similar effect took place in the Netherlands, although on a much more modest scale, in the form of the repatriation of a couple of hundred thousand people from Indonesia. This is illustrated on page 88. The first and larger stream took place in the first years after the War and adds to the birthrate peak in that period. The second and smaller stream came at the final rupture between the two countries in 1958.

MILLIONS

14
12
10
8

— NET INCREASE IN POPULATION OVER 12 MONTHS PRECEDING 1.1 OF THE YEAR MARKED

• • TOTAL POPULATION ON 1.1 OF THE YEAR MARKED

THOUSANDS

240
220
200
180
160
140
120
100
80

YEAR

1946 7 8 9 50 1 2 3 4 5 6 7 8 9 60 1 2 3 4 65

It is clear that a sizeable addition of adults to a population has a completely different, and furthermore short-term, effect than a peak in the birthrate.

A further influence of a similar demographic nature should also be considered. Due to the vagaries of war in the early seventeenth century, the southern part of the country with a Roman Catholic population was administered, by the protestant Dutch Republic, as occupied territory. The official emancipation of Roman Catholics was guaranteed in the constitution of 1815, but it took almost 150 years for this underdeveloped region to contribute in all walks of life in proportion to its population. This is shown, for instance, by the fact that only in recent years has the Roman Catholic share of first-year university students reached the national average. This implies that in the postwar period the Netherlands could make use of an appreciable hidden reservoir of untapped talent and energy.

Before summing up, it seems proper to pay some attention to the branches of industry prominent in the Dutch scene. We find oil and petrochemicals, fats and foodstuff, and electronics in firms which rank among the largest in the world; in somewhat smaller organizations, but still large, rayon, heavy chemicals, aircraft, mechanical engineering and shipbuilding. None of these branches is subject to the atomic competition of classical economic theory. The notion of oligopoly describes the competitive situation much better. This does not imply less severe competition than in the former case. Perhaps it is logical that the most of these branches are centered on products that require aggressive marketing and that are not hampered by chauvinistic emotions on the part of the buyer.

As regards industrial R and D in a country like mine that has been traditionally open to the competitor from abroad, it is finally the competitive situation that determines its intensity. This means that every firm is compelled to engage in R and D on a scale which is not too far off the average for corresponding industry branch, if it wants to remain independent in the long run. The aspect of R and D in which it differs from the many other measures to be taken by an industry in order to stay alive lies in the time scale; it needs more foresight by management.

The economic optimum of R and D expenditure in established branches of industry depends on the competitive situation. Individual firms adapt more or less closely to an average value. Between branches, however, very large differences in average R and D intensity can be observed. This leads to the conclusion that the optimum amount to be spent on R and D within one nation depends very strongly on the composition of industry of that nation.

In conclusion, I see the following elements as essential in the successful transformation of the Netherlands into an industrial nation: 1. social stability; 2. no timidity in entering foreign markets; 3. stimulating effect of foreign competition at home; 4. boost from repatriates from Indonesia; 5.

general recognition, already prior to World War II, of usefulness of industrial R and D; 6. availability of engineering and scientific talent; and 7. fairly sound educational facilities, with the proper level of interaction between society and industry.

**Chapter 10**

# Performance in Technological Innovation in the Industrially Advanced Countries

*Keith Pavitt*

The following paper reviews and speculates on some of the results of a study, undertaken by the Directorate for Scientific Affairs of the OECD, which attempts to compare ten industrially advanced countries' performance in technological innovation.[1] Given the nature of the audience to which the paper is addressed, and the necessary limitations placed on its length, the paper stresses empirical and policy considerations rather than theoretical and conceptual ones; and it comments on the degree to which the results of the study support, refute or reconcile the abundant, necessary, but sometimes conflicting, 'conventional wisdom' which surrounds this field of enquiry.

The author is indebted to his colleagues, Sergio Barrio, Menahen Carmi and John Ricklefs, all of whom were involved in the study, and all of whom have made very useful criticisms and contributions related to this paper. However, neither they nor the OECD necessarily subscribe to the views expressed herein, which are the sole responsibility of the author.

### International Comparisons

In an area evolving as rapidly as that of private and public policies towards science and technology, international comparisons of a quantitative and a qualitative nature are inevitable and (if properly made) useful. Quantitative comparisons between countries have been based mainly on research and development statistics, the density, accuracy and comparability of which have increased enormously over the past five years. Both at the national and the international levels, these comparisons have had a considerable and positive influence on policy formulation. But, as their authors have pointed out on several different occasions, they suffer from one inherent limitation: namely, they compare 'inputs' of scientific and technological resources and not 'outputs' of scientific and technological knowledge and its application.[2−5] It has been argued in some quarters that the relationship between 'inputs' and 'outputs' – in other words, the efficiency of the process of research and its application – varies considerably amongst countries, and that international comparisons between R and D inputs are therefore not very useful. It was partly in response to this criticism that the OECD was asked to try to compare industrially advanced countries' economic 'output' of research and development activities: in other words, their performance in technological innovation.

### Invention, Innovation and Diffusion

It is a useful oversimplification to divide the process of technological innovation into three parts:

(1) *Invention*, which occurs when the feasibility of a new product or production process is postulated or established.

(2) *Innovation*, which occurs when, for the first time, a firm sells a new or better product or uses a new or better production process, with resulting commercial success.

(3) *Diffusion*, which is the process – after innovation – whereby a new or better product or production process is produced or used by a wide number of firms; diffusion can take place within a country and from one country to another.

R and D activities are an important input to each of these parts of the process of innovation. Invention depends heavily, although sometimes indirectly on research activities in universities, government laboratories and the central research laboratories of large firms. Innovation nearly always requires industrial research – and particularly development – activities, which may nonetheless account for only 20 per cent. of the total costs of an innovation.[6] And the process of diffusion also entails industrial R and D activities related to the absorption and improvement of an innovation[7] or to its independent redevelopment. Little precise information exists on the deployment of advanced countries' R and D activities amongst these three stages of the innovation process. Statistics collected in Japan suggest that the main focus of Japanese industrial R and D is the absorption and improvement of innovations originated in other countries.[25] It would be useful to collect similar statistics for the U.S.A. and Western European countries.

Surveys undertaken in the U.K. and the U.S.A. do, however, show that a high proportion of industrial R and D activity is directed to new and better products rather than to new and better production processes.[8-10] The same pattern probably exists in other industrially advanced OECD countries, where no such surveys have yet been made. Thus, there is probably less than half a truth in the conventional economist's idea of a firm producing the same products and undertaking research and development in order to increase the productivity of its manpower and its equipment, and to economize on the use of bought-in materials.

Probably more important are firms' R and D activities aimed at making products with better performance/cost characteristics either before or not too long after their competitors: in other words, R and D activities aimed at product differentiation in conditions of imperfect competition. When, as is often the case, these new and better products are immediate goods which are bought and used in the production activities of other firms and industries, they contribute to productivity increase throughout the economy.[11] It is probably through this latter mechanism that R and D and technological innovation make their most important contribution to measured productivity increases.

### Measuring Performance in Innovation

Comparing the performance of the industrially advanced countries in technological innovation was not a simple task. There existed no coherent and universally accepted body of economic theory or of statistics which enabled a straightforward and uncontroversial measurement of technological innovation. Previous studies had attempted to measure the rate of innovation in specific firms, and to compare the rate of innovation and diffusion within specific industries and specific countries.[12-14] But this was the first attempt to compare performance in innovation and diffusion amongst the whole of the manufacturing industries of the advanced countries.

As such, the methods and results of the analysis can justifiably be criticized on both conceptual and statistical grounds. Suffice it to say here that the author is well aware of the limitations of the methods used, and that similar problems of direct and accurate measurement exist in many other branches of the applied social sciences, especially when one attempts to define and measure a social phenomenon for the first time.

Six independent statistical indicators were in fact used to measure the industrially advanced countries' performance in innovation: (1) the location of 110 significant innovations since World War II; (2) monetary receipts for patents, licences and technological know-how; (3) the origin of technology imported by Japan; (4) the number of patents taken out by each country in foreign countries; (5) export performance in research-intensive industries; (6) export performance in research-intensive product groups.

The main results of this analysis are summarized in Table 1 where, for each indicator, Column A shows the absolute performance of ten industrially advanced countries, and Column B ranks the countries' performance, after correcting for differences in the size of the countries concerned. There is a statistically highly significant degree of concordance amongst the countries' rankings in each of the indicators used. Since the statistics for these indicators

Table 1. Indicators of Ten Industrially Advanced Countries' Performance in Technological Innovation

| Indicators of performance in technological innovation / Country | (1) The location of 110 significant innovations since World War II | | (2) Monetary receipts for patents, licences and know-how (1963-4) | | (3) The origin of technology imported by Japan (1960-64) | | (4) The number of patents taken out in foreign countries (1963) | | (5) Export performance in research-intensive industries (1963-65) | | (6) Export performance in 50 research-intensive product groups (1963-65) | |
|---|---|---|---|---|---|---|---|---|---|---|---|---|
| | A. Absolute number of innovations | B. Ranking when corrected for country size | A. Absolute receipts from six major countries (in $ million) | B. Ranking when corrected for country size | A. Absolute number of technology import agreements (1960-64) | B. Ranking when corrected for country size | A. Absolute number of patents taken out in foreign countries (in thousands) | B. Ranking when corrected for country size | A. Share of 10 countries' exports in research-intensive industries (Percentage) | B. Ranking when corrected for country size | A. Share of 10 countries' exports in research-intensive industries (Percentage) | B. Ranking when corrected for country size |
| Belgium | 1 | 5 | 7.9 | 6 | 12 | 8 | 1.8 | 10 | 3.5 | 9 | 3.0 | 9 |
| Canada | 0 | 10 | 6.2 | 8 | 21 | 6 | 1.9 | 9 | 3.4 | 9 | 2.9 | 9 |
| France | 2 | 9 | 46.3 | 5 | 63 | 7 | 9.3 | 6 | 7.7 | 6 | 6.5 | 7 |
| Germany | 14 | 4 | 49.4 | 7 | 255 | 4 | 29.9 | 2 | 22.1 | 2 | 21.1 | 2 |
| Italy | 3 | 7 | 9.9 | 9 | 24 | 9 | 4.6 | 7 | 5.9 | 6 | 5.7 | 6 |
| Japan | 4 | 8 | 5.9 | 10 | n.a. | n.a. | 3.5 | 8 | 5.3 | 8 | 5.9 | 7 |
| Netherlands | 1 | 6 | 26.0 | 2 | 51 | 2 | 6.4 | 3 | 5.3 | 4 | 5.9 | 5 |
| Sweden | 4 | 2 | 7.1 | 4 | 33 | 3 | 3.8 | 3 | 2.8 | 5 | 4.0 | 3 |
| U.K. | 18 | 3 | 76.1 | 3 | 121 | 5 | 15.2 | 5 | 14.2 | 3 | 13.9 | 3 |
| U.S.A. | 74 | 1 | 348.7 | 1 | 1,218 | 1 | 56.3 | 1 | 30.0 | 1 | 31.1 | 1 |

*NOTES*

For indicators (1), (2) and (3), ranking in Column B was derived after dividing Column A by working population in manufacturing industry.

For indicators (4), (5) and (6), ranking in Column B was derived after dividing Column A by share of 10 countries' exports in all manufacturing industry.

For indicator (5), research-intensive industries are defined as aircraft, chemicals, drugs, instruments, and electrical and non-electrical machinery.

For indicator (6), 50 research-intensive product groups chosen at random from all manufacturing branches.

Source: *Relazione Generale sullo Stato della Ricerca Scientifica e Tecnologica in Italia*, 1968. Atti Parlamentari.

were selected independently, it can be claimed that the rankings give a fairly accurate picture of the industrially advanced countries' performance in innovation.

The indicators show that, in absolute terms, performance in technological innovation reflects the size of countries: the U.S.A., followed by France, Germany, Italy, Japan and the U.K., followed by Belgium, Canada, the Netherlands and Sweden. Indicators (2) and (3) suggest that the U.S.A. has been responsible for between 50 and 60 per cent. of all innovations in the ten countries concerned. In *per capita* terms this is higher than any other country. But it should be remembered that a similar percentage of economic wealth is also concentrated in the U.S.A. In other words, relative to other industrially advanced countries, U.S.A. productivity in producing innovations appears to be no higher than in producing, say, steel and motor cars.

A detailed breakdown of the 110 innovations comprising Indicator (1) of Table 1 shows that, in general, U.S.A. innovations have been particularly important in new product areas developed since World War II (e.g. computers, numerically controlled machine tools, semiconductors, titanium), whereas the other industrially advanced countries have been relatively stronger in longer existing product areas (e.g. consumer electronics, iron and steel, pharmaceutical products, bulk plastics).

There are also significant differences in performance in technological innovation amongst the other industrially advanced countries, once population differences are taken into account. Within Europe, Germany, the Netherlands, Sweden and the U.K. have had a stronger performance than Belgium, France and Italy. Both Japan and Canada belong to the latter group, while incomplete data suggest that Switzerland belongs to the former.

Although no attempt was made to compare the ten countries' performance in invention, examples were found to confirm the widely held view that, by comparison with the U.S.A., Western European countries have been relatively stronger in invention than in innovation. In computers, scientific instruments and the fabrication of titanium, European inventions have later become American innovations.

The results of this analysis are unlikely to cause any big surprises to those familiar with international developments in industrial technology. The measured weakness performance of Japan hides the fact that her innovative capability is increasing very rapidly. The overall performance of the U.K. is strong, once one recognises in any analysis that the U.K. has neither the size nor the resources of the U.S.A. A recent policy report by the U.K. Government recognises this fact explicitly for the first time.[15]

## Measuring Performance in Diffusion

It was not possible to make such a statistically detailed comparison of the industrially advanced countries' performance in the diffusion of innovations, mainly because of the insufficient number of empirical studies comparing the levels and the rates of diffusion of specific new technologies in different countries. However, it was possible to make rather broad comparisons of the levels and rates of diffusion of four important technologies: man-made fibres, plastics, computers and nuclear energy. The comparison suggests that the process of diffusion tends to begin earlier in the U.S.A., which reaches higher levels of diffusion well ahead of the other industrially advanced countries. At the later stages of the diffusion process, however, Western European countries and Japan tend to catch up with the U.S.A. level of diffusion, the rate of increase in diffusion in Japan being particularly rapid.

## Growth Implications of Present Patterns of Innovation and Diffusion

What have been the effects of the above patterns of innovation and diffusion on the industrially advanced countries' economic performance? The short answer is that the relative concentration of innovative activity in the U.S.A. has not had harmful effects on the economic growth of the other advanced countries, because innovations originating in the U.S.A. have been rapidly diffused in these other countries.

For a country of the size, the level of wealth and the policy objectives of the U.S.A., a high rate of innovation and early diffusion was necessary in order to satisfy emerging consumer demands, to increase the productivity of expensive manpower, to compete successfully in international markets against countries with lower manpower costs, and to meet the technologically stringent requirements of defence and space programmes.

Other industrially advanced countries which are smaller, and where the level is lower, did not have the resources to originate such a high proportion of the world's innovations, nor were they obliged to, since they could import innovations already developed in the U.S.A. and elsewhere. Their economic growth performance, and the satisfaction of new consumer demands, depended much more on the speed and effectiveness with which they imported and diffused other countries' innovations than on the number of innovations that they made themselves. The importation of U.S.A. innovations by the other industrially advanced countries, as reflected by U.S.A. receipts for patents, manufacturing licences and technological know-how, increased by a factor of more than three between 1957 and 1965; and over the same period the proportion of American originated innovations imported through inward direct investment by U.S.A. firms, rather than through licensing agreements, increased from 44 to 71 per cent. in the case of Western Europe, from 75 to 90 per cent. in the case of Canada, and from 15 to 25 per cent. in the case of Japan.[16]

In other words, U.S.A. innovations have been very effectively transferred to the other industrially advanced countries, and to Western Europe and Canada largely through direct investment by American-based multinational firms. This process, coupled with the relatively rapid rate of diffusion of innovations, has been one important factor in the strong growth performances of Japan and most Western Europe countries since World War II. Until Europe and Japan reach the same level of economic wealth as the U.S.A., it is through the same mechanisms that new technology will have its greatest impact on their economic growth performance. And the size of this impact should not be underestimated. A recent study which compared the growth performance of the U.S.A. and a number of European countries suggests that up to between 50 and 60 per cent. of the difference in productivity between the U.S.A. and Western Europe may be due to a 'lag in the application of knowledge',[17] an important element of which is the lag in the diffusion of innovations.

Unfortunately, this paper will say little more about the diffusion of innovations in the industrially advanced countries or about the factors which determine the effectiveness of the diffusion process. This is because there is insufficient empirical knowledge to justify any generalizations in an international context. One should mention, however, that E. Mansfield has made an extensive summary of U.S.A. studies on the process of diffusion in U.S.A. industry and agriculture,[18] and that a study is now being undertaken by G. F. Ray of the National Institute for Economic and Social Research, London, who, in collaboration with five other European institutes, is comparing the levels and rates of diffusion of ten innovations in Western European countries.*

Such studies are particularly necessary in order to put the U.K. growth performance in a proper perspective. As we have seen, the U.K. has a relatively strong performance in innovation. There is as yet no evidence that its performance in diffusion is uniformly weak, and it imports as many American-originated innovations as other industrially advanced countries of equivalent size. Yet this must be reconciled with a weak growth performance. C. Freeman has already set out some possible explanations, which range from weakness in following up the early stages of the innovation and diffusion process to factors quite unconnected with innovation and diffusion.[5]

## Why Have an Innovative Capability?

The remainder of this paper will concentrate instead on innovation rather than on diffusion, on its relevance to the industrially advanced economies, and on some of the factors which influence the effectiveness of the process of innovation. We have seen that a strong innovative capacity has been necessary

* Published since this paper was written: National Institute for Economic and Social Research, London, 1969.

for the U.S.A. for reasons of economic growth and trade performance, and also for political reasons. We have also seen that a strong innovative capacity has not been necessary for the economic growth of the other industrially advanced countries. But a number of other reasons can be advanced for having a strong innovative capacity in these other countries.

The first reason is political and industrial. In firms in the high technology industries, a strong innovative capacity is necessary for competition in international markets. Lack of it means bankruptcy or loss of control. Innovative capacity in these industries is therefore a very relevant subject to industrial managers, politicians and defence planners. However, what conclusions they reach will be based largely on political, personal and professional value judgements, and will thus not be dwelt upon here, except to say that no European country – and not even Europe as a whole – can be technologically autarchic, except at huge and intolerable economic cost.

The second reason is the contribution of an innovative capacity to a country's balance of payments. There is in fact little doubt that a strong innovative capability, particularly in the high technology industries, leads to a healthy balance of trade in these industries. However, some economists would argue that the resources devoted to a strong innovative capability would have a higher balance of payments return if deployed elsewhere. Furthermore, there has in fact been no correlation in the industrially advanced countries between a strong innovative capability and a strong balance of payments, largely because many factors other than a country's innovative capability have an important impact on its balance of payments.

Finally, the extent of the balance of payments advantage will depend on one important factor in addition to the strength of a country's innovative capability relative to its competitors: namely, the way in which innovating firms decide to exploit an innovation in foreign markets. Whether these firms decide to export, to license or to invest directly abroad; and when they invest directly abroad, where they decide to invest, what markets they decide to exploit from a given foreign investment, where finance is raised, what is done with the resulting profits, and where components, machinery and equipment are purchased – all these factors will influence the degree to which a strong innovative capability strengthens a country's balance of payments position. In spite of these reservations, however, the balance of payments argument for a strong innovative capability is probably a valid one, especially when the innovative capability already exists.

The third reason for a strong innovative capability in a number of industrially advanced countries appears obvious, but is so important that it needs to be stated. The greater the amount and the geographic spread of the production of innovations, the greater the use of inherent human abilities, and the greater the amount of new technology from which all countries can benefit.

The fourth reason is that a strong innovative capability is relevant to a healthy fundamental research effort in many areas. In the industrially advanced countries, the relationship between fundamental research and industrial innovation is, should be, or probably will be closer than is generally thought. It is no accident — and it is not irrelevant to recall it here — that the countries which in the past have had a strong performance in innovation have also been the countries where scientists have consistently won Nobel Prizes. If, as seems likely, a continued and strong performance in Nobel Prizes reflects a generally healthy fundamental research activity in a country,[19] then one must explain this relationship.

In modern economies the relationship is not simply one where fundamental scientists make discoveries which industrialists then exploit. It is also one where firms which have a strong performance in industrial innovation tend to grow and to be profitable, thereby creating demands for more knowledge, and for more qualified research workers, scientists and engineers, demands which can be satisfied only by strengthening fundamental research and educational activities in the sector concerned.

This relationship can be illustrated by developments related to computers over the past thirty years. In the 1940s and the early 1950s, France, Germany and the U.K. probably made as many important contributions to computer science and technology as did the U.S.A. But in the 1950s and 1960s it was in the U.S.A. that a large, commercially viable computer industry was created, which in turn further stimulated the development of U.S.A. computer science and education, with the result that, today, computer science in the U.S.A. is certainly much greater in volume and probably higher in quality than in Western Europe.[20]

All this is not to argue for an indiscriminate allocation of large amounts of resources to fundamental research, nor to suggest that the primary purpose of stimulating technological innovation should be winning Nobel Prizes. The important point is that the creation or the maintenance of a strong innovative performance will of necessity require and create a strong, and closely coupled, fundamental research activity within firms and within the universities. Without the existence of a strong innovative activity, and of strong coupling, related fundamental research activities are likely to be weaker.

There is a fifth reason which is often advanced to justify the need for an innovative capacity in a country: namely, that it is necessary in order to be able to assimilate successfully innovations imported from other countries. However, one doubt can be cast on this hypothesis. Most of the examples that are cited to uphold it assume a relationship between independent institutional entities: for example, between independent companies in the plastics industry,[14] or between Japanese firms and firms in other countries from whom they have bought licences. But once this assumption is relaxed, the need for an indigenous innovative capability may not be a real one. Canada, for example, has successfully assimilated foreign technology without a strong innovative capability, but through heavy direct investment by U.S.A. firms and with a highly educated labour force. In other words, the successful absorption of technology developed elsewhere does require an innovative capacity if the absorbing institution is independent, but not necessarily if it is not independent.

### Some Characteristics of Countries with Strong Innovative Capacities

So much, then, for the reasons for having a strong innovative performance in a wide number of industrially advanced countries. Some of these reasons are political, some industrial, some economic and some scientific and cultural. But one lesson is clear from the experience of European countries since World War II. A strong innovative performance will continue if, and only if, the innovations are those as defined earlier in this paper: namely, commercially successful ones. The remainder of this paper will speculate on some of the conditions necessary in a country for commercially viable innovative activities. This will be done by confronting the measured performance of the industrially advanced countries as presented in Table 1 with some of the other characteristics of the countries concerned, and which are often advanced as being important for successful performance in technological innovation: namely, level and pattern of R and D expenditures, number of large firms, level of income per head, size of national markets and level of defence and space activities.

The results of this analysis suggest that by far the most important characteristics for strong innovative performance in a country are a strong R and D activity concentrated in industrial firms, and the existence of a good number of large firms. The importance of R and D activities will hearten those who have persisted in believing that international comparisons of R and D activities do mean something. The results also confirm at the level of a country what has already been proven by studies at the level of individual firms: namely, that there is a close relationship between inputs of R and D resources and outputs of innovation.[21] In addition, the fact that R and D financed and undertaken by industrial firms reflects innovative performance more than total R and D activities tends to support those who advocate some redeployment of R and D resources out of government laboratories into industry.

The importance of the existence of large firms to a country's performance in technological innovation may lend support to the present policy of the Ministry of Technology and to the activities of the Industrial Re-organization Corporation. On the other hand, it can be legitimately argued that big firms should become big because they are commercially and managerially success-ful, and not because of government intervention. In any event, the contribution of large firms appears to be in contradiction to the numerous and recent examples, cited in one U.S.A. report, of specific innovations, and even whole industries, where the most important innovations came from small firms and individuals rather than large firms.[6] This contradiction is apparent rather than real. The importance of large firms in industrial innovation certainly does tend to confirm the conclusion of another U.S.A. report that one of the most important elements in the American innovative capability is the large, multi-disciplinary research laboratories of industrial firms which are capable of turning their attention to and solving a wide range of technological problems.[22] But the observed importance of small firms and individuals in the innovation process, together with the results of thorough empirical enquiries by E. D. Roberts into the origins of small science-based firms in the Boston area,[23] suggests another important function fulfilled by large firms: namely, to create a capability embodied in scientists and engineers who go out to start up their own firms in order to apply and exploit commercially the technological − and sometimes the market − knowledge that they have acquired in large firms.

If one accepts that this is the case, then policy makers and students of science policy should be asking themselves two sets of questions. First, why do large firms not apparently succeed in exploiting effectively all the capabilities of their scientists and engineers? Is it because they are badly managed? Is it because large firms do not have the financial or managerial resources to exploit all worthwhile innovative opportunities open to them? Or is it because of the extreme difficulty of predicting the future technological and market potential of any new piece of knowledge? If this last cause does happen to be the most important one, then some of the more novel and ambitious concepts of R and D forecasting and planning may well need to be revised, and public policy makers will need to create a flexible environment which ensures the widest possible number of avenues for technological knowledge to be exploited commercially.

Second, European policy makers must ask themselves why small science-based firms have not developed as rapidly in Europe as the the U.S.A. It seems clear from the above analysis, although some have advocated otherwise in the past, that since World War II small technologically intensive firms must *follow* the existence of technologically strong, large firms. In this context, is the real problem in Europe one of lack of risk capital? Or is it the lack of a strong technological capability within large firms? Or written and unwritten rules and traditions which discourage scientists and engineers from starting their own firms? Or lack of a market for the products that science-based entrepreneurs would normally produce? Here one can only ask these questions, but they certainly deserve an answer.

Surprisingly enough, none of the other three factors (i.e. the size of national markets, the level of income per head and the level of defence and space programmes) appears to have had the same close relationship with *over-all* innovative performance as the existence of large firms and of strong company financed R and D. Indeed, when the U.S.A. is excluded, there is no discernible relationship between countries' size of national market and defence R and D and procurement on the one hand, and innovative performance on the other. However, although this may be true for *over-all* innovative performance, studies of innovation in certain specific industrial sectors have shown a positive relationship between innovative performance, government procurement and the size of national markets, in cases where governments have been important customers for the products concerned and have applied 'buy national' policies, and where the technologies involved have been relatively expensive.

This pattern suggests that, in many cases, large firms with strong innovative performances can overcome tariff and non-tariff barriers, and penetrate foreign markets, thereby avoiding any difficulties caused by the restricted scale of national markets. It also suggests that large firms have the greatest difficulty in doing this when the international market consists of a number of governments, each practising 'buy national' policies. Finally, and perhaps most important, it suggests that such a government policy may be effective in the U.S.A., where the market and innovative resources are large enough to allow simultaneously the advantages of scale and competition, but it is not a policy that works in individual European countries where neither markets not resources are big enough.

For European industrialists this probably means that, in many technological and product areas, plans for commercializing innovations on a European or a world scale need not necessarily wait for the completion of a fully integrated European customs union (a fact that some U.S.A. firms discovered years ago). It also means that, even with the existence of a European customs union, European firms with sufficient size and innovative capability can penetrate other markets, and – like Rolls Royce – the U.S.A. market. Finally, it means that Western European governments must consider how to modify their practices for the procurement of technologically sophisticated products, so as to reap fully the benefits of sufficient scale and competition, in such areas as aircraft, computers, power generating, and telecommunications equipment.

Finally, there is the contribution to differences in countries' innovative performances of differences in management. Studies of specific industries undertaken at the OECD and elsewhere suggest that U.S.A. managers keep 'lead times' between invention and innovation shorter than their European counterparts, and that they succeed better in coupling technological, production and market factors, both in choosing R and D projects and in getting results applied.[14, 20] In addition, research programmes and literature on the management of research and innovation are much more abundant in the U.S.A. than in other industrially advanced countries. However, none of this is new, and little more can be said here about inter-country differences in the management of innovation, except that it is a very important but sadly neglected subject in Europe, where a great deal more analysis and fact-finding needs to be done.

Related to the question of management is the influence on performance in technological innovation of the nature and the level of population of the labour force. Statistical comparisons between countries' educational and innovative performance must be approached cautiously, given a certain lack of international comparability of occupational data collected in census surveys, and of equivalent educational qualifications.[24] Nonetheless, the data do tend to confirm that by comparison with Western Europe and Japan, the U.S.A. has more university graduates in general and more science graduates in particular. It also has more engineering graduates, if those with post-secondary, non-university qualifications are excluded, but fewer if they are included. And the U.S.A. has a large number of managers with university qualifications as a percentage of the total labour force.

### Some Concluding Remarks: Areas for the Study

It is hoped that the contents of this paper have shown the usefulness of trying to compare the industrially advanced countries' performance in technological innovation. The actual results of the comparison will probably not cause many surprises, although both students and practitioners of technological innovation will criticize the validity of the statistical indicators used. The contention that the most important components of a country's innovative capability are its industry financed R and D and its large industrial firms – or, in other words, the capability for international, oligopolistic competition through research and product differentiation – will certainly provoke argument. And even those who agree can justifiably argue that this paper gives little indication as to what scientists, managers and government policy makers should do to create these essential conditions for success.

In fact, the most important conclusion of this paper is that, particularly for Europe and Japan, we still do not have enough detailed and systematic information and analysis of the processes of technological innovation, and of the factors that affect the efficiency of these processes, to be able to formulate sound policies. There follows, therefore, a list of studies that would be particularly timely and relevant, and many of which would benefit from being undertaken on an international, comparative basis.

1. The inter-institutional mobility of scientists and engineers, and the factors affecting the creation and success of small science-based firms: important work has been undertaken in the U.S.A. on this subject, but very little in Europe and Japan. This paper has already asked some of the questions that need to be answered.

2. The role of R and D in government laboratories, and the utility and feasibility of redeploying such R and D resources into industry: this is a problem of particular relevance to Canada, France and the U.K.

3. Economic, organizational and behavioural aspects of the management of R and D and technological innovation in industrial firms: in particular, the management problems facing European and Japanese firms in what will increasingly and inevitably be an international framework.

4. The relationship between research, innovation and the strategy of the firm: important work has been done in the U.S.A. showing a firm's objectives, its technological capabilities and its environment can be and have been effectively linked together [26] Similar work needs to be undertaken in Europe and Japan, where the natures of firms' technological capabilities and environments are very different.[27]

5. Statistics on the *objectives* of R and D in different industries and in different countries: for example, the relative balance between products and processes; between minor improvements, major improvements and breakthroughs; between 'offensive' strategies, 'defensive' strategies, and 'absorptive' strategies; between consumer, industrial and government products; and between invention, innovation and diffusion.

6. The problems related to international technological co-operation: particularly in Europe, technological co-operation involving governments will sometimes be necessary in order to overcome the limited size of national resources and national markets. Yet European technological co-operation has not, to say the least, been conspicuous through its success. It is a sad reflection on attitudes and institutions in Europe that relatively little objective and detailed analysis has been made of the reasons for past difficulties, and the conditions for future success.[28]

7. Continuing studies of innovation and its diffusion on an industry, national and international basis.

Finally, a word on the purpose of research and technological innovation in the industrially advanced countries. One important purpose always has been international competition in military weaponry. More recently we have seen the emergence of large-scale research and innovative projects related to international competition in national prestige. And some have lamented, others rejoiced, that the award of Nobel Prizes has also become a factor in national prestige. Now the analysis in this paper suggests that economically oriented R and D is increasingly related to competition in international markets, and that success in this objective is intimately related to a healthy effort in fundamental research.

In other words, there appears to be precious little R and D in the industrially advanced countries, other perhaps than in medicine and agriculture and in certain sectors of fundamental research, that is not stimulated or conditioned by international competition of one sort or another. Certainly, within this system, scientists can, and will, continue to pursue knowledge 'for its own sake', and international interdependence and competition will ensure a rapid adoption and diffusion of innovations and increasing material well-being – at least in the industrially advanced countries, although not necessarily in the less developed ones.[29] But it is relevant to ask if this system is entirely a satisfactory one. Could not science be made to contribute more effectively to other objectives through other stimuli? It is also relevant to ask the historians of science whether this close coupling between science, innovation and international competition is a new phenomenon, or whether it has been with us for a long time.

## Summary

Most international comparisons of scientific and technological resources have been in terms of 'inputs' of resources to scientific research and development. A recent OECD study attempted to make an international comparison of one part of the 'output' of R and D activities: namely, technological innovation and its diffusion amongst ten industrially advanced Western countries. It found that the U.S.A. has the strongest performance in innovation, both in absolute terms and relative to total population. In Western Europe, the relative performances in innovation of Germany, the Netherlands, Sweden, Switzerland and the U.K. have been stronger than those of Belgium, France and Italy. It also found that innovations are diffused earlier in the U.S.A., but that – in the later stages of the diffusion process – Western European countries and Japan tend to catch up with the U.S.A. level of diffusion. (No evidence was found of U.K. weakness in innovation and diffusion by comparison with other countries of equivalent size.)

The relative concentration of innovative activity in the U.S.A. has not had any harmful effects on the economic growth performance of the other industrially advanced countries, because innovations originating in the U.S.A. have been diffused rapidly and effectively in other countries, increasingly through direct foreign investment by U.S.A. based multi-national firms. The reasons for having a strong innovative capacity in Western Europe and Japan have little to do with requirements for economic growth. They have to do with industrial, political, balance of payments and scientific factors.

The most important factors related to a strong innovative performance in a country appear to be the existence of strong R and D activities financed by industrial firms, coupled with the existence of large firms. The size of national markets appears to be an important factor mainly when technology is expensive and governments are the main market.

Further studies and analysis are necessary for sound government and industrial policies in Europe. Also, historians of science and technology should be asked if international competition has always been such an important determinant of national R and D activities.

### References

1. 'Member Countries' Performance in Technological Innovation', *Gaps in Technology Between Member Countries: Analytical Report*, Vol. III. To be published by the OECD, Paris.
2. *Proposed Standard Practice for Surveys of Research and Development*, OECD, Paris, 1962
3. C. Freeman and A. Young, *The Research and Development Effort in Western Europe, North America and the Soviet Union*, OECD, Paris, 1965
4. *The Overall Level and Structure of R and D Efforts in O.E.C.D. Member Countries*, OECD, Paris, 1967
5. C. Freeman, 'Research Comparisons', *Science*, 27th October, pp. 463-468, 1967
6. *Technological Innovation: Its Environment and Management*, U.S. Department of Commerce, 1967
7. For a demonstration of the economic importance of industrial R and D activities related to the improvement of an innovation, see: J. Enos, 'Invention and Innovation in the Refining Industry', *'The Rate and Direction of Inventive Activity'* Princeton University Press, 1967
8. *Surveys of Business Plans for Research and Development Expenditure*, McGraw-Hill, New York
9. *Industrial Research in Manufacturing Industry, 1959-60*, Federation of British Industries, 1961
10. S. Myers, *Technology Transfer and Industrial Innovation*, National Planning Association, 1967
11. A. D. Little, *Patterns and Problems of Technical Innovation in American Industry*, Report to the National Science Foundation, U.S. Department of Commerce, 1963
12. W. F. Mueller, 'The Origins of Basic Inventions Underlying Du Pont's Major Product and Process Innovations, 1920-1960', *The Rate and Direction of Inventive Activity, op. cit.*, 1962
13. E. Mansfield, *Industrial Research and Technological Innovation*, Norton, 1968
14. C. Freeman, 'Studies of Innovation in the Plastics, Electronics Capital Goods, and Chemical Plant Industries', published in the *National Institute Economic Review*
15. *Technological Innovation in Britain*, Report of the Central Advisory Council for Science and Technology, H.M.S.O., 1968
16. 'Scientific and Technological Capabilities and International Flows of Goods, Technology and Capital', *Gaps in Technology Between Member Countries: Analytical Report*, Vol. IV, op. cit.
17. E. Dennison and J. Poullier, *Why Growth Rates Differ*, The Brookings Institute, 1967
18. E. Mansfield, 'Technological Change: Measurement, Determinants and Diffusion', *Report of the National Commision on Technology, Automation, and Economic Progress*, Appendix II, Washington, 1966
19. J. Ben-David, *Fundamental Research and the Universities*, OECD, Paris, 1967

20. *Technological Gaps Between Member Countries: Electronic Computers,* To be published by the OECD later in 1969

21. E. Mansfield, (1964). 'Industrial Research and Development Expenditures', *J. Political Economy*

22. *Applied Science and Technological Progress,* A report to the Committee on Science and Astronautics, U.S. House of Representatives, by the National Academy of Sciences, 1968

23. E. D. Roberts, 'Entrepreneurship and Technology', to be published in W. H. Gruber and D. G. Marquis (Eds.), *The Human Factor in the Transfer of Technology'* M.I.T. Press

24. 'Member Countries' Educational Capabilities', *Technological Gaps Between Member Countries: Analytical Report,* Vol. I, *op. cit.*

25. 'Japanese Businesses Show Proficiency in Using Foreign Technology', *The Japan Economic Journal* (10th October, 1967); A Baba, *National Policy of Research and Development,* Council for Industry Planning, Tokyo

26. H. L. Ansoff, *Corporate Strategy,* Penguin, London, 1968

27. For some preliminary ideas, see article by the author in *Long Range Planning,* September, 1969

28. It is also worth noting that *critical* study on the problems of European technological co-operation is being undertaken *outside* official organizations (e.g. by Christopher Layton; by Jean Monnet's Action Committee)

29. C. Cooper, 'Science and Underdeveloped Countries', *Problems of Science Policy,* OECD, Paris, 1968

## Discussion

The discussion concentrated on questions of stock and flows of techno-logical resources. Lord Bowden suggested that outstanding economic growth in some countries owed a good deal to the manpower resources which they had attracted from the rest of the world. Countries were not wholly independent of each other and some had drained and used the assets of others, perhaps unknowingly, to the detriment of the country from which they came. Were the growth rates of the U.S.A. and Canada correlated with their intake of skilled manpower from Europe? Such an effect was dramatically apparent in West Germany whose growth, until the building of the Berlin Wall, was associated with its ability to draw on almost the entire output of the universities of East Germany.

Professor Burke, himself a subject of the brain drain syndrome on three occasions, thought it was wrong to regard the international movement of skilled manpower as 'exploiting other countries' assets'. The movement was voluntary, and as often caused by adverse conditions in the country left behind (which were known) as due to attractions of the new country (which were, to the individual, highly uncertain). Professor Burn pointed out that if workers moved it was from places where they were not being effectively used to places where they would be. In this sense, aggregate productivity was increased by the transfer. But, he went on, this transfer of resources could not alone explain the North American advance. The origins of this far pre-dated the migrations of which Lord Bowden was speaking.

Dr. Gellman drew attention to the fact that the U.K. had lost managerial as well as technical people. He suggested that tax policies within a country played a great part in stimulating or restricting entrepreneurship, hence affected the flow of these types. Dr. Knoppers, himself a participant in the flow, agreed that its social and economic origins were very complex. He had been attracted by the attitudes to innovation and research which he found in the U.S.A.

Mr. Maddock drew attention to Mr. Shanks' paper which had found deficiencies in the administration and control of government science. These criticisms, in his view, were not entirely accurate. He explained some of the ways in which the Ministry of Technology was already streamlining and controlling the government research effort. He listed the Programmes Analysis Unit, the critical examination of aircraft projects, the cutback in nuclear investment and the change within the industry to a more commercial structure, together with several other examples of the ways in which central research spending was being controlled. Nor was government expenditure excessively concentrated. The OECD had reported that the proportion of government research money spent in industry in the U.K. was the same as that in America, and both were higher than in any other country.

The discussion then turned to the relationship between natural resources and innovation. Mr. Wolff raised the question of the position of economic strength which countries with large natural resources would be able to exert in the future, as the present predominant position of the highly developed countries with few natural resources became eroded, that is as technological differentials were evened out. Mr. Pavitt offered an historical interpretation of the present situation. Most of the concern about relative national technological strengths came from countries such as England, France and Germany — those which used to be able to do everything and now no longer could. In contrast Sweden, the Netherlands and Switzerland, for example, had realised 50 years ago that a complete technological coverage was impossible and so had concentrated their resources effectively in specific areas and specific world markets. The intermediate size countries could learn much from the historical example of these small nations. Professor Burke added that two of the recent best performers (Japan and Denmark), as well as Germany in the last century, could be said to have been propelled to their high level of performance by their meagre resources. History would not tell, of course, if such motivations would prove effective in the future, but Israel seemed quite ready to gamble on it.

Mr. Bodington returned to the problem of skilled manpower, by pointing out that resources were today becoming more and more a question of people. If you lost people, you lost resources. Therefore, we should devote more effort to identifying future 'key people', training and developing them, and finding the most effective use for their talents. Dr. Woodroofe accepted the paramount importance of manpower as a resource. One reason for the shortage during periods of strong economic expansion in the U.K. was, he suggested, because, unlike Italy and some other European countries, we did not have a large pool of labour which could be drawn from an inefficient agricultural industry in times of industrial expansion. Hence we were faced with the requirement to implement techniques of mechanization far more productively. We were failing to concentrate adequately on patterns of utilization of labour.

# Political, Social and Economic Aspects

# Chapter 11

# The Role of Government

*J. C. Duckworth*

## Introduction

We may conveniently discuss the role of Government in encouraging technological innovation and the growth of the national economy under two heads — firstly, direct intervention in selected fields, and secondly, the creation of a sympathetic environment by fiscal or other means. Some activities, of course, may have effects in both areas, but the two aspects will be discussed separately and then some general remarks made comparing their relative effectiveness. It is clear, however, that innovation and growth, as well as our present standard of living, are dependent on factors which have been operating over many decades. The starting points, and the opportunities for Government action, therefore vary from country to country and I do not believe that growth rates over recent years should be over-dramatized. In particular, other social considerations are extremely important, but are not the subject of this paper.

## Direct Intervention

Historically, Government has taken direct action to encourage innovation in those areas where it has assumed an executive function. For many hundreds of years this was almost entirely in the defence field. Even here, the initiative until recently largely was left to private industry — Government exerting its influence by its purchasing policy (often very reluctantly as, for instance, in the case of the Parsons steam turbine!). In the last half-century or so, however, the cost and risk of developing weapons or weapon systems has increased so that Government in the main has to fund not only the purchase and the development of the weapon, but also much of the advanced applied research on which new systems depend increasingly. In recent years, Governments have extended their executive functions beyond the military field to different extents. Almost universally, however, education has been recognized as a proper field for direct Government intervention, originally for social reasons, but now because it is realised that a properly educated and trained population is a country's main national asset.

We will be discussing the educational system later, but it is so important a part of Government's role that I cannot entirely ignore it here. In terms of economic benefit, it does not appear that in this country we have the right balance of expenditure to suit present needs, either within the educational system itself or in its total relationship to use of scarce manpower resources within the nation as a whole. As regards the first point, a modern industrial society requires a high level of general education, whereas traditionally we have concentrated on a system which gives the very best to relatively few. In other industrialized countries it is noticeable how many graduates are working on the 'shop floor', and this, in my view, is an important factor in breaking down the 'two opposing sides of industry' attitude, which is at the root of many of our problems. As regards the second, economic and social factors in the past have led to a situation in which far too small a proportion of the best university and schools output has gone into industry. Government plays a major part in deciding the balance in these factors, and since the health of the economy depends ultimately on the availability and training of the right intake for industry and commerce, the role of Government is a vital one.

Outside the defence and educational fields, the direct intervention of Government in this country has grown rapidly since the last war. Government responsibility for development in civil aircraft and atomic energy arose from defence activities; in addition, Government has largely assumed responsibility for the rate of innovation in other wide areas by nationalization of various key industries and by expansion of its social services. There is no real evidence that publicly controlled bodies have shown greater ability to innovate than private industry, and indeed the difficulties inherent in relationships between monopoly purchasers and their suppliers, and the inertia of large organizations exposed to conflicting policies rather than normal commercial pressures, have on the whole had the opposite effect. Moreover, concentration of immense development resources on particular industries, such as aircraft and atomic energy, without an adequate return on these resources, especially in respect of exports, has had the effect of encouraging and magnifying the unbalance of the educational system by reducing the flow of high grade personnel into potentially more profitable activities. However good management may be down the line, Government has not shown itself able to demonstrate the flexibility necessary at top management level to meet changing situations. Before taking control of the commanding heights of the economy, it is as well to find out first how to manage them efficiently!

Another area in which the Government has a vital role to play in encouraging innovation and growth is by the easing of problems of job transferability from older to more productive industries, e.g. by adult retraining programmes, assistance to mobility, and generally by reducing the temporary personal disadvantages sometimes involved in improving the national welfare. Much of the necessary action may be indirect rather than direct, i.e. by legislation, but retraining schemes particularly require direct action by Government and much is already being done in this country in this field.

A further line of activity, less direct but still involving Government expenditure, was started after World War I by the creation of the Department of Scientific and Industrial Research, in recognition of the fact that Government had an interest and responsibility in furthering innovation in civil industry. As we have heard, after the last war, the NRDC was created to exploit inventions arising from universities, research councils and Government establishments and to provide finance for development. Later still, the Ministry of Technology was formed with wide responsibilities for the encouragement of technological innovation, followed by the creation of the Industrial Reorganisation Corporation to encourage the reconstructing of industry to achieve greater efficiency.

### Indirect Action

The use of incentives by Government to encourage innovation and economic growth is of long standing, though the deliberate use of fiscal means for this purpose is perhaps of more recent origin. An early example of Government incentives of this kind was the establishment of the patent system in the U.K. in the time of the first Queen Elizabeth, under which the crown granted monopolies to encourage manufacture of new products within the realm. The patent system, modified and extended, remains one of the main means by which Governments encourage innovation and economic growth. Indeed, usage of the system is now so overloaded that serious efforts are at last being made to develop it as an international system rather than a number of national ones.

The panoply of investment grants, taxation incentives and regional schemes employed by most Governments is of relatively recent origin — at least on a large scale. For the first time deliberate attempts are being made by many countries to devise fiscal systems which will encourage innovation and economic growth. A study of these systems would be too complex and lengthy a matter for this paper and this conference, but it does appear that the present U.K. fiscal system has a counter-productive effect in this respect. So far as my own organization, NRDC, is concerned, far more effort than seems reasonable is devoted to the effects of taxation on the prospects of potential projects, and to means of minimizing tax liabilities. It has been pointed out also that individual inventors are discouraged by our taxation system from developing their ideas in this country. In general, the U.K.

taxation system appears to be designed to an excessive extent to stop-up loopholes and to 'be fair' rather than to encourage the creation of wealth. Clearly, changes in the taxation system will not alter attitudes and so create wealth overnight, but in my view the necessary change in the environment, starting from the education system onwards, can only take place in an atmosphere where the creation of wealth is given a higher status in our society, and for this I believe radical changes in the taxation system are a prerequisite.

Action by Government in the military sphere has already been discussed briefly under the previous heading – Direct Intervention. However, military and para-military expenditure can have indirect influence by the much-discussed effect of fall-out or spin-off. It seems certain that early accounts of the benefits of spin-off were optimistic, but it is true that projects of this kind often involve development of the most advanced technology and that the industries involved can benefit – not only from overseas sales of military products, but also from developments which can later be applied to the civil market. As a means of stimulating the civil economy, military or para-military spending is undoubtedly inefficient, but if it is on a large enough scale it can still have major consequences, as can be seen by the domination of some markets by U.S.A. firms. Moreover, though it is inefficient, it is usually publicly acceptable, whereas the much smaller expenditure required to achieve the same result by more direct means would probably not be so. Indeed, the search for efficient and publicly acceptable means of achieving the same objective, without huge military expenditure, is one of the major problems of Government today. A satisfactory mechanism has to be found, and then a satisfactory means of managing that mechanism.

## Discussion

Governments of all the industrially developed countries appear to have reached the conclusion that both direct and indirect means, as described above, of Government assistance are necessary to encourage innovation and industrial growth. Even if all reasonable fiscal means – incentive grants, taxation allowances, regional grants – are in operation, some projects are too large or too long-term to be undertaken by private sources of finance. There appears to be no difference in principle between Governments in this respect, though there are wide differences in emphasis and in means of implementation.

In this country there is little doubt that in the post-war years too much emphasis was placed on 'science', and more latterly 'technology', without a full appreciation of the financial and other resources needed for engineering design, production and marketing of products and processes. Unfortunately, this trend coincided with the national philosophy which had grown up, in the years when we could afford it, of the superior status of cultural, rather than productive, activities. Efforts to change the educational system to give a better balance are under way, but in the meantime it is hardly surprising that the slogan has emerged that we are good at inventing but no good at exploiting the results of our inventiveness. Though I believe this to have been much exaggerated, it would be somewhat surprising if it were not to some extent true, since such a small proportion of the better brains have gone into industry over the last century or so. Our real need is for a large proportion of our best people to have a general training, including science and engineering, and then to become business entrepreneurs — and one of the most important objectives of Government should be to encourage this trend, to dispose its resources accordingly and to create the best possible environment in which such enterprise can flourish.

The most immediate problem of the U.K. Government in this area is to use to maximum effect the resources of the Government R and D laboratories. Some of these were created to meet defence requirements, some were set up as part of the old Department of Scientific and Industrial Research, either as general industrial laboratories or to carry out research into particular areas where Government had a 'user' interest, as for example in fire prevention and control. In the war years the defence laboratories, and in the post-war years the Atomic Energy laboratories, attracted a disproportionately large number of top-class science and engineering graduates, who have subsequently been shielded from market pressures. It is generally agreed that the Telecommunications Research Establishment — now the Radar Research Establishment at Malvern — was one of the most successful war-time establishments, and in my view this was not primarily because it comprised able scientists but because it was always fully aware of the 'market needs' of the time. This was an achievement of the war-time Superintendent, Mr. A. P. Rowe, which I do not believe has been fully recognized. His initiation of 'Sunday Soviets', at which senior service personnel discussed their needs with scientists, and his encouragement of the idea that the scientists and engineers should not confine themselves to specifications written by the services but themselves should investigate the problems and propose solutions led, I believe, to the outstanding success of the establishment, and is a classic example of the effectiveness of a market-oriented development team.

An appreciation of civil, rather than military, markets is generally a much more complex and difficult problem. Moreover, the defence establishments have a management structure appropriate to the solution of a limited number of major problems. The number of civil markets which are sufficiently large to justify such a management structure are strictly limited. The development of atomic energy was one, and the Atomic Energy Establishments could be set up on the pattern of the Defence Establishments. The problem of diversification of such establishments to civil markets is, therefore, not only one of switching resources but also must involve major structural changes, including the redeployment of large numbers of staff. Whether or not this can be done, and whether or not the obvious advantages of maintaining at one centre large groups of scientists and engineers can more than offset the difficulties of making them sufficiently responsive to market pressures, has still to be proven.

It is clear, however, that a real problem does exist to which there is at present no completely satisfactory solution. The rate of technological development and innovation, with the magnitude of projects and their long 'pay-off' time, which appears most advantageous to the nation as a whole is generally greater than that which commends itself to individual firms. NRDC has attacked 'his problem on a relatively small scale by supporting development work in the firms themselves, and the requirement that the Corporation should pay its way ensures its close attention to the market needs. However, the more favourable the environment that is created by indirect Government action, e.g. by fiscal and labour policies, then the more will industry be able to undertake from its own resources and the less will be the need for direct Government intervention. But it is likely that it will be nationally advantageous – at any rate, every industrialized nation appears to think so – to undertake some projects which are too large or too long term, or both, to be financed from private sources. To sum up, therefore, it is industry which in general has the knowledge of markets, and it is industry which should be best suited to select future applied R and D areas. Government must first create the environment in which industry will do as much as possible itself, and then find effective means of supporting specific long-term and large projects without itself too closely 'calling the tune'.

## Summary

Government investment in science and technology is accepted without question in some fields, e.g. in defence and as an essential part of the educational system. The wider responsibilities of Government in attempting to stimulate innovation in civil industry – by means other than the creation of a favourable climate through fiscal policy – were recognized many years ago by, for instance, the setting up of the National Physical Laboratory and the Department of Scientific and Industrial Research. Since the last war Government has intervened more directly in civil industry both by national-ization and also in particular fields such as atomic energy and aircraft, but until the advent of the Labour Government in 1964 it was confined to specific fields except through the activities of NRDC. The heavy con-centration of Government expenditure on technology in limited areas, without the application of normal commercial criteria, has had unbalancing effects which are incalculable but almost certainly disadvantageous to the economy as a whole. Efforts are now being made to 'diversify' the Government's attempts to encourage innovation, and to use the Government establishments to greater effect. It is clear, however, that a really effective means of using Government resources with full regard to market requirements has not yet been found, and that much also remains to be done to create the most suitable climate for an innovating society.

## Discussion

How is it possible to achieve maximum return from Government expenditure on research? Dr. Goldman acknowledged that national laboratories in the U.S.A. had problems similar to those in the U.K., and suggested that their efforts should be deployed to solving social, rather than industrial, problems, for instance, urban sprawl and desalination of water. Mr. Duckworth pointed out that, in fact, some of the Government laboratories have attempted to do just this, although the field still presented many difficulties, for example, how could Government be an intelligent buyer? Lord Jackson warned that it was more than a question of simply finding the problems and deriving solutions. Solutions were of no use unless carried through to economic exploitation. 'It is difficult', he said, 'to see how the translation of good ideas into productive usage can be achieved, unless the men responsible for the solutions follow them through to the market'.

These comments drew attention, said Mr. Maddock, to the need for interplay of many different disciplines in the new technologies. This meant that multi-disciplinary centres of science were needed. MIT, Stanford and Caltech provided this kind of service in the U.S.A. and it was the intention that establishments like Harwell in the U.K. should do the same, operating as they did on a commercial basis. Lord Bowden suggested that a great source of weakness was that we had not in the U.K. linked universities with industry in the same way as America and, for instance, Holland had done.

Dr. Jones examined the logic of Government finance for research in industry. Since Government funds for industrial research derived originally in large part from incomes, corporate and personal, earned in industry, might it not be possible that a better outcome would arise if a proportion of this money was not collected in the first place, so that industrial firms might spend it themselves on innovation? Mr. Duckworth commented that the over-all tax burden on industry was much the same in this country as in others, though collected in different ways. He agreed that industry was probably best suited to do the R and D work for many areas, but felt that there were specific long-term projects which only Government could support adequately.

Mr. Maddock pointed out that the really large Government expenditure was not on research but on defence, education, health, and so on. Dr. Goldman observed that the impact of these expenditures on industry could be enormous. Many of the large technology-based companies in the U.S.A.

got their first start from defence funds used to buy their products. Was the U.K. deploying its major Governmental expenditures in the right way to give the private sector a similar boost? Querying whether the same could happen in Europe, Mr. Pavitt pointed to the size of the American government market which gave the advantages of competitive contracting procedures. This did not always happen in the U.K. This could constitute a case for widening the market, perhaps on a European basis, to introduce competition and advantages of scale. It should be borne in mind, however, that European government markets were less technologically sophisticated than in the U.S.A., which meant that potential commercial spin-off was often five years behind the U.S.A., i.e. too late.

Mr. Freeman, introducing what was to be one of the key topics of the Symposium, said that he felt the participants had so far concentrated too much on economic aspects. There was a danger, he said, in identifying economic growth with human happiness. In very poor countries there was a close approximation, but the more removed an economy became from primary poverty the less useful was economic growth as a measure of social achievement. As an example, he pointed out that in medical research many achievements had a negative effect on the growth of the GNP. 'It may well be that certain very important goals which may be pursued by innovation, will not come at all within the economic growth goal.'

Dr. King supported this view. He asked whether technological innovation was possible, or desirable, except as part of a totally innovative society, one with both technical and social innovation. Without this linkage there might be disruption of society as a result of increased wealth, and he suggested that student unrest, the demand for participation in industry, 'the neuroses of the lonely housewife in the mechanized kitchen', were indications of a failure so far in this sense. In accepting the new kinds of social responsibilities, Government would have to understand the need to balance technological innovation with other factors, to relate it to social, educational and economic factors in order harmoniously to release its potential for real wealth.

# Chapter 12

# The Role of
# the Educational System

*H. S. Wolff*

I work in a branch of technology which, in Britain at any rate, is somewhat of a 'Cinderella' in comparison with the 'big business' from which many of the contributors to the Seminar have been drawn. It concerns the application of engineering thought and engineering practice to the problems of human biology, and especially to those of medicine. Because there are comparatively few practitioners of biomedical engineering, people like myself may find themselves having to be inventors, designers, market researchers, teachers, politicians and salesmen, all rolled into one if an apparently promising innovation is to take root and reach the point of profitable exploitation.

Such multifarious activities inevitably bring one into contact with representatives of the various sections of the population, who must each play their part if the innovation is to succeed. Such authority as I assume in talking about the role of the educational system is based on my inevitably superficial analysis of the difficulties I encounter in trying to introduce new devices into the medical field, and some experience of rather unorthodox teaching of post-graduate students. My remarks will be confined almost completely to engineering or technological education.

At last, four distinct classes of recipients for technological training can be recognized — and for these, four quite distinct educational processes are required. First, there is the conventional engineering training leading to a specialist qualification. Secondly, and more controversially, a shallower and more widely based course to train the problem analyst and problem identifier. Thirdly, technical support personnel must be provided to make, maintain and install the products of technological innovations. Lastly, and most important of all, a climate must be created amongst the population who use the devices either for their own benefit or the benefit of others which recognizes a good innovation as such, and in which there is enough understanding and feeling for the technology to make the new device work.

## The Graduate Engineer

He emerges from the university, or the technical college, almost innocent of the real world outside. This is not his fault: often he will have been taught by people who have never been outside, and who moreover, and perhaps correctly, decide that the length of the course is only just adequate to instil the ability to derive commonly employed concepts from basic principles. Unfortunately, such teaching does not make the student an engineer, and even less a potential innovator, because he has not been given the mental sub-assemblies from which a new idea could be constructed. To take an example from mechanical engineering: does anyone give a course of lectures which describe the principal methods of converting continuous motion into discontinuous motion (cine projectors, bacon slicers), or the means available to allow a wheel to turn freely in one direction, but not in the other? To know about these things is just as basic, and often much more relevant, than being able to derive the equations for the period of a compound pendulum from first principles.

Whatever a student is taught, he must be able not only to reproduce the material, or even slavishly to apply it: if he is to innovate, he must understand to the point where the knowledge becomes an integral part of him. To be able to teach in this way intuitively is probably rare: because not only must the deep level of understanding exist in the teacher, but also he must be able to establish contact with the students, some of whom require practical analogies, and others a more abstract treatment for the vital 'click' to occur.

There must be, therefore, a greater emphasis on the actual mechanics of teaching, quite apart from what is taught, if the innovative ability of the engineering graduate is to be raised.

## The Problem Analyst, the Problem Identifier, the Organizer of Solutions

I have not thought of a name for this class of individual, but I am absolutely convinced that at least in the field of biomedical engineering his presence is essential. His education would have been equivalent to a first degree in a life science of pre-clinical medicine, plus an exposure to a wide range of technologies, to the point of realizing their significance, and being able to think in terms of their potential range of application. I would use such an individual in the first case as a problem analyst who provides the link between the biological problem and the various specialist engineers who should contribute their skills to the construction of a new instrument or device.

No single engineer is likely to have a sufficient knowledge in fields other than his own to provide or even conceive the solution to a complex problem, nor is he likely to be able to assess the biological acceptability of his solution. On the other hand, no biologist or doctor is likely to be sufficiently learned in even any one technological speciality to design competently within it. There has to be somebody, therefore, who conducts the orchestra of engineering specialists, and interprets the score in the light of the biological requirement.

Another function of such an individual is to identify solutions to problems which have not hitherto been explicitly recognized. What I mean by this is that the gap between what a prospective user of technology knows to exist, and what actually exists, may be so great that the 'not asking for the unknown' effect begins to operate. Most people are not capable of formulating problems unless they are aware, at least in a general sort of way, that a solution exists. There is, therefore, a requirement for a 'prospective technologist' who is aware of the current state of the art, and can thus identify sections of his chosen field of application, where innovation made possible by developments in technology can be brought to bear.

Universities are traditionally resistant to training people over a broad field but to little depth. This resistance is reinforced by the implication that such people, whether problem analysts or the organizers of the specialist skills of others, would automatically be 'boss' people who would have positions in an organization superior to those of the traditional university specialist. In a sense, this would be true because they would be trained for an essentially managerial function. If a course in technological orientation could be made a post-graduate one, following perhaps a more specialist course in the target subject, then the operation might not be so distasteful to the authorities. However, no such course exists, and I am convinced that the lack of the kind of people I have described represents a considerable obstacle to technological innovation.

### Support Personnel

The motor car without the garage mechanic would very soon literally become a non-starter. In a field such as bioengineering, there is virtually no mechanism for the formal training of support personnel. This position is serious because not only is the user of the technological product often almost entirely without technical training or even interest, but also the rate at which devices are being introduced in relative terms is high. A further problem is that in some instances the intellectual qualities required for quick fault diagnosis may be comparable with those required of the university graduate, and these moreover have to be allied to often not inconsiderable manual dexterity. Yet the individual in terms of status and pay will rank well below the graduate. Two things will have to be done: first, courses will have to be designed deliberately for what might be termed 'a technological middle class', the members of which are not specialist material. In the U.S.A. plans are being put forward to train 10,000 BMETs (Biomedical Engineering Technicians) by the middle 1970s, using two-year courses in technical colleges. These people must be made to feel important, paid adequately, and their prospective employers must be made to realise that they represent the oil on the cogs of a technological society. Secondly, the equipment designer must learn to design around the intellectual and manual skills of the support personnel, and it should be part of his training to appreciate what these skills are.

## The Target Population

An innovation will only be successful if somebody makes use of it. If it concerns only a small number of people on a production line or a highly trained group of computer operators, the problems are small because they can be motivated and trained to use the innovation relatively easily. If, on the other hand, the target population consists of nurses, teachers or social workers, who are numerous and whose whole motivation may be to keep technological intrusion out of a person to person relationship, then the problem becomes much more serious. I regard these motivational reasons as the principal obstacle in the way of introducing technology into those spheres where even minor advances can result in benefits quite out of proportion to the complexity or cost of the devices which are involved.

There seems to be three ways in which the resistance to technological innovation can be overcome. First, the technology must be tailored in such a way that after explanation it becomes quite obvious that its only purpose is to permit the user to give a better service, and thus to do more for his patient, pupil, etc. A patient monitoring system does not replace the nurse, it gives her more acute and extra senses: eyes in the back of her head: and possibly more time to *care* for her patient, as only one human being can for another. In the same way, a teaching aid should enable the teacher to achieve more often the sudden flash of comprehension in his pupil, which represents his motivational reward.

Secondly, and this applies most strongly to hospital equipment, failure of the machine must not leave the user in a completely helpless position. To give an example: an intravenous drip, used very commonly in the hospital ward, must be one of the most unreliable pieces of equipment which has ever been designed. The drip rate can change, the needle can block, the reservoir may be empty, but because the nurse knows exactly the remedies to apply so as to put the device back into action, she does not develop any resistance against its use. If a piece of electronic or other technological equipment fails for reasons which fundamentally may be more serious, she has to call in the help of somebody else. I believe that it is possible to have a design philosophy for even quite complex equipment, which makes it possible to apply simple logical processes to fault finding well within the mental and manipulative capabilities of the nurse, which will identify the particular module of the equipment which has gone wrong, and allow her to replace it. When the day dawns on which the night nurse can say to the ward sister that she has had some difficulty with the heart rate channel at 3.00 a.m., but had identified a defective rate meter module and replaced it by a spare, then I think we will have overcome one of the larger psychological obstacles which we face at the moment.

To design equipment which has the inherent capability of indicating its own faults is not at all easy, and the decision to make equipment which exhibits these qualities has to be taken at a very early stage in the design. I believe that it is an important part of the function of the innovator in the social, medical and educational fields to design the equipment in such a way that the user maintains almost complete mastery over it so as not to interfere too much with his own motivational processes.

The third way of overcoming the obstacles for innovation will be, of course, to raise the overall standard of technological awareness in the target population. This can only be done by an early exposure to technology in school and during professional training. The nurse, the medical student, the social worker and the teacher must grow up with the conviction that technology is man's servant, but that man can only maintain his mastery over it by knowledge and understanding.

On the other hand, the innovator must not fall into the all too common trap that technological feasibility automatically implies desirability. His general education must give him the will and judgement to discipline himself at times so as not to innovate for its own sake, and to bear in mind that technological innovation must not result in human degradation.

## Discussion

Lord Jackson expressed agreement with Mr. Wolff's central thesis, but also drew attention to the practical difficulties in its implementation. It was a question of finding teachers who could teach in the way required; and people with this ability were, he felt, at present rare. But a more important point was the relation between the numbers of scientists and technologists on the one hand, and technicians, on the other. 'We are not the only country which, in my opinion, is, and has been, devoting far too much attention to the production of an increasing number of scientists and technologists. We are overlooking the fact that in some respects a greater shortage exists at the technical supporting manpower level.' Lord Jackson mentioned other European countries which, he felt, had approached this problem more fruitfully. Mr Wolff thought this was as much a problem of national characteristics as of the educational system, that to produce or work in a 'subservient category of people' was against our national nature.

Mr. Goldsmith questioned Lord Jackson's response to the paper. Lord Jackson, he said, had agreed with Mr. Wolff that the education of scientists and engineers was lacking. But as a teacher had he no further reply? Lord Jackson responded that the reason why the kind of education required was not being provided adequately was because too many of the teachers had an insufficiently broad or multidisciplinary experience, though many of them were aware of this deficiency in themselves. Many of the techniques of teaching and examination, he added, were artificial. And this problem was not restricted to engineering, or even to this country. It lay in the fact that the simplest things to teach, and to examine, were the precise-answer questions, which were inevitably only tenuously linked to the real world.

Mr Wolff took up a concept introduced earlier in the day, that of 'peripheral innovation'. He had coined the phrase 'Unexciting Research Into Necessary Equipment (URINE)' to describe 'one of the most neglected forms of the application of technology to medicine'. It was based on the observation that there was no organized system for applying technology to undramatically disabled people, and he gave as example the problem of improving the mobility of a wheelchair within the confines of a small home. Mr. Pavitt suggested that the reason why this field of innovation was almost totally unexplored was that the needs had not been articulated: government and institutions were not writing specifications, industry was not being prodded from outside to recognition of these markets. Mr. Wolff added that 'the prestige to be got from transplanting a kidney is infinitely greater than helping any number of old ladies in their homes'. The other reason, he felt, was that the market was often regarded as commercially unattractive. It was seen as a field which did not lend itself to standardized production: that it was almost necessary for a systems analysis to be carried out for each individual case. He believed that a kit of supportive devices could be designed involving locomotion, cooking, etc., which by their large scale applicability could provide very attractive markets. However, he was able to report that he had been successful in persuading a new Canadian medical school at the University of McMaster, in Hamilton, Ontario, to undertake this kind of responsibility for its local population. The school would include a bio-medical engineering department, with bio-medical engineering 'home visitors', people able to do just this systems analysis of individual cases.

Dr. Fryers pointed out that in this field it was impossible for a firm to obtain protection, or to command a price, for its products commensurate with their value. He suggested that relying on institutions such as universities to innovate would not in the long run be so efficient as would be the introduction of a climate where profit could be made out of providing services of this kind, so that industry could respond.

Dr. Archer brought together the two themes of the role of the educational system and what the Symposium had agreed was the under-emphasis on 'URINE'. While the scientific and engineering disciplines were by now relatively well developed and sophisticated the discipline of social engineering was, he said, still very much their poor relation. Social engineering was concerned with 'how to structure a situation so as to profit from it'. It was the analytical approach to the balancing of factors such as 'who is going to profit from what, who is going to pay for what, what is the effect of purchase tax, statutory requirements, demarcation between professions or unions, how should the paperwork, and the prescription, procurement and supply machinery be organized', and so on. This approach was as much a part of the problem as the mechanical engineering, or the physics, or the production engineering. Yet, said Dr. Archer, our social engineering 'is dismally under-developed'. He suggested that peripheral inventions of the kind under discussion would advance very much more rapidly if social engineering were introduced as a part of the syllabus for technological courses.

Mr. Teeling-Smith linked the advancement of socially desirable inventions firmly with increase in total wealth. It was, he said, precisely developments of this sort which could be tackled only from 'new money'. It was in this context that the sort of mechanism to which Dr. Fryers had referred would apply. We must do things with technology, he continued. 'We have got to harness it to this simple, home-spun type of innovation, which is going to make life better for a greater number of people, particularly in an ageing population, and we have got to pay for this innovation by also harnessing technology to increasing national wealth.'

Mr. Freeman again suggested that there was danger in linking human happiness too closely to economic considerations (see Discussion Session 3). He had remarked that there were certain kinds of innovation important to human happiness which would not arise from the market system as it now operated. These were cases, he said, where 'social benefits may be very great in relation to social cost, but private benefit may be less than private cost'. There might be areas where it would be possible to make such innovation work by social engineering of the type Dr. Archer mentioned but there were some others where it had never worked — crime prevention, pollution, city transport, town planning, and possibly some bio-medical engineering problems — and where it might never work.

Chapter 13

# Market Analysis
# and Marketing

*Aaron J. Gellman*

Innovation is a process. With technological innovation, the process is virtually always a complex one beginning, perhaps, with painstaking basic research or with an unanticipated flash of insight. The process, then, ranges through the applied R and D stages and, with success, ultimately to large scale production and widespread use.

## Resources for Innovation

In aggregating the total resources necessary to carry through the process of technological innovation in a significant number of cases, it has been determined that only from 5 to 15 per cent. of the expenditures are associated with the R and D phases, with the remainder necessarily allocated to the more mundane, but nevertheless essential, tasks of production engineering, tooling up and marketing. Within the 85 to 95 per cent. of the resources committed beyond invention and R and D on the way to innovation, in most cases market analysis and marketing take a significant portion. What is more important, market analysis and marketing are often crucial to the success of the innovation, and are indispensable to maximizing the profitability of an organization engaging in technological innovation in the first place.

Yet the role of market analysis and marketing explicit in support of technological innovation seems little appreciated by those involved as innovators and by senior policy-making and decision-making executives; students of the process of innovation also display a similar blind spot, as evidenced by the notable lack of material on market analysis and marketing in support of innovation in the rapidly growing literature on technological change and innovation. It is especially painful to record that it is a rare university curriculum in industrial management, economics or engineering which takes note of innovation as a process, much less as a process involving critically a special sort of market analysis and marketing effort. (Small wonder, then, that the bulk of top managers and officials do not recognize the entrance of an 'innovative process' since they are the products of such educational experiences.)

## Motives for Innovating

What are the innovating organization's motives, aside from the ancient (and largely valid) economist's assumption of profit maximization? In some instances the innovation is essential to the survival of the organization; perhaps a threat has been posed from a source external to the organization, and this requires a reaction in the form of a successful technological innovation, unless the organization is to suffer grievously, if not fatally. More common, and more relevant, innovation is a means — perhaps the only means — for achieving some overall organizational growth objectives, which increasingly are being set forth implicitly or explicitly in an overall strategic plan. Where growth is a prime objective, the market analysis carried out in support of innovation relates to identification and classification of markets expected to show rapid expansion in the time period for which the organization's plan was developed. In the U.S.A. today, such analysis would certainly turn up 'hardware' for education, leisure time products, medical service automation devices, and a host of others. Of course, not all such general market areas will be relevant to the capabilities of the firm as presently constituted, but the market analysis should begin from a general overview and be particularized thereafter. (It is worth noting that, especially in a large organization, an activity explicitly devoted to identifying growing areas of the economy can be useful to those framing merger, acquisition and diversification policies. Especially in the U.S.A. in recent years, innovation through acquisition or merger has become increasingly common and often starts with just this sort of general economic pulse-taking.)

Again, especially in larger firms with growth objectives to be met primarily through internal expansion, it is imperative to identify the most rapidly growing markets, and isolate those which can be served more effectively (and profitably). The simple mathematics of growth can shake a manager quite effectively: a $100-million firm with an overall (and modest) revenue growth objective of 10 per cent. per year without regard to inflation must find *net* additional revenues of $10 million. As a practical matter, revenues from new activities must be well in excess of $10 million, due to the erosion of prices on some products and the withdrawal from the market of still others. Should the firm decide its programmed growth is to be achieved primarily through successful technological innovation, the task the next year will be to develop products which will generate some $15 to $20 million in sales, and in each successive year the objective will be even greater in absolute terms.

**Market Analysis Required**

The character of market analysis related to innovating is largely of a different genre as compared with more routine sales of promotion matters. In the latter case, the fine and tedious details of price and income elasticity, consumer reaction, advertising programmes, etc., occupy the analyst, often requiring figures to the fifth decimal place since margins may have worn quite thin where the product has been in the market for some time, or where it is being introduced to meet a competitive situation which *per se* implies margins more nearly in the 'normal' range.

By contrast, the analysis in support of innovation is concerned with everything routine market analysis requires, but far more besides. Since any innovation worth undertaking should have dramatically greater than 'normal' profit margins associated with it initially, it is usually not worthwhile to be quite as precise in the more mundane areas of market analysis. Instead, the analytical resources should be devoted to broadening the scope of the analysis to identify all the various barriers to innovation, and to developing strategies to surmount them.

Illustrations of the two classes of market analysis can be drawn from the aircraft manufacturing industry of the U.S.A. in the late 1950s. First, while considering the market for piston-engine aircraft one manufacturer concerned itself with the effect of a price reduction on the demand for such aircraft, and sought to determine the impact that possible rate reductions, posted partially because of reduced aircraft capital cost, would have upon the demand for travel and airfreight service. In contrast, another manufacturer contemplated the development and introduction of the first American commercial jet: although concerned about product price and airline fares and rates, the market analysis effort was directed heavily towards determining the reactions of the Federal Aviation Agency's safety people who would have to set rules for an entirely new regime for air travel; of airport operators, who would face noise and runway length and strength requirements of a different order; of the general public, who would find jet travel an entirely different experience from flight in propeller-driven aircraft; of various labour groups that would have to work with, or on, such vehicles; and of financial and insurance organizations faced suddenly with financing a larger fleet of aircraft, many of them with capital costs three or more times greater than those of aircraft previously in service.

In the latter example, it is clear that the market analysis of technological innovation extended far beyond the mere 'target' of the innovation, the individual or organization that had to make an affirmative investment or expense decision for the process of innovation to be complete. Similarly, if marketing in support of innovation is defined as any effort which promotes the innovative product (or service), it becomes obvious that such marketing efforts are far broader, and have substantially more breadth and depth, than those necessary to maintain or even expand the sales of an established product, which itself may at one time have been highly innovative. Put another way, in a conventional marketing programme the effort is directed largely, if not entirely, at the buyer or investment decision-maker to the exclusion of virtually everyone else. Where innovation is concerned, with the sometime exception of consumer products, the target of the innovation is not alone, or even principally, the focus of the marketing effort. As implied above, enthusiasm, acquiescence or at least neutrality often must be cultivated in others who are not users or consumers of the innovative product or service if the innovation is to be successful.

### Dynamic Market Analysis

Where the prospective technological innovation involves significant resources, the associated market analysis must be dynamic in character and, generally, should look a considerable period into the future. The effect of the innovation on the structure and behaviour of all relevant markets should be considered specifically. For example, introduction of the revolutionary high-speed, automated machine tool would certainly induce countermoves by other machine tool producers. Perhaps prices of substitute equipment would fall; there might be consolidations among the other companies, or one of them might seek to acquire or merge with the innovator. Again, perhaps competition would be capable of offering quickly nearly identical units at the same or a lower price: in the former case, splitting the market; in the latter, creating the prospect of reduced profits for the innovator.

What would be the reaction of the unions should reliance on highly skilled machine tool operators be dramatically decreased and the labour market severly dislocated? And what about the markets in which products turned out by the machine tool are sold? It is possible that those firms acquiring the machine tools would choose to exploit their lower-cost position by reducing prices and driving competitors out of these markets, thereby setting the stage for higher prices and profits for themselves in the future: in the process, succeed in substantially concentrating the buyer power which the innovator faces in the future, which again might mean reduced profit margins in the long run.

### Mental Attitudes and the 'Innovation Quotient'

Whether one is advancing a technological innovation which is demand-stimulating or cost-reducing, or which promises both happy results, the mere expectation of profitability is simply not enough to guarantee the project will be a success. It may well turn out that the targets of the innovation either cannot be convinced of its inherent attractiveness and profitability for themselves, or they just do not care. The latter situation is encountered perhaps most frequently in nationalized or government regulated industries, and generally is found only in highly concentrated industries. The market analysis in support of technological innovation, therefore, should always attempt to measure the propensity to innovate (or to accept innovation) of the targets of the innovative process. Setting aside programmes associated with consumer products where market research, test marketing and other techniques are comparatively well developed, market analysis in support of innovation should ascertain as quickly as possible if there is a reasonable propensity to innovate on the part of the target(s) so that the probable acceptance of the innovation is sufficiently large to justify commitment of the considerable resources required to develop the product. Indeed, it has been suggested that in planning a programme of innovation and in allocating resources among various alternative projects, as well as in pursuing established projects, the 'Innovation Quotient' (i.e. IQ) of actual and potential targets of innovation ought to be estimated.

In general, it is possible to rank industries and firms as having low to medium IQs and to make basic decisions as to whether to attempt to produce technologically innovative equipment for them based in part on such judgements. Consider the railway industries in the U.S.A., for instance. The American railway, for myriad reasons including the mutual interdependence of over 100 individual carriers, is among the lowest IQ industries and firms. Therefore, it would be a rational decision for a firm facing the possibility of developing, producing and marketing a specialized and innovative item of equipment for railways to decide to place its resources in some other innovative activity because of the low IQ of these particular 'targets'. Indeed, there are cases on record where technologically innovative hardware with capital return periods of from six months to three years has been unsuccessful, largely because of the low IQ of railways of the U.S.A., that is the widespread and seemingly inherent unwillingness to try something new and different.

**Inside Marketing**

It was noted earlier that the marketing effort in support of innovation is frequently, if not usually, directed at people and organizations both inside and outside what might be considered the 'normal' innovative process loop. Such marketing efforts should be extended most certainly within the innovating organization to all those who have the power to sustain, curtail or expand the resources devoted to any particular innovative project, and to the process of innovation in general. In marketing the innovation it is wise, if not essential, to maintain enthusiasm for the project at both line and staff levels, and from the top down. Interest must be maintained at as a high an organizational level as is justified by what supporting market analysis shows the potential profitability of the project to be.

Marketing inside the organization is often (inappropriately) swept away as being part of 'company politics'. But marketing both the innovative process and specific innovations within the organization is always important, and often crucial, to the success of the innovation, since significant resources must be committed by the company to the process of innovation. The problem of marketing innovative projects within the firm is compounded by the very nature of the innovative process, where there surely will be failures in some projects and seeming waste of resources, even though the expectation is that those innovations which are successful and generate profits will do so handsomely and provide an abnormally high rate of return on the entire effort.

In keeping before relevant echelons of management in the innovating firm the potential return to each innovative activity, more than routine progress or status reports are required. The best methods of marketing the innovation internally, and the type of information employed to maintain enthusiasm, depends upon the bias and style of the organization and its executives. Allocation of the innovator's own marketing resources to such activities will be determined importantly by the size and structure of the firm, but it is the rare organization with a programme in support of innovation where the very highest executives do not wish to monitor progress of such project, if only informally.

Of course, senior management's interest in innovation projects and their willingness, even eagerness, to accept communications out of channels when related to such activities, stems significantly from the excitement often generated by innovation: excitement for those engaged in carrying through the process, for the financial community, and, hopefully, for the profit and loss statement. Moreover, the excitement of the process of innovation can be a powerful force not only in obtaining resources, but also in maintaining enthusiasm among all who are involved anyway in working through the process. Exploitation of this excitement in the process of innovation is an important responsibility of the managers of innovative activity, and should be viewed properly as a marketing technique, where the object of the effort is internal to the firm. The same technique also, on occasion, may be enlarged to include suppliers to the innovation programme where their co-operation is essential to the success of an innovation, or of a whole programme.

### R and D Personnel and the Process of Innovation

It is often thought that personnel carrying out R and D work, which is expected to produce the basic raw material of profitable technological innovation, are themselves essentially disinterested in problems of the organization outside the R and D area, and are put off most especially by any consideration related to the market for, or market-ability of, the output of R and D activities. Recently, in a number of cases it has been demonstrated thoroughly that a great proportion of the people engaged in such pursuits do wish to make profitable the organization's investment in the innovative process. It is not merely a question of job security in a market for R and D personnel, such as persists in the U.S.A. There are myriad instances where first-rate scientists engaged in basic research in the corporate environment in the U.S.A. have taken special pains to carry out work which might lead to the solution of a corporate problem, or which enlarge the firm's market, all this without any requirement to do so. They may even enlarge the firm's horizons, or induce a redefinition of the firm's *raison d'être*. In some respects, then, the market analysis in support of innovative activities should be made available, at least to some extent, to the R and D staff members who want such information, along with other people involved in the general management of such R and D facilities, and those responsible for allocating resources to and within the R and D organization's infrastructure.

**Timing the Innovation**

A principal focus of market analysis in support of innovative activity relates to the timing of the market introduction of the new product or service. The history of technological innovation is replete with instances where the right product was introduced at the wrong time, either too early or too late in terms of requirements or tastes. While too early introduction may not be fatal to the ultimate success of an innovation, it will usually substantially reduce the profitability of the innovation, as the often considerable investment in the innovative process, including tooling and possibly inventory, will remain unproductive until the market is ready. Far worse, of course, is the situation where the innovation is too late to generate the demand necessary to make the project profitable: industrial requirements, or consumer preferences, have gone 'beyond' the innovation and no opportunity for its profitable exploitation remains.

**Definition of the Relevant Market**

In support of the analysis of markets for innovative products, and to assure a proper marketing effort subsequently, it is necessary to define the relevant markets which the firm seeks to serve. For example, what is the relevant market from the point of view of the organization? What share of this market is to be captured and held by skilful exploitation of the process of innovation? When should the market analysis and subsequent marketing effort be directed at the customer, when at the customer's customer? Usually, it is wise to identify those organizations among the possible targets of the innovation which have the highest IQ. Moreover, the frequent mutual interdependence of organizations on the demand side of the equation should be recognized as well.

## Summary

In summary, it is necessary to recognize that technological innovation is in fact a complex process requiring a substantial breadth and depth of resources, especially if innovation is relied upon as a means of achieving growth, or even for maintaining a firm's relative position in the economy, or of an economy's relative position in the world.

It is essential to recognize that a significant portion of the resources necessary for successful innovation are associated with market analysis and marketing, and that a lack of activity in this area, or inappropriate efforts, can seriously jeopardize the success of specific innovations and of a broad programme of innovation. In carrying out the market analysis, the proper focus of the subsequent external marketing programme should be identified even as marketing efforts are being directed at targets within the innovative organization. There should always be regular communications between those involved in the market side of the problem and those involved in generating the raw materials of innovation.

It is well to note also that there are a number of popular notions about innovation which do not stand up under the cold light of an analysis of the process of innovation. Specifically, the concept that if one builds a better mousetrap the world will beat a path to one's door is a dangerous one upon which to base decisions relative to the allocation of scarce resources to innovative activities. Even the better mousetrap requires substantial market analysis and marketing efforts, not only to support its introduction but also to maximize the profits which can be derived from the innovation. Similarly, the notion that 'nothing can stop an idea whose time has come' is absurd. The best way to stop an idea (or innovation) may well be through failure to recognize the frequent critical importance of market analysis and marketing in carrying through the process of innovation.

## Discussion

Mr. Pavitt asked how market research could best be used in the case of radical innovation. The Sony Company of Japan was developing a small portable television set, but was informed by market researchers that it would not sell in the U.S.A. Yet 3,000 television sets were sold on their day of introduction. Similarly, IBM's original analysis of the possible computer market indicated a much lower demand than actually developed. Were there, he asked, any drawbacks with existing marketing research methods, and how did one deal with them?

The main problem, said Dr. Gellman, was that we were trying to make a consumer market research do the job in a technical field where it was not wholly adequate. We made insufficient use of such techniques as revealed preference. He was amazed how often companies failed to use these, even when multi-million dollar projects were involved. The difference in approach he suggested, lay in the terms 'market research' and 'market analysis'. Market research approached a market which already existed: market analysis determined whether or not there was a market.

Professor Burke queried whether it was ever really possible to ascertain revealed preference (the possible existence of a market) without a product and with people who had no experience of the utility of the device concerned. To the first part, Dr. Gellman replied that recent work in America demonstrated that it was not necessary actually to have the product in order to test preferences. The second part, he acknowledged, presented greater difficulties. One had to attempt to create a surrogate of the experience in the mind of the target of innovation 'in order to elicit and gauge his response'. 'This is', he added, 'a very young quasi-science.' Professor Burke commented that he felt the method was perhaps, as yet, less valuable than the services of its enthusiastic proponents.

Dr. Woodroofe accepted that there was a difference between the consumer goods fields, with which his firm was primarily concerned, and those of more technical or industrial commodities. The ratios of expenditures were different. For consumer goods, early bench-testing was a comparatively small expenditure. Pilot production was more expensive, but putting the product on the market, or marketing, was enormously expensive, so that a firm could not afford to proceed without consumer-testing the product, even if it was a product which had never been known before. So the company implemented techniques, such as concept-testing. He was sure that such techniques and the methods they involved could usefully be extrapolated to areas other than the consumer goods field. Dr. Gellman, while acknowledging that Dr. Woodroofe had not suggested this, warned against the supposition that techniques could be directly lifted from the consumer goods to the industrial goods field. He gave as an example the dissimilarity of the possible trades union responses to technical innovation. How well the innovating firm coped in advance with these potential problems could play a significant part in the success or failure of the innovation.

In answer to a question from Dr. Peccei, Dr. Gellman said that the time scale which a firm utilized for planning its market analysis was a function of the resources which it had to devote to innovation, the nature of the industry in which it operated, and the definition of its markets. Having clarified these factors, an overall rational judgement could then be made only in the context of the individual company's corporate plan.

Mr. Wolff asked if there was not a form of marketing which the Symposium so far had neglected. What about that company which began marketing with the firm conviction that its product was fundamentally necessary and good for the population? As an example he suggested the marketing of the birth-control pill in India. In those circumstances, no amount of preference testing would have given the right sort of answer. Such a firm have to start off with 'a sort of missionary zeal'. Was this not a form of marketing also worth exploring, particularly on a governmental scale where one was marketing for a social purpose? Dr. Gellman replied that this illustrated one of the proper and noblest roles of government, to step into the picture where the innovation's pay-off to society must be taken into account to make the act of innovation worthwhile and profitable.

# Chapter 14

# The Investment Decision

*Duncan Burn*

I am asked to talk about 'The Investment Decision'. But a technological innovation needs not one but a series of expenditure decisions, which are all investment decisions. The number of decisions needed varies, but the series is often spread over a long period, and decisions at successive stages are not necessarily made by the same person or group. At the beginning of the series you have the initiation of a search, which can be more or less specific in its object, or the decision to develop further an invention which is in its infancy. Decisions to continue (or discontinue) through various development stages follow up to the first commercial production, and finally the wide diffusion of the innovation.

The efficiency of the operation depends on the choice of the persons who make the decisions (which is partly an outcome of institutional structure), the criteria these persons use, the stimuli which motivate them, and the controls exercised by economic and social institutions.

Inventors rarely have access to or control of investment resources, so that the relevant investment decisions are almost all made by people who are not inventors – for example, by managers, bankers and institutional investors, ministers, civil servants and heads of Government agencies.

The impact of an innovation on economic growth is greatest at the end of the investment chain – when commercial applications starts, and when application is widely diffused. It is quite possible for commercial application to occur in a different country from the country of the initial investments, and diffusion can occur in many countries simultaneously.

We can distinguish usefully between what may be called different orders of innovation. The first motor car, the first aeroplane, the first turbo alternator, the first jet engine, were clearly of immense significance, but they had little effect on economic growth. They have been followed by innumerable improvements resulting in constantly higher efficiencies, and such improvements involve innovation in varying degrees – advances in metallurgy and metal shaping, for instance, inventions and developments of other materials with special properties, advances in electrical and electronic devices, and so

*139*

on. This process of cumulative innovation clearly has a much greater impact on economic growth than the primary, seminal, innovation when first launched, but the cumulative process is less conspicuous and dramatic, and commonly less imaginative.

Against this background it is not surprising that there is no close correlation between the expenditure on R and D in a country and the same country's rate of economic growth. Such figures as there are will be familiar, and although the margin of error must be large and the figures are not quite up to date, they no doubt provide a sufficiently reliable tough indicator. The U.S.A. spends far more on R and D, both absolutely and as a proportion of national income, than in any other country. The U.K. spends substantially more, absolutely and as a percentage of national income, than any other European country, and more than Japan (though by 1963–1964 Japan employed more people than the U.K. on R and D). But the main Continental industrial countries have had a far higher rate of growth than the U.S.A. or the U.K., and the rate of economic growth in Japan has far exceeded even that of the most successful Continental economies. The U.S.A. growth rate, which has exceeded the British, has been significantly lower than the rate in Germany, France, Italy and, above all, Japan.

But, of course, a great deal of the growth on the Continent and in Japan has depended directly on U.S.A. innovations – licenced, or exploited by U.S.A. companies through overseas subsidiaries. Much has depended also on U.S.A. example. Despite the nationalism which disfigures many discussions of policies for innovation, there is a large if rather one-sided international interchange, and U.S.A. capital and technology has flowed to countries where other factors of production are attractive; where labour, for instance, is relatively cheap, and where there is favourable access to markets. Investment in the final stage of innovation, diffusion, is presumably proportionately high in the countries which benefit from the inflow of U.S.A. technology; but the figures would hardly come into R and D statistics.

What part, if any, of the excess of Continental and Japanese growth rates over the American can be accounted for by the flow of U.S.A. innovation and capital is obscure. The U.K. after all has also benefitted from the flow, but has a lower growth rate than the U.S.A. This has an air of paradox.

If we turn to the U.K. position, I would start by emphasizing that lags in technological development are no recent development. The *Report on Technological Innovation in Britain*,[1] published in July 1968, speaks of 'the lead taken over the past two decades by the U.S.A. in technological innovation': but this is misleading. The Commissioners of the 1851 Exhibition remarked – as I recalled in an article published in 1931 – that countries which lacked cheap fuel or raw materials tended 'to depend more on the intellectual elements of production than in this country'.[2] The lead of the U.S.A. in the use of labour-saving devices and mass production methods — standardization, interchangeable parts, automatic special-purpose machinery for a remarkably wide range of products and purposes, including packaging, and their lead in economy in the use of fuel and iron which were relatively costly in the U.S.A. — was acknowledged between 1850 and 1870. The immense strength of U.S.A. engineering, which lies at the root of so much of U.S.A. success, rests on a history of cumulative innovation which has given her technological primacy in many fields for over a hundred years. The objective significance of this naturally grew as U.S.A. industrial output outstripped that of all European countries, first individually then collectively. In the early stages, innovation was not based on work in laboratories: but since the electrical age — since the '90s, that is — it has been so increasingly.

Already in the 1850s the reasons for U.S.A. leadership in the branches of industry where it was established were being set out in terms surprisingly close in many respects to our present explanations — the large rapidly growing market, receptive of innovation, and with a high general standard of living; the energy, enterprise and ingenuity of the people, to which immigration from various sources contributed; the mobility between employments, the readiness of the workmen to welcome change and all labour-saving contrivances; an unlimited belief everywhere in progress; the rapid spread of knowledge of innovations through the voluminous and universally read press; and all the qualities that spring from a 'universally high' level of education. I emphasize this history of lags and explanations because, obviously, there is a danger in trying to account for and remedy a state of affairs which in important respects is a century old on the assumption that it is only 20 years old. If this error is made, you may easily attach too much importance to influences which are symptoms rather than causes. The U.K., at fairly frequent intervals, has patched her education system to meet foreign competition — it has always been the easiest and normally the least painful thing to do — without in the end removing the technological gap. It has been part of the process so interestingly discussed on a broader canvas by Professor Ben-David.[3]

We are not concerned here with all the factors which may have checked the growth rate in the U.K. The statistics referred to above, however, suggest that the productivity of R and D in the U.K. may be relatively low, and this requires analysis. No comprehensive assessment is feasible. But there are a number of pointers — which all seem to point in the same direction. I will list a few, with references to structural features in the organization of R and D which may be relevant.

In the steel industry, where innovation has been conspicous since the war, the sources of all the major changes have been outside the U.K.: engineering changes mainly in the U.S.A., metallurgical mainly on the Continent. There has been a large government-assisted Research Association in the U.K. industry. If we turn to the development of large turbo alternators, where there have been great cumulative innovations in the last 15 years, the lead in size of units and thermal efficiencies has been in the U.S.A. In the U.K. there have been for most of the time twice as many firms engaged as in the U.S.A., all having to carry the growing development costs for large units which are bought in smaller numbers, and to invest in extended manufacturing capacity to handle bigger machines and components. In addition to the R and D of the firms, the Central Electricity Generating Board (CEGB) rapidly expanded its R and D facilities, increasing still further the fragmentation of research in this industry. Recent mergers will presumably greatly lessen this.

The building of power stations has normally taken much longer in the U.K. than in most other leading industrial countries — up to a year or 18 months longer. It has been the same with steel or chemical works. For the productivity of R and D this means high costs in the final stage, delay in getting the first returns on the whole series of outlays, and delay in obtaining feedback which will help further development. These factors are important moreover at the stage when R and D really affects growth. (I am not referring here to delays which occur because things go wrong: that is another story.) In nuclear energy there have been delaying factors due to the organization, and to centralization, which led to concentration on a narrow front, inappropriate in a new technology when it was unwise to dispense with variety in the experimental phase. Developments which now look particularly attractive were slowed down. There was heavy spending on multiples of one uneconomic type of plant, when a wider range of experiment would have been stimulating and fruitful — and cheaper.

This is a complex story not susceptible of brief description, which I have explored at length elsewhere.[4] But it drew attention to the contrast between the way in which the U.S.A. and U.K. governments have managed their R and D spending. Both have enormous R and D budgets, increased greatly since 1939 by defence projects. The U.K. government has used its resources largely in Government establishments or authorities; the U.S.A. has spent most in sub-contracts to firms and universities, and has set out to divest itself of responsibility for R and D for commercial purposes — such as nuclear generation of electricity — as quickly as it can. This has been rewarding in several ways: the work has benefitted from the commercial standards and experience of the firms; from the competition between them; from their concern with time, their need of profits, their need to be successful quickly for survival and growth. The proliferation of commercial projects by State subsidy has been avoided. The good firms, of course, have benefitted directly from orders and have grown progressively stronger, and the results of government-sponsored R and D, which can be useful for other industrial purposes, flow readily into such uses.

The British arrangements have resulted in an extraordinary situation, where the people who take major decisions do not stand or fall by the outcome of these decisions. Ministers who take decisions on atomic power programmes have moved on to other ministries, or out of office when the outcome of their decisions is known; their association with decisions is soon forgotten. Civil servants who advise them have power with no formal responsibility and they, too, will have done many other jobs before the outcome of the decisions is known. Within the Atomic Energy Authority (AEA), a very large body, there have been conflicting views on policy and the right technical choice. The ultimate decision then must be made by the Chairman, who is also the chief link with the Government. The Chairman and all members of the Authority are appointed by the Minister. Like Ministers they come and go, though not so frequently – but none of them has so far remained in office long enough for the full effect of decisions in his time to be clear. Risks of personal loss and exposure to competition are largely absent in this structure.

Recent British policies on mergers and the reorganization for atomic energy appear to reflect some reaction against both fragmentation and centralization. The policies will result in redistribution of investment decision making and executive control at some points. There is some approach to the view that what is wanted is better investment in R and D. It should be possible, that is, to get a higher rate of growth from a smaller input of R and D investment. (The same conclusion is appropriate for investment more generally.) This does not mean necessarily that a lower rate of investment in R and D is desirable, or that a higher rate might not be justified. It does mean that higher quality, not quantity, should be the first priority: quality judged by commercial results. Firms would undertake R and D to the extent that it was profitable to do so. Prestige for ministers or research teams would not count in the sum.

It has been argued strongly that manpower shortage is a serious restraint on R and D in Britain. The 'brain drain' casts doubt on this. It is interesting that the numbers employed in R and D in Germany (187,000 in 1963–1964) have been conspicuously lower than the numbers in Britain (289,000 in 1963–1964).[5] So long as many R and D workers are employed unproductively it is impossible to form a judgement on this. It is probable that wasteful use in some industries (in atomic energy at some periods, for example, and probably in aircraft) has led to scarcities elsewhere. It may be that the proportion of scientists to engineers is relatively high and could reflect attitudes which keep R and D productivity down; the engineer has never been as highly regarded in the U.K. as in the U.S.A. These problems are outside the scope of my paper.

The slow, perhaps belated, gravitation in the U.K. towards U.S.A. methods of organizing R and D, with larger firms, more devolution of state-financed R and D into industry, possibly less state R and D expenditure, less fragmentation and less centralization seems logical if the object is to make R and D productive in the U.K. as it is in the U.S.A. Two obvious points arise, however. This development naturally meets opposition from those, including many scientists, who find the idea of a market economy distasteful. And we have to ask how well the system can work in the U.K.

With regard to the first, the U.K. alternative has clearly not worked well: the market is a means whereby consumers can express their preferences continuously and as they change, whether because the alternatives or their own tastes change, and whereby also pressure to efficiency (including creativeness) is continuously exerted on producers. The market does not work perfectly and needs intervention, but this is well understood. Conceptually, it can be a means of sensitive adjustment: no one has to pretend that he knows what is comprehensively the public interest, to be imposed on consumers.

I must deal with the second point at greater length. Can it be assumed that large firms, to quote Dr. F. E. Jones' stimulating paper on *Science Policy*, will 'undertake the optimum amount' of R and D 'consistent with viability and growth'.[6] I would not know how to measure the optimum amount, but this apart, we have to recognize from our own and American experience that large firms can become unadventurous in assessing and undertaking research projects. Mr. Peterson makes some interesting references to this in his contribution to *Innovation and Profitability*.[7] One safeguard is that big companies compete with each other, within and across industry boundaries; this can be significant more easily in the larger U.S.A. market than in the British. Few British firms compare with the biggest U.S.A. firms: ICI does, but no other British chemical firm is in the same league. There is a real problem here if we are thinking of the market stimulus to R and D investment. It is not equally serious in all sectors: where it occurs the best safeguard may come from encouraging foreign competition and foreign links, depending on international companies. My impression is that inter-governmental activities are likely to be less fruitful, less straightforwardly economic in their aim to bring this about and so less helpful to growth, than arrangements made between firms on their account.

In the U.S.A. exceptional small firms exploiting a single innovation and growing fast — Xerox and Polaroid are examples — have also provided a spur to the big firms. With our rather imperfect industrial capital market such firms might find difficulties in their earliest stages in the U.K.

The changes occurring in Britain, still very tentative in some aspects, do not offer automatic success. Even if competition is stimulated the extent of the response will depend on the quality of management in the large firms: its skill in integrating marketing and research, in selecting creative leaders and spotting winners, in eliminating delays in development, and in cutting out wasteful research, which I suspect is quite plentiful. Note that nearly 40 per cent. of the 600 top executives of the leading U.S.A. corporations in 1966–1967 had technological degrees, and over one-half of the younger executives who would succeed them had such degrees.

We must ask, too, whether what I have called 'traditional restrictive attitudes' will have a frustrating effect. The distrust of the market and marketing, and of profits, for example, the assumption that the 'pure' scientist is always more distinguished than the applied, can obviously be disturbing both inside a firm and as a source of government policy. If prices and profits on new products are depressed by government action, firms will be less able to finance further development from their own cash flow or to attract funds from the market. If.this means that investment requires much government aid, the purpose of diverting more research from government to industry will be partly frustrated. The U.S.A. gains from the fact that almost all who are involved in directing firms, or working in them, or shaping policies towards industries prefer the same system and want it to work well.

I have referred to the risk that price and tax policies may inhibit research. (The risk is particularly conspicuous in regard to pharmaceuticals where the argument for low prices is emotive, the State is the major purchaser, and the pattern of consumption is determined not by the ultimate users but by doctors.) I would complement this by saying that it is doubtful whether R and D should be encouraged by special tax allowances. We are not concerned to stimulate research in firms for its own sake, but only where it is a good investment. Government grants for investment are naturally attractive to industrialists; but except on a relatively small scale they are likely to distort development. I was interested to see that Mr. Peterson and his colleagues in reporting to the U.S.A. Secretary of Commerce 'could not convince themselves that major tax incentives were really the way to foster innovations' in the U.S.A. though they saw a case for special treatment of small newcomers.

### References

1. *Technological Innovation in Britain*, Report of the Central Advisory Council for Science and Technology, HMSO, July 1968, p. 1
2. D. L. Burn, *American Engineering Competition, 1850–1870, Economic History*, January 1931, pp. 292–311
3. Joseph Ben-David, *Fundamental Research and the Universities*, OECD, 1968, p. 87
4. Duncan Burn, *The Political Economy of Nuclear Energy*, I.E.A., 1967
5. *The Overall Level and Structure of R and D Efforts in OECD Member Countries*, OECD, 1967, p. 14

6.   Dr. F. E. Jones, *Science Policy*, a paper to the Science and Technology Seminar arranged by the Conservative Party Technology Committee, November 12, 1968, p. 4

7.   *Innovation and Profitability*, Science of Science Foundation, 1969, pp. 11–12. Also p. 6

Chapter 15

# R and D Policy and
# Economic Growth

*H. Aujac*

We were asked for some remarks on three sorts of problems: Can one show a strict correlation between a country's R and D expenditures and the growth rate of its GNP? Is it possible to measure in terms of national accounting the consequences on economic development of a major innovation? Do certain policies aiming to improve rapidly the technological level of a country not risk proving opposed directly to this by contributing to ruin the whole economy?

I consider now an answer to the first question. As we know, in the U.S.A. the value of both parameters is very high. But our British friends tell us that in the United Kingdom R and D expenditures are at a high level whereas the growth rate of the GNP remains low. By contrast, France provides an example of a country with low R and D expenditures (until recently) but whose rate of expansion kept relatively strong. But it is easy to find countries in which R and D expenditure and GNP growth rate are equally low. Thus, showing a correlation between R and D expenditures and the growth rate of the GNP is rather tricky.

But it seems necessary to ask ourselves why we are trying to prove such a correlation: is it not in order to quantify another correlation, that between the extent of technological innovation and the raising of general welfare? This last proposition has been long considered as obvious even before Schumpeter's analyses of the 'dynamic entrepreneur'. But can we consider it as equivalent to the first: high R and D expenditures automatically bring about a high growth rate for the GNP? It seems not, and for several reasons.

(a) Only very cautiously can one relate intimately R and D expenditures and the extent of technological innovation. As recorded by current statistics, R and D expenditures seem a poor indicator to real R and D activities, and the connection between R and D activities and technological innovation is very complex.

Statistics at present being what they are, obviously the amount of R and D included in the major public projects, and particularly in the aerospace and military projects, is much more easily taken into account than the corresponding expenditures by the many private firms working for civilian demand. 'Development' is of course an important part of the activity of any firm, but it is very difficult to evaluate in accounting terms. To be clear on this, we need only consider the perplexity of managers in medium and small firms when they have to fill in question forms concerning their R and D expenditures.

Moreover, the percentage of R and D expenditure in the major public projects, especially in the aerospace and military fields, is always remarkably high whenever the missiles or weapons in question are modern. These projects end up in the production of protypes, reproduced sometimes in only very small quantities. As a consequence, the proportion of R and D in the total cost of such a project is incomparably greater than it is in an innovation destined for the civilian market; in this last case, the R and D expenditures are amortized on mass production.

So the value of R and D expenditure is only a very imperfect indicator to the volume of R and D activities. But it is also particularly dangerous to relate the value of R and D expenditure and the extent of technological innovation. France is a good example of a country which produces many inventions which often become technically interesting prototypes. But only with great difficulty are these inventions transformed into innovations, and the prototypes much too seldom find their way into industrial production. In order to compare from one country to another the efficiency of R and D activities as related to technological innovation, it would be useful to have specific indicators as to the intensity of innovation. The percentage of new products in the turnover of a given industry could be an example of such an indicator.

To summarize thus far: we cannot relate the value of R and D expenditure and the extent of technological innovation, because the value of expenditure is hardly representative of the volume of activities, is much too sensitive to the existence of public projects in the aerospace and military fields, and is very differently related in various countries to technological innovation.

(b) Will we be luckier in trying to find a clear correlation between the growth rate of the GNP and the improvement of general welfare? First, we must recognize clearly the source of most difficulties: the growth rate of the GNP is generally measured at constant prices. Thus, the growth rate obtained is related closely with the price structure used as reference prices.

From a theoretical point of view, general interdependence absolutely forbids separation of the analysis in terms of quantities produced and exchanged from the analysis in terms of prices, and also from the analysis in terms of users' preferences. Thus, the growth rate obtained by calculation at constant prices is of very questionable value. If we were to use suitable units, such as the employment level as Keynes recommended or socially useful work as Marx recommended, our result would be quite different. The value of the GDP, in a full employment period, would be equal always to unity, and the growth rate consequently would be equal always to zero.

In practice, it may be possible to have a less negative attitude. For instance, if the economy develops in a manner which we may call 'intensive', characterized by a mere increase of traditional demand with no major change in the structure of this demand, or any deep change in production techniques, then the GNP can be a useful indicator, giving a sufficiently true idea of the evolution of welfare. One can then admit that the structure of constant prices can represent, even over an import time gap and with a sufficient degree of approximation, the social preferences and the state of technical development reached by the economy.

Unfortunately, the GNP has proved unable to account, even very approximately, for other types of growth, and in particular for those characterized by the massive appearance of new products and techniques and by the rapid obsolescence of the older products and techniques. In this case, the development of the statistical series concerning quantities and prices, necessary to follow the evolution of the GNP, becomes nearly impossible. The series of price indexes, in particular, lose much of their meaning. The gap rapidly widens between the classifications of products and techniques on one hand, and their real content on the other, as the classifications remain rigid while their social and technical content changes rapidly.

Thus, whilst we were prepared to be satisfied with using the GNP, as a more or less valid indicator of the evolution of welfare, such a use becomes impossible for precisely the type of development characterized by rapid technical evolution.

These various remarks concerning the relation between the value of R and D expenditure and the intensity of technical innovation, or between the GNP growth rate and the evolution of welfare, are perhaps a first explanation of the surprising results given by the comparison of R and D expenditures and GNP growth rates in various countries.

Whatever the level of development the economy of a given country may have reached, the adoption by the authorities of large public projects in the aerospace or military fields, especially if they concern new weapons or missiles, necessarily provokes a massive increase in the recorded value of R and D expenditure. If the economy is in conditions of underemployment, the adoption of such projects also provokes a rapid increase of the GNP. If the economy is in full employment conditions, the adoption of such projects can only be at the expense of welfare, even if the defective manner of measuring the GNP and its development seems to indicate that one can have both butter and guns at once.

The above should invite us to caution; but we shall not conclude that we should give up hope of analysing, and perhaps quantifying, the effect a well thought out R and D policy can have on economic growth. We wish merely to keep in mind that the economist's duty is to make it clear to the public authorities that the methods at present available in this field are defective, and that new methods must be invented.

We come now to the second problem: is it possible to measure in terms of national accounting the consequences on economic development of a major innovation? This question is evidently connected with the first question. We have insisted long enough on how little we thought the GNP could give a suitable image of the development characterized by rapid technical progress and therefore our answer will be rather negative. But we would like to make our reasons for pessimism clear. Some of these concern the very conception of economic development.

Practically, we shall show our reasons with the example of a major innovation which has already been made, such as one of the major innovations the influence of which was decisive on economic development in the last century: steam engines, organic chemical industry, electricity, etc.

If we state the problem in this way, 'What were the consequences on economic development as a whole of one of these innovations, and is it possible to measure them in terms of national accounting?', what can we answer?

The innovation has taken more or less a long time to diffuse and to affect the different sectors of the economy. Because it was a major one, its diffusion finally gave birth to a completely different society from the initial one.

If we were to describe this history of a major innovation from the point of view of the ease of showing up and measuring its consequences on economic development, we should distinguish three periods.

Period A corresponds to the birth and first life of the innovation: it then seems to develop parallel to general economic development and practically independently. Defining and quantifying the consequences of the innovation on the general economy is easy, but these consequences are pretty negligible, as during this period the innovation and the economy develop independently.

But a moment comes when the rate of diffusion of the innovation is such that it provokes a qualitative change of society. Then begins a period we can call C. The influence of the innovation on the economy is then decisive, but the extent of the diffusion and the importance of its effects are such that it becomes nearly impossible to isolate them and even more so to measure them. The innovation has transformed the quality of growth, and economic development has absorbed and made its own what was still an innovation in the former period.

There is a transition period B, during which coexist certain characteristics of the old economy, which still ignores the major innovation, and certain characteristics of the future economy, as the innovation will have built it, at least in part. In this period, measuring the consequences of the innovation is very difficult and rather purposeless.

In brief, measuring the consequences of the diffusion of a major innovation on economic development is a problem the nature of which changes according to the reference period chosen to analyse its consequences. We can hardly escape the following dilemma. Either the innovation is still in the very first stages of its diffusion — and we can perhaps hope to measure the present consequences of the innovation, but these can only be negligible. Or we are faced with a major innovation already clearly appearing as such. Its consequences are then obviously most important, but it becomes impossible to define and even more to measure them, as the innovation and the economic evolution have become an inseparable unity. The conclusion would be different and more optimistic if the innovation were a minor one and its lifetime short.

And now, trying to evaluate in terms of national accounting the possible consequences of a major R and D project, and no longer those of an existing innovation, clearly raises incomparably greater difficulties.

What should we conclude from a practical point of view, for example, in trying to use the cost-benefit method to enable the selection of the most profitable R and D projects for economic development? It hardly seems possible to express in terms of national accounting the benefit part of the cost-benefit method, unless the innovation is a minor one, and unless its probable lifetime is short considering the likely changes in the economic and social environment. Once again we will have to find something else, and we already know that this 'something else' will have to consider a series of qualitative factors which national accounting ignores.

We would now like to evoke a problem concerning economic policy in the field of technological development. When public authorities try to modernize the national economy from a technical point of view by aiding the development of activities with a high R and D content, what can they do?

Schematically, we can say they have a choice between two policies. They can either try to develop the technological dynamism of all enterprises, for instance through a policy of tax exemption for R and D, or of accelerated amortization, and so on, or else they can choose a selective policy. In this case, the public authorities can aid a particular sector the position of which is thought strategic from the point of view of technical development, or they can create from nothing a new activity by means, for instance, of a large public project, and so on. The choice between these two policies is a practical question of utmost importance. Experience will soon show up the advantages and drawbacks of each policy. Meanwhile, we can make some remarks.

The first type of policy, which concerns every firm, has usually rather unspectacular results, at least in the short run. However, it seems to have the advantage of giving an opportunity to every firm really capable of seizing it, because the firm is in a situation enabling it to use techniques and to diffuse products with a higher R and D content, and because its management has organized itself in consequence. Thus, it is in all economic sectors that the firms which are capable of it succeed in their technological mutation. At the end of this transformation, the chances are that we shall find, at a higher level of technology, a relatively balanced economy, all the parts of which are more or less coherent from the point of view of their technical development.

The second policy, consisting in developing, for instance, by means of large public projects, new activities with a high R and D content, has the advantage of giving tangible results very quickly, but it also runs risks in contributing towards dislocating the national economy. The new highly technological activities develop independently from the more traditional activities precisely because the difference in technical level between these two sorts of activities is too great. The new activities implanted in this way develop as parasites at the expense of the national economy as a whole.

The nature of the risk thus appears clearly. The traditional activities see their international competitiveness decline gradually and dangerously; as a result, the new activities lose their natural development basis, and to continue they must try to become satellites of more advanced foreign economies. At this point, the ruin of the national economy is completed, through the dislocation of its constituent parts: the traditional activities are slowly dying, the new activities can no longer develop. This situation is not unlike that of an underdeveloped country which wishes to acquire an aerospace or nuclear industry for reasons of prestige, but which, after such an effort, must sacrifice the more traditional productive investments although they are essential for improving the living standard of the population. Even very great industrial countries seem, *mutatis mutandis*, to be faced with the difficulties of this sort.

We have considered extreme solutions in order to show the danger of policies of R and D when they are used without certain precautions. For instance, it seems absolutely indispensable to see to it that the new activities induced by the large public projects should not be on too high a technological level compared with the productive sectors. Maybe some of the political reactions we are witnessing, and which have an appearance of anarchy, only express an obscure intuition of the risk the State can make society take through an inadequate policy concerning R and D and technical progress.

Indeed, the risk is not only economic, it is also social and political. A given society can absorb, without excessive stress, only a given rhythm of technical progress, and only a technical progress of a particular nature, suited to that society.

M. Claude Gruson, who created the Department of National Accountancy of the Ministère des Finances, and played a very important part in perfecting the methods of French planning, recently wrote, 'Where do rational management techniques lead to when their application reaches beyond advanced firms into economies which comprise declining sectors (which nevertheless remain indispensable) and in which men are working whose possibilities of adaption are weakening (but who must live)? It must be said with force: if these techniques become dominant, they will build a society which will be radically and irretrievably refused'. After having shown that the direction and rhythm of technical progress imposed by the competitive market does not always benefit the large mass of the population, he concluded on the necessity of a national plan with the object of creating conditions such that each individual could reap the benefit of technical progress. 'But, with this object in view, the national plan must be conceived as something more than a mere technical instrument for enlightened management. It must be conceived as a political project.'

## Chapter 16

# Technological Innovation and Added-value

*L. Bruce Archer*

Most innovators see the achievement of innovation as almost justification enough for their endeavours. The community, too, in the shape of commercial firms, charitable foundations and government agencies, seems to be willing to support artists, researchers and inventors in almost anything they desperately wish to do, provided they seem desperate enough to do it against all the odds. The conventional wisdom postulates that, as a general rule, what *can* be done, *should* be done. And, of course, history is on the side of the conventional wisdom. After all, Nature relies for progress on random mutation and survival of the fittest.

It is, therefore, not surprising that even modern studies on technological innovation are not entirely free from the assumption that research is of itself 'a good thing', to be conducted in the vague expectation of some future benefit. Perhaps the truth of the matter is that the wheel (or whatever) has been re-invented every day since the beginning of intelligent life and will continue to be re-invented every day until the end of intelligent life, the critical moment being the occasion when the world was ready to notice and exploit the invention. The instinct of man to support invention may be the instinct to keep all possibilities in being against the day when one possibility might become a necessity. Perhaps the oversight in the conventional wisdom is failure to recognize the importance of the role of, not the inventor, but the man who notices what the inventor is up to, and turns it to good effect. That, at any rate, is the implication behind several recent analyses which point out that the British economy and British business exhibit comparatively slow growth despite a high investment research.

Clearly, innovation does not contribute to an economy simply by being — it must also be exploited. Leaving aside for the moment the question of how to exploit it, let us ask the question: How exactly does technological innovation (if exploited) benefit a business or an economy? What, indeed, *is* technological innovation? In the context of this paper, the term *technological innovation* is taken to cover new or improved industrial products or commercial services, new or improved materials, new or improved processes and any other change arising from the application of organized knowledge to the production and supply of goods and services. Since the purpose of any normal business (in a capitalist economy, anyway) is to make profit, and since the purpose of any national economy (whether capitalist or not) is to generate, or at least to conserve, wealth, anything that benefits a business or economy does so by favouring the accumulation of profit and/or the creations of wealth. How does technological innovation favour the accumulation of profit or the creation of wealth?

In general, any successful commercial transaction constitutes the supply to a buyer of some product or service which has a greater value to the buyer than its cost to the supplier. The *price* at which the exchange takes place will lie somewhere between that value and that cost. Where the product or service has a greater value to the buyer than the price he paid for it, particularly where he puts it to some purpose himself, then the buyer has profited. Where the price at which the product or service was sold is greater than its cost to the supplier, then the supplier has also profited. Business, especially manufacturing business, is not necessarily a zero-sum game. New wealth can be injected into the economy at the same time. In the context of both business and the national economy, the usefulness of technological innovation is therefore to create, or to increase, the differential between the value of goods and services, and their cost; or to stop an existing differential from eroding under the ravages of competition, market saturation, changes in consumer needs or just plain boredom. A beneficial innovation will add more to value than to cost, or cut more from cost than from value. The cost-cutting bit is easy enough to comprehend. It is on questions of adding value that we get into difficulty.

If a prospective purchaser is offered two alarm clocks, alike in all respects except that one is a better timekeeper than the other, he will presumably choose the better timekeeper. An innovation that leads to a more accurate alarm clock will therefore tend to add to its value. The extent to which the purchaser will be willing to pay a higher price for that added value will depend upon his circumstances and temperament. It will also depend upon both the increment of improvement and upon the base from which it is measured. If the increment is too small or the base line too high, the added-value will be negligible. Hence, once the line of development of a particular feature has reached a diminished level of return in this way, the manufacturer will turn to other means for reducing costs and/or adding value.

The value attached to a particular property or attribute of a product or system will vary from person to person, circumstance to circumstance and from time to time. The purpose of market research, test marketing and so on is to find out who values what, and how much, in particular circumstances at a particular time. It is possible, nevertheless, to identify certain general attributes which tend to add value to most people in most circumstances. For example, as in the case of the clocks, added utility, all other things being equal and within limits, will tend to add value in the eyes of the prospective purchaser. Of course, economists will argue that anything that adds value adds utility, but in this context utility means useful properties such as extra capacity, extra power, added durability, a wider range of application, and so on.

But it is also observable that there are other attributes which add value to commodities, but which only an economist could call utility — the sensual gratification given by a piece of music on a disc, for example, or the pattern on a piece of textile. Much of the attention we pay to sensual gratification, style and finish we call aesthetics. The aesthetic appraisal of a product or an environment is as much intellectual as sensual, of course, but we can use the term aesthetics here to mean all those emotional responses generated by the automatic and intellectual appraisal of the impact of the physical properties of the product on the sense organs of the observer. Thus, all other things being equal, and within limits, added aesthetic quality as well as utility will tend to add value to a commodity in the eyes of the prospective purchaser.

Another class of value-inducing attributes is that of social gratification. A product or service may give the user a sense of status, or security, or of being appreciated. It may serve as an outward and visible symbol that he belongs (or aspires to belong) to some in-group. Some people would say that the whole purpose of society is to give people security and the opportunity to be what they want to be, so the attribute of social gratification in a product or service is not to be despised. So, all other things being equal, and within limits, added socially enhancing qualities will tend to add value.

Again, it is a matter for common observation that the laws of supply and demand not only affect price, but also value. Where a product or service is valued mainly for its utility, scarcity may only affect value in the rather limited sense that it permits the user to command a premium on *his* goods or services. There is no question, however, that the rarity of an antique, or the novelty of a toy, or the originality of a high fashion garment, which in each case is also a kind of scarcity, adds materially to the value of the product. These are all circumstances where aesthetic and social qualities are important. The effect is surprisingly general, however, and we can postulate that, all other things being equal, and within limits, the quality of rarity (in all its senses) will tend to add value to a product or service.

Paradoxically, in most circumstances, a prospective purchaser will set a higher value on that which he can receive on demand than that which he has to wait for, perhaps because he is conscious that there is many a slip 'twixt cup and lip. So, all other things being equal, and within limits, added availability of a product or service tends to add value. The marketing man's dream is therefore a high value, low cost, unique product, available off the shelf and sold at a price which will command the optimum size of market. Whatever the professional innovator may think about it, the economic aim of the transaction is usually to sell at a price which more nearly represents value than it does cost.

The state of the art of handling such variables and of revealing people's value systems is still extraordinarily primitive. Nevertheless, it is possible to go some way towards describing their relationships. Firstly, the merit in the eyes of a prospective purchaser of the commodity in question reflects the amount present of particular properties.

$$O = fP$$

where $O$ signifies varying degrees of merit
and $P$ signifies varying states of some property.

It is convenient to express $O$ on the scale 1 (unity) = total satisfaction or perfect merit, 0.5 = threshold between acceptable and unacceptable degrees of merit, and 0 (zero) = total lack of merit. $P$ would be expressed on whatever ratio, ordinal or cardinal scale was appropriate to it.

The overall merit of the product or service reflects the set of merits in respect of various properties, weighted according to the importance of each of the properties in the eyes of the purchaser.

$$\text{Overall merit} \rightarrow \{(r_{O_n} \cdot O_n)\}$$

where $r$ signifies an importance rating.

In order to be able to express formally the relative merits of alternative products, an index of merit can be constructed thus:

$$M = \frac{\Sigma(r_{O_n} \cdot O_n)}{\Sigma r_{O_n}}$$

where $M$ signifies the index of merit.

Here again an index of 1 (unity) will represent perfect merit in respect of all properties considered and 0.5 will represent the threshold between acceptable and unacceptable overall merit.

One of the properties considered by the puchaser would be the price he would have to pay and this might be weighted very heavily or quite lightly, according to circumstances. The supplier, on the other hand, would be interested in additional properties of the product or service, such as the use it would make of his resources, the advantages of keeping the workshops turning over, the return on capital invested and the risk of its paying off.

Merit in respect of investment expediency, for example, might be expressed thus:

$$O_E = 1 - \frac{F + S(1 - \theta)}{2\theta R}$$

where $O_E$ signifies degree of merit in respect of investment

and $F$ signifies the marginal cost % of finance

and $S$ signifies the loss % of capital invested, if a failure

and $R$ signifies the return % on capital invested, if a success

and $\theta$ signifies the probability of success.

Here again, 1 (unity) represents perfect merit, 0.5 the threshold, and 0 (zero) total lack of merit. The overall index of merit would take this into account, suitably weighted, alongside the merits in respect of other properties, as before. We are thus not entirely without means of expressing the crucial relationships. A commercial transaction can only take place if the conditions represented by the indices of merit are sufficiently attractive to each party to persuade him to clinch the bargain. Clearly, the exploitability of any technological innovation depends upon its impact on the overall merits of products and services, which in turn hangs on the degree of merit it imparts to the properties modified, the amount of importance attached to these properties by the prospective user, the counter-effect on other properties such as cost, the importance attached to *these* properties, and its expediency related to risk.

Perhaps the key to the whole problem of exploiting technological innovation lies in this question of risk. It is characteristic of the mechanism of the money market that capital tends to flow to the lower risk investments. The laws of supply and demand apply to capital as much as to anything else. Hence investors jostling for the security of low risk enterprises have to be content with low interest rates and investors adventuring in high risk enterprises demand high interest rates.

Whether a technological innovation is financed by bank or other institutional loans, or by public investment, or by the allocation of existing resources, the return required must in the long run reflect the risk of the enterprise. If it does not, capital will tend to flow in or out until the laws of supply and demand force the interest rates up or down. Where a high risk enterprise is undertaken on a developer's existing resources, he will tend to limit his investment to a given fraction of his total resources, so that a total loss would not unduly affect his overall return. In all cases, therefore, there is a direct relationship between the residual uncertainty at the end of a development project and the cost of servicing the capital resources employed.

Since, on the other hand, the cost of achieving greater certainty is itself a call on resources, it is clear that the development activity must be conducted on such a scale or with such efficiency that the justifiable cost (appropriate to risk) of servicing capital plus the cost of design and development is equal to or less than the margin between the selling price and the manufactured and marketed cost (see Figure 1).

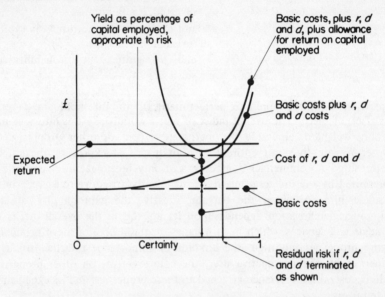

The research, design and development activity should not normally be continued beyond the point when total costs, including an allowance for a return on capital appropriate to the risk involved, match the expected return.

Figure 1

Going into production with residual uncertainty — that is to say, taking a gamble — may well result in higher profits and quicker returns if it succeeds. There is also a higher risk of total loss. Paying the price of making sure, or spreading the cost of a more elaborate design and development programme over a larger number of products, generally results in greater certainty of a smaller profit and with delayed returns.

The evidence of studies such as *Technological Innovation: Its Environment and Management*, indicates that 5–10 per cent. of the cost of technological innovation goes on research leading up to the basic invention; 10–20 per cent. on design, prototype construction and making the idea work for some useful purpose; 40–60 per cent. on production development, production planning and making the idea work under commercial conditions; and the remaining 15–30 per cent. on manufacturing and marketing start-up expenses. Unfortunately, this distribution of cost is not generally recognized, or if recognized is not generally acted upon, particularly by British industry. In far too many cases, firms contribute directly or indirectly to research on quite an adequate scale, encourage new design and invention in every way, and when a prototype is ready for the board to inspect, they think they are home and dry. In fact, they are probably less than one-third of the way home. Too often, having passed the design for development, they become steadily more and more disillusioned as time goes by, and money is spent, whilst the product remains unready for the market. Too often, at just the wrong moment, they give up hope and abandon the project when a few months would have seen it through. This failure to devote the right level of intellectual effort and the right scale of resources to the post-prototype stages has already been well documented. Just two aspects of this failure are worth remarking.

Clearly, the conventional wisdom referred to at the beginning of this paper is no longer acceptable. Random mutation and survival of the fittest, although Nature's way, is an extremely expensive way of ensuring the presence of an invention when the need arises. The advance of technology (to return to the field of our own enquiry) has reached a point where the philosophy of 'what *can* be done, *should* be done' is not only profligate but downright dangerous — as witness recent controversies on the wisdom of proceeding further with biological weapons systems, organ transplants and genetic engineering. The really intractable problems before us now are not problems of means but problems of ends. We can achieve almost anything we want to achieve, if only we set our minds to it. Where failures occur — and far too many failures, lapses and abandoned projects do occur — it is more often from a mistaken understanding of values or a mal-assignment of resources than from a fundamental inability of human resources to meet the cases if they were fully applied. In other words, our failures are mainly failures of entrepreneurship.

Thus in industry, as in biological life, it takes two parties to bring a viable new system into the world — the innovative or seminal role, and the entrepreneurial or ovular role. And just as it generally requires the presence of several million sperm to ensure an adequate probability of fertilizing an egg, the industrial situation has until now required the presence of untold quantities of bright ideas to bring off a viable industrial innovation. The tendency of present thinking is to suggest that a higher success rate is more likely to be achieved by improving the ovular, entrepreneurial, function than by specifically encouraging the rate of flow of seminal ideas.

Entrepreneurship is of two kinds: technical entrepreneurship which recognizes and turns the innovative idea to some valuable purpose and makes it practicable and cheap enough to be produced commercially; and marketing entrepreneurship which recognizes or stimulates needs, divines the viable price and constructs the conditions necessary to effect the transaction. Perhaps the biggest single cause of failure to reap adequately the potential business or national economic benefits of technological innovation is a failure to concert the activities of the technical entrepreneur and the marketing entrepreneur: in other words, inadequate vertical integration of the exploitational effort. It has long been remarked that R and D, production, marketing and finance personnel do not understand one another's vocabularies, manners of reasoning or goals. Research people do not even understand development people. The one thing they have in common, if only they could recognize it, is a commitment to the task of adding value to resources, albeit at their respective conceptual, entrepreneurial or realisational stages.

The administrative trick of organising the innovative effort vertically, so that all divisions of a business enterprise see clearly their respective commitments to innovation, as well as to production, might go some way towards improving the incidence of successfully exploited germinal ideas. A proper recognition, especially by engineers, of the Janus-like quality of entrepreneurship — technical entrepreneurship looking towards science but thinking about realisation, and business entrepreneurship looking towards society and still thinking about realisation — might go even further. But most effective of all would be the application of more and better scientific thought to the collection of data and the building of models for the complex but vital interplay of perceived qualities, value, price, cost, risk, the rewards of risk, and the cost of reducing uncertainty. The fact that such research is not undertaken reflects both *within* industry, and *about* industry, the low prestige attached to entrepreneurial and implementational endeavour. If the conventional wisdom should be inverted to become 'What *should* be done, *can* be done', then the man who turns invention to good effect must enjoy greater influence, resources and honour. A good way to begin would be to conduct serious research into the mysteries of added value, and the art of producing it.

# Discussion

Mr. Duckworth offered some statistical illustration of Dr. Archer's 'sperm-and-ovum' analogy of the proportion of original ideas required to give rise to one successful completed innovation. In the 20 years of the NRDC's existence it had taken 10,000 submissions from institutional sources and 10,000 from private sources. Of the former, about 30 were now making money in terms of tens of thousands of pounds, three were making hundreds of thousands, and only one was making millions. From the private sources, the proportions were lower.

He went on to expand the meaning of his earlier reference to the time-scale of our present economic problems. He assured Professor Burn that, in fact, he was lumping a large span under his term 'the imperial past', and that there was no disagreement between them that the origins of present unfavourable international comparisons could be found in the last century. He agreed with Professor Burn that some inertia in the British system had prevented us from adapting as early as we should have to the new requirements of international competition. But we were starting out from a somewhat different position from many of our competitors. We had the bigger job to do in reorganizing the structure of our society and getting used to being a competitive nation.

Professor Burke commented on Professor Burn's remark that inventors were rarely self-financing. This, he said, was a recent phenomenon. Of the cases in 'The Sources of Invention' 35—40 per cent. had financed themselves to a stage which today would be impossible. He felt that one of the few certain conclusions to which the study of innovation led us was that the process was getting so expensive that it could now only rarely be afforded by the individual. Professor Burn agreed, but pointed out that even in the relatively early days of the industrial revolution outside resources were often needed, and he quoted the example of James Watt who was supported by Boulton and indirectly by the banks. In heavy industries, he said, total self-financing had certainly ceased by the 1850s.

# Discussion

*General Discussion of Matters Arising from the Day's Proceedings*

The general threads of the closing discussion were the differences between nations in innovative success and postulation of causative factors.

Dr. Pannenborg, commenting on the role of government, suggested that a way in which direct government action should be used was through the educational system to bridge the gap between university and the industry. This was an urgent necessity, for, he noted, industry in the U.K. was being starved of talent. Mr. Duckworth added that the government itself had contributed to this starvation by retaining far too many people in universities and in other professions outside the industrial field. He agreed it could act directly to alter the educational system to provide the people industry needed. But it could only indirectly influence their decision to enter industry, and this it could do by creating the right climate for an innovating society. For example, a change in taxation systems would not cure all our ills, but nevertheless would help to create a climate of incentive.

The tendency to regard industry as not entirely respectable had been a general European phenomenon, commented Dr. King. He described how the Swedes had attacked this some years ago. Industry was observably bereft of first class brains so a group of top industrialists deliberately created 'a cult of industrial snobbery' by establishing the Royal Academy of Engineering Sciences. The King was its patron. Through the activities of the Academy, the computer and concepts of automation, for instance, had been put over at an early stage of their development, and because of this patronage their importance was early accepted in Sweden.

Professor Oshima, commenting on taxation systems, referred to the tax exemption in Japan for R and D expenditure. This had been intended to promote industrial R and D. But this policy was now being somewhat questioned as individuals reached higher levels of income and found the progressive taxation system impacting harder on them than before. The government was now accused by the salaried class of giving too much benefit to industry. This illustrated the importance of the social background.

As a suggestion of how bold creative thinking should approach the restructuring of society, Mr. Bodington expanded his concept of a massive central investment in computers to which all would have free access. Such a total information bank would have enormous industrial benefits, induce extensive technical education, and facilitate the dissemination of information crucial to the solution of a wide range of problems. Professor Burn warned that often the demand for information was an excuse for doing nothing. He also commented that he knew of many firms which had bought computers only to find they were not of central value. Mr. Bodington agreed, but pointed out that such misusage was one of the problems which he wished to solve. He viewed the computer as the analogue of the machine between 1770 and 1800. Mr. Duckworth said that there was little evidence that government could do this kind of thing intelligently. In activity of this kind, it usually succeeded only in distorting the market without strengthening the industry, as, he suggested, had happened in aircraft and atomic energy.

Mr. Goldsmith raised the question of the fundamental differences between the cultural and social 'natures' of nations. He had been impressed, he said, with the example of the teabag in Japan and the fact that native green tea would never be put in a bag and used in this way, though foreign-grown tea was. This led him to suggest that the comment by Dr. Gellman was not entirely valid that if all nations had organized themselves in the same way as Japan none would have progressed. 'We must recognize', he said, 'that different nations can never approach the teabag in the same way, and possibly what we ought to be concerned with is finding out about our own native teabags.' This might then lead us to some further insight into the kind of socio-cultural complex which lay behind innovation.

Mr. Wolff, who was, he said, looking for correlations, put forward the hypothesis that the mix of population might be a causative factor. Japan was the country with the longest-standing homogeneous population. The U.S.A., in contrast, had a mixed strain of population. Could it be, he asked, that the mixed strain animal was highly innovative conscious because of the variety of genetic material, while the homogeneous population was successful in other ways?

Dr. Woodroofe pointed out that a fact which must be considered in this context was the increasing consistency of the pattern of life throughout the world. In some measure this stemmed from the growth of American companies and the spread of their products throughout the world. However, they had made important mistakes by failing to recognise cultural differences.

Dr. Goldman took up the point of the international spread of American industry. Why was this, he asked? It should not seem so inevitable. Some of the most important technological developments had been made on the European side of the Atlantic. But often they had been exploited only in the U.S.A. He cited the float-glass process which Pilkington licenced in the U.S.A. and suggested that the royalty received was small relative to the value of the

*Discussion*

product. He pointed out how the Ford Motor Company in America had, after extensive research effort, been able to make the glass meet the varying specifications of the American market — something which the Pilkington company had not done in Great Britain but which, he suggested, it could have done.

Dr. Knoppers said that it was necessary for innovating companies to enter the American market in order to maintain a competitive lead for their products. But this was a very expensive process and could mean for some companies that licensing out was necessary.

Dr. Pannenborg thought that these patterns also had something to do with the psychological barriers, a lack of self-confidence to enter the U.S.A. market. Dr. Fryers agreed, pointing out that the U.S.A. market was 10 times the size of the British, therefore the scale of risk was very much greater. But Dr. Gellman was not convinced. There had been no period since the war, he said, when American interest rates had not been much more favourable than European, and enterprises had not been easier to finance in America. Dr. Charpie, supporting this point, disputed the notion that the scale of the U.S.A. market was either a particular advantage to the American company, or necessarily a deterrent to overseas firms. The point of maximum risk in introducing a new product was, he said, long before it reached the maximum potential market. 'No innovations are introduced to "the American market" ', he said. They were introduced to selected customers in selected regions, and the problems in this crucial early stage were certainly not those of managing the total American market. In his view, the availability of capital in the U.S.A. was a more important factor behind the American success; another was the fact that a successful climate bred success. Dr. Peccei pointed out there were factors other than market size which could deter European companies from entering the U.S.A., for instance anti-trust legislation.

# Industrial Aspects

# Chapter 17

# A Management View of Innovation

*Antonie T. Knoppers*

There are as many management views of innovation as there are managements. Each is a synthesis of hopes and doubts superimposed upon experience. A common view, one held by all major corporations, simply does not exist, although a common rhetoric in praise of innovation is not hard to find. Even if we single out a particular company, we still cannot isolate a single management view. In most companies, management is of many minds about innovation and its obligation to support the innovative process. As a rule of thumb, this ambivalence increases as a company becomes more complex and richer. Only the smallest companies, embryonic enterprises with no assets, hence, nothing to lose, can consider innovation an unmixed blessing.

For most corporations, the relationship between management and innovation has many of the earmarks of the more celebrated relationship between a vigorous young man and a lovely young lady. Management, by stages, is curious, talkative, flirtatious and not a little frightened. Management may get cold feet and flee, only to find to its chagrin that it cannot live without the lady. And so begins a touch-and-go-marriage, full of adoration and recrimination, between two partners who feel they need each other ... but who also cherish dreams of their former independence.

In the two decades since World War II, many corporations have found technological innovation to be a key to remarkable growth. On this one subject of growth management, truly, has a unified point of view. Therefore, it has a consuming interest in innovation. At the same time, management realizes that for innovation really to contribute to growth, it often must sail close to some dangerous financial shoals. This is management's dilemma. While innovation sometimes yields fabulous returns, it usually is costly and it can be disastrous. Moreover, innovation is never the only source of growth. Higher income often can be achieved by added promotional emphasis, acquisitions and other more tried-and-true methods. Therefore, the challenge for management is to see clearly how innovation can best fit into a corporation's overall concept of growth. What emphasis should innovation be given when it must compete for resources with production costs and marketing expenditures and even with proposed acquisitions or dividends?

Management, in short, must define its long-range objectives. Properly done, this process is not merely extrapolation, with today a miniature of tomorrow. Rather it is a process of search which begins with an appreciation of the complexity and rapidity with which our environment changes. Trends affecting our business must be probed for implications which then modify our goals and strategies. This makes it possible to answer the basic question: 'What should we become, given our strong points and our weakness?'.

Somehow, marketing must make an accurate assessment of what the public wants or, at least, is ready to accept. The Galbraith thesis that corporations can be quite effective in stirring up consumer demand can be taken just so far. Enough highly promoted failures exist to prove conclusively that the man on the street is a different animal from the rat in a Skinner box. The *New York Times*, describing Professor Galbraith's recent confrontation with his British critics, reported one memorable example where the public called the shots. This was panty hose. It was pointed out to Professor Galbraith that here, at least, was a case where the ladies insisted and won out in the face of a demurring industry.[1]

From management's point of view, marketing, for all its variables, is considerably more comprehensible than the intellectually foreign work of research and development. Yet R and D must be integrated with the marketing inputs if innovation is to succeed. Schematically, it is simple: the top management group works out corporate strategy and assigns priorities; within this framework, the 'marketers' define needs and opportunities, and R and D delivers the merchandise. It makes for a neat chart. But in practice, the process is never simple.

Management makes more than a commitment to research. Just as fundamentally, it must make a commitment to the type of research. Will the main thrust of the company's effort be fundamental in nature or essentially an effort to modify existing ideas? The choice, whether to work towards peripheral or core inventions, is a major decision for any management, although to a certain degree it is influenced by the type of industry involved. In mass consumers' goods industries, peripheral improvements are the order of the day. On the average, one finds few revolutionary improvements in the changes in new automobiles, artificial fibers, toothpastes, breakfast cereals, cosmetics — and even in major segments of the electronics field.

This is partially because core innovations are truly rare and very hard to come by. But it also reflects a deep-set attitude on the part of much of management. Donald Schon went directly to the psychological crux of the matter. He noted that management will always praise innovation, but that it also cannot fail to see innovation as the enemy of planned activity.[2]

Management, understandably, is uncomfortable with the idea that a discovery from its laboratories could force a costly reorganization and reorientation of its manufacturing and marketing structure. But it likes even less the idea that a competitor's discovery could do this. Hence, the paradox of companies that pursue research but construct all kinds of financial and organizational barriers to preclude excessive research successes. To fall back

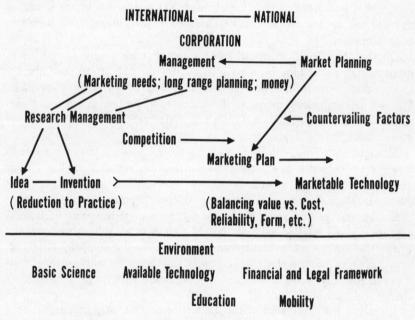

Figure 1. A 'neat' chart

on my metaphor, many large corporations, for all their elaborate research commitment, resemble overpowered automobiles that are being driven in high gear with the handbrake on.

One need only start to list the practical and experimental applications for the laser to sense how profoundly upsetting to the state of the art involved a core invention can be. In some technical areas, small companies, working within the intellectual ferment of the core invention itself, are ideally positioned to exploit genuine breakthrough discoveries. Some of these small, research-intensive companies have prospered handsomely, especially in two or three university-associated sites in the U.S.A. Time and again, small, research-based companies have made big corporations sit up and take notice.

Management of major corporations must decide whether it wishes to go the route of basic research, with all of the expense and uncertainty that this involves; or would it rather 'counterpunch', simply reacting to the demonstrated successes of others? If the choice is for basic work, in addition to justifying the expense, management must also live with the realization that the time lapse between invention and product may be very great and the payoff may not be commensurate with the importance of the discovery. Neither cryogenics nor holography is a new concept. The enormous commercial potentials of both are obvious. Yet neither has begun to realize its inevitable commercial success because of very difficult technical problems of development.

On the other hand, industrial laboratories that are deeply committed to fundamental studies have been conspicuous for their ability to react quickly to core discoveries in their general field, regardless of where these are made. The Bell Laboratories response to the discovery of the laser is a case in point. Anyone familiar with research within the pharmaceutical industry could cite many others.

Management's first obligation is to recognize its own role as a catalyst in creating an ambience where research can flourish, and this implies a basic understanding of the R and D process. Management must be genuinely involved. Michael Shanks summarized this very perceptively in writing: 'Research has proved most successful where management has been most emotionally and intellectually committed to its success. It has also flourished where there is a certain fluidity and flexibility in the company structure, which permits the interplay of personality and ideas, and where management is psychologically ready to alter existing plans and patterns to accommodate change and innovation.'[3]

Invention itself, the start of the innovative process, may be rational or it may be haphazard. The Edison inventions, combinations of two or three known effects into a practical product, were rational inventions; Fleming's discovery of penicillin's antibiotic activity was chance. In modern invention, the two frequently interact serendipitously, as in the invention of xerography. Carlson's five steps were the picture of rationality; the addition of selenium to the process, the key to its high efficiency, stemmed from instinct rather than from logic.[4]

A major factor in the inventive process is recognition, the ability to see objects or effects in a new context. An elderly Viennese microbiologist told me last year that, for two decades, he had thrown away culture plates as contaminated when they showed the same effect as later stimulated Fleming. Moreover, the concept of antibiosis was known even to Pasteur and his pupils. Fleming's contribution, and it was a contribution of genius, was recognition.

Luck undoubtedly plays a role in invention. But luck, in this case, is not merely random good fortune; it has characteristics of a personality trait, combining the faculty of recognition with other less-definable factors, such as a sense of timing and an instinct for success. Moss Hart, the playwright, underscored an identical success factor in other professions when he wrote: 'Every successful person I have ever known has had it — actor or businessman, writer or politician. It is that instinct or ability to sense and seize the right moment without wavering or playing safe, and without it many gifted people flicker brilliantly and briefly, and then fade into oblivion in spite of their undoubted talents.' [5]

The demand for talent in the R and D process extends far beyond the invention stage. It must be understood that the 'D' of R and D — development — often is equally high in its requirements. Problems of development can be monumental. As a general rule, the development process is far more expensive and far more time consuming than bench-level pioneering. Developmental work, as the American space programme so clearly illustrates, can have the excitement and drama of fundamental research.

Innovation demands that corporate management have qualities of recognition and imagination similar to those it requires of its R and D scientists and engineers. Management must have the judgement to balance research input with marketing input. The problem is one of cancellation of variables: the rough odds for success that can be assigned to a project must be weighed out against the predicted economic potential of an untested end product.

While this may sound like a corporate blindman's buff, management is by no means completely in the dark in undertaking such assessments. It has at its disposal such techniques as simulation and technological forecasting, neither, of course, free of uncertainties, but both possessing a sophistication that the uninitiated seldom imagine.

Much useful work has been done in searching for a valid methodology for technological forecasting. Some approaches, such as the Delphi technique and Trend Extrapolation, have shown particular utility, especially in the materials field and certain performance applications.

In all of forecasting, we are developing an increased appreciation of our limitations as seers. We are aware that planning strategies must be multi-dimensional, crossing back and forth over functional lines within a corporate organization. Marketing strategies, of course, have financial implications; research strategies can accelerate obsolescence of existing plants and have important manpower implications. Knowing such things, we can plan accordingly.

Far more difficult to plan for is the impact of outside forces upon a company's operation. Much of our planning postulates a constant value system for the society for which we are producing goods and services. Yet signs are everywhere that social values are undergoing a far-reaching transformation. In the context of this change, technological forecasting and corporate planning are valuable but imperfect tools. A modern management must be as alert to their potential as it is aware of their obvious limitations.

Most of the significant actions which management takes, or plans to take, have impact extending some years into the future. Capital asset commitments are obvious examples of decisions with long-term implications, but marketing strategies, training programmes, staff additions, product line extensions, R and D programmes are all examples of other decisions which also shape the future well beyond the year of implementation.

Furthermore, the year of initiation of a programme is often not the year, nor the period, during which the returns from the programme effort can be measured usefully. In addition, programmes introduced today must actually be addressed to business conditions as they are judged to exist some time in the future. This, of course, is brought about by the changes which will take place in the operating environment, as well as the lead time necessary for the impact of the programme to develop.

For all these reasons, we at Merck have felt it necessary to plan our growth and operations with a 5-year perspective. The system we have established, called the Integrated Planning System, calls for an annual re-assessment of:

1. the environmental trends affecting our business;
2. our goals and major strategic programmes and the assumptions which underlie them;
3. the Action Programmes affecting both our current on-going operations and the Development Programmes established to provide for changes;
4. the resources needed to fund our Action Programmes.

When we have done this for the 5-year period ahead, we then prepare a detailed programme for the first year – a programme organically linked with the remaining four years of the Integrated Plan. We call this first year our Profit Plan: in other companies, this is referred to as the annual budget.

The strong and distinctive features of our Integrated Planning System are that:

1. it is forward plan which seeks creative solutions to achieving growth consistent with appraised environmental change;
2. it permits balanced judgement of the claims on corporate resources for both current operations and development programs;
3. it provides for functional coordination among marketing, production and administration in the Action Programme of the enterprise;
4. it provides for annual reassessment of all planning elements;
5. it relates current budgets to future growth planning.

Planning in a modern sense is useful to any industry and indispensable to an innovative one. Planning gives management the framework it must have to coordinate research, marketing, finance and production effectively. As a corollary to its planning function, the successful company of the future unquestionably will make far broader use of R and D techniques of problem analysis in other company functions such as finance, manpower development and advertising.

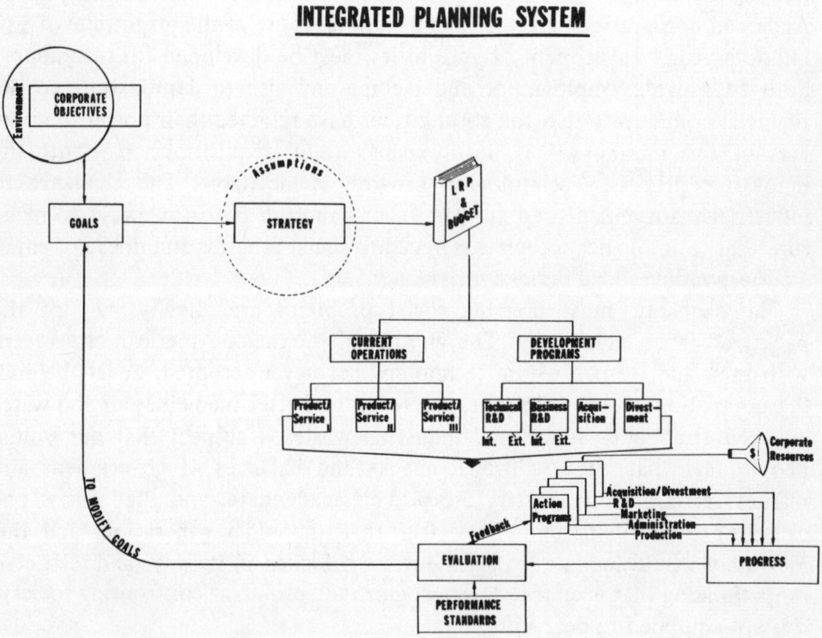

## INTEGRATED PLANNING SYSTEM

Figure 2. An integrated planning system

One obstacle to innovation with which every management must come to grips lies deep within its own psyche. It is the very human tendency to oppose newness. As Dostoevski said: 'Taking a new step, uttering a new word, is what people fear most'. Management knows the same paralysis, which it can always rationalize and which can be described equally well as 'failure of nerve' or 'failure of imagination'. These are Arthur Clarke's terms. The malady, of course, can be diagnosed only in retrospect.

In my view, we should not see each failure by management to seize a research opportunity as another paradise lost. A healthy scepticism by management is often as much a virtue as a vice. Present events are proving that technology is not always self-regulating in terms of its responsibility to society, and that it sometimes needs a period of social assimilation.

Therefore, a built-in braking mechanism may even be socially useful. Competitive pressures will always make certain that the technological genie does not remain bottled up. The very serious question is whether the balancing factors that have protected society in the past are adequate now for this vital function.

The financial leverage on society that today is in the hands of the management of major corporations is without parallel. Professor Robert Heilbroner, in a 1968 review, pointed out that the sums that accrue to American corporations after dividends and taxes are of the magnitude of $30 billion a year.[6] Investment opportunities must be developed for this money, both to provide employment and income and also to demonstrate to the financial community that the corporations have retained their power to grow. Part of this money will go into expansion and acquisitions, part into the innovative process. Technological progress is inevitable. The challenge to industrial management and to our social structure is to find ways to make sure that technological progress is keyed to social progress and does not entail a corresponding social regression.

Many of our most pressing social problems are already part of the backwash from technology. The ghettos of the major American cities teem with men and women whom technology has never accepted, or left behind; the population pressure, in part, is a result of better medicine; air and water polluted from auto fumes and industrial wastes. I suspect that our young people feel that the traditional checks and balances of government and market restraints on industry are proving inadequate, and that this is one cause of their alienation. They feel that the older generation, and this inevitably would include management, is so locked in its ways and restricted in its thinking that even if it does recognize the problems confronting society, it is not equipped to deal with them.

I would like, in my own mind, to know with certainty that these misgivings are misplaced. This is not easy in the face of the evidence. Industry is not involved in the way it must be involved in the solution of these problems; yet without participatory involvement, its capacity to survive as an independent institution may be in serious jeopardy. The dilemma is that industry, as a financial institution, must respond to the demands of the marketplace. Yet in the areas where it can be most useful, social priorities are hard to reconcile with harsh economic imperatives.

Beyond the question of social injustices, industry must also wrestle with the broader question of the impact of its products on society as a whole. Is it morally correct to build atomic power reactors close to populated areas when questions exist in some qualified minds as to their safety and even their vulnerability to sabotage? Is it correct to build atomic reactors and allow their deadly refuse to amass, when no one has an adequate answer to the disposal of these wastes nor assurance that answers can be found?

This apocalyptic example obviously goes well beyond the bounds of the type of problem most management will be called upon to deal with. I mention it to illustrate the degree to which the present has ceased to be a time for complacency. The future will be even less tranquil. All of industry must expect to swim in strong social currents. Industrial management, with its prime responsibility for innovation, must learn to consider both the effects of society upon its products and also the effects of its products upon society.

Managements that traditionally have seen innovation only in terms of a competitive edge might well be advised to weigh them instead on the scales of social contribution. It is on this basis that they will be judged.

My view is that management will emerge successful from the difficult period of testing we are entering if it looks first to the public and then to its laboratory. Industry, in a small sense, is the master of the public's destiny, but the public is the complete master of industry's destiny. As Henrik Ibsen wrote in a less dangerous time: 'I hold that man is the right who is most closely in line with the future . . .'.

### References

1.  'Panty Hose Fitted to Economic Ideas', *New York Times*, March 22, 1969
2.  Donald A. Schon, *Technology and Change*, New York, Dell, 1967
3.  Michael Shanks, *The Innovators*, Harmondsworth, Penguin, 1967
4.  'Profiles', *New Yorker*, April 1, 1964, pp. 46–88
5.  Moss Hart, *Act One*, New York, Modern Library, 1962
6.  Robert L. Heilbroner, 'The Perils of American Economic Power', *Saturday Review*, August 10, 1968, pp. 21–24

# Chapter 18

# Innovation and Coupling Systems in Research and Development

*C. Freeman*

### Invention and Innovation

One of the greatest difficulties confronting studies of innovation is to devise some measure of efficiency in innovative work, that is, to relate 'input' and 'output'. Schumpeter made the valuable distinction between 'invention' and 'innovation', which has since been generally adopted by economists, although not quite in the original form. It is a vital distinction because many 'inventions' may never lead to an innovation. Since he regarded 'inventions' as exogenous to the economic system, Schumpeter stressed the *decision* of the entrepreneur to commercialize an invention as the decisive step and defined the entrepreneur as the 'innovator'. Today, when a great part of inventive work is in-house, the expression 'management of innovation' is often applied to the whole process from laboratory to industrial use. But it is also used in the more specialized sense of the first *commercial* introduction or use of a new product or process. Taking this second meaning, innovation may be regarded as the ultimate aim of most applied research and experimental development, and the success of a particular R and D programme in principle may be measured by the economic benefits arising from the innovations. When the goal of the innovative process is not an economic one, a similar assessment may nevertheless usually be made in terms of 'effectiveness'.

The distinction between inventions and innovations is extremely important for policy for science and technology, as it is theoretically quite possible for an R and D laboratory or system to have a large flow of inventions, or publications, or other information output, but for few innovations to result from this flow. If the information output is regarded as a goal for its own sake, then this may be a satisfactory state of affairs. But this is rarely the case with applied research and experimental development. Hence the critical importance of coupling systems in the network of R and D laboratories and institutes.

The intermediate information output of the R and D industry, like all knowledge, may be used many times over (being indestructible) or not at all. It may be used with very short time lags or very long ones. It may be used abroad before it is used at home. It may be published, or it may be kept secret. If published, it may be widely diffused or barely noticed. In a highly structured science it will normally be abstracted, but the most radical advances often depend on crossing these structural boundaries. The information flow in technology differs substantially from that in science, and formal publication systems are usually less important in technology.

Success in innovation depends on combining inputs from a variety of sources, often including some from outside the formal R and D network. To assimilate this information it is not usually enough to have a good information and documentation service, although this is important, it is also necessary to have direct contact through people. The importance of this direct transfer of knowledge through people has often been demonstrated, but two illustrative examples may be cited:

(1) The war-time radar programme: an extremely successful series of innovations arising from government, industrial and university co-operation.

(2) The Scottish electronics scheme in the 1950s: a series of failures arising from lack of communication, not only between government and industry but also within firms between different departments.

It is only by measuring *innovations* directly or indirectly that the efficiency of the system in generating *final output* can be assessed. For *ex post* studies the measurement of intermediate output itself often involves reference to final output. For example, lists of 'important' inventions or 'key' patents can only be made *ex post* using the criterion of successful innovation to estimate 'importance'. Most histories of 'inventions' are actually histories of 'innovations'. It is the benefit to society, however measured, which is the ultimate criterion of R and D output.

## Cost-Benefit Analysis of Innovations

If a flow of successful innovations is considered as the ultimate aim of the R and D system, then these may be measured in terms of their contribution to specific goals, in relation to their cost. The measures used in this type of assessment may vary with the policy goal. For example, those reductions in mortality or disease attributable to specific innovations might be a criterion for effectiveness of medical R and D, whilst increased destructive power of new weapons systems might be the criterion for military R and D.

It is not possible within the scope of this brief paper to review methods of measuring the effectiveness of military R and D. But it is important to note that analysis of the cost-effectiveness of new weapon systems, during and since World War II, played a major part in the development of techniques of operational research and systems analysis, which have since found much wider applications. Here the discussion concentrates primarily on economically-oriented R and D and on 'welfare' R and D.

For economically oriented research, the appropriate criteria might sometimes be cost reductions in the case of process R and D, or contributions to market growth and profitability in the case of new product R and D. The type of measurement which is relevant, will vary with the level of decision-making and with the type of innovation. At the level of the firm a great deal of detailed information will be available, which can be used both in *ex ante* and *ex post* project evaluation, but cannot normally be used at a higher level of aggregation. In a market economy the main criterion may well be profitability of innovations. At the level of the industry, or the government, it may be possible to assess external and secondary benefits arising from an innovation, or external costs, which are disregarded at a lower level. The method of assessment may also vary with the type of economy: in a market economy the competitive position of the firm will be a relevant dimension, but this may not be so in a socialist economy. Just as with industrial productivity measurement, techniques which are appropriate in one firm or for one type of output may not be relevant for another.

Unfortunately, very few studies have been published relating to the project or programme evaluation of enterprise-level R and D, *as it is actually carried out*. There are plenty of papers and books prescribing ways in which it *ought* to be carried out, but there is some evidence that these techniques are not very frequently applied in practice,[1] except perhaps in the socialist countries, where in some industries they are used systematically. What little evidence exists suggests that most firms find it hazardous to measure costs or benefits whether *ex ante* or *ex post* and that qualitative judgments are widely used.

Two well-known cost-benefit studies of important individual innovations are those of Griliches[2] and of Grossfield and Heath.[3] The frequency of their citation is a tribute both to their quality and to the extreme difficulty of assembling the relevant data for such analysis. One of the principal merits of both these studies was the care with which they attempted to measure the social benefits arising from the diffusion of the innovation. In the case of the potato harvester, Grossfield was able to estimate the total savings arising from the difference between hand-picking and mechanical harvesting, whether these benefits accrued to the manufacturers, the farmers, or the consumers. He was also able to demonstrate and measure approximately the cost of the contribution of the National Institute of Agricultural Engineering and the NRDC itself to the success of the innovation. But both he and Griliches encountered difficulties in calculating the cost of 'failures', i.e. parallel or abortive attempts to make similar innovations, and research in related fields which made an indirect contribution. These difficulties of selecting, isolating and measuring the appropriate 'costs' are multiplied many times over in the case of most industrial and agricultural innovations. Researchers usually find that, although occasional individual projects readily lend themselves to cost-benefit analysis, most do not.

This is probably one of the main reasons for the scarcity of practical examples of cost-benefit studies and rate of return studies at enterprise level in market economies. Other major factors are company security and a certain reluctance to subject past experiences to impartial scrutiny. Difficulties in quantifying costs and benefits are stressed also very strongly by Mansfield, who has contributed the most important econometric studies in the field of industrial innovation.[4−5] Like many economists he is sceptical of the results so far achieved by a 'production − function' type of approach.

### Indirect Measures of the Output of Innovations

Mansfield's studies of size and growth of firm in relation to innovation, timing of innovations and rate of diffusion of innovations show that, because of data limitations in calculating rates of return on R and D investment, the effect of successful innovation on a firm's growth rate is one useful alternative measure of R and D success. He found that the average effect of a successful innovation in the steel and petroleum industries was to raise a firm's annual growth rate by 4 to 13 percentage points. Very striking differences were also found between the growth rates of innovating firms and those of other firms of comparable initial size. In the coal and petroleum industries he found that the larger firms made a disproportionately large share of the principal innovations in relation to their market share, but not in the steel industry. These estimates were made on the basis of direct identification and listing of 'important' innovations from technical journals and correspondence with firms. In the course of his studies he was also able to develop useful models designed to explain the diffusion of process innovations.

Other economists have attempted to relate industrial R and D expenditures and innovations to world market performance. It can be argued, at least for capitalist countries, that the world export market provides a fairly severe objective test of the innovative success of a firm's (or an industry's) R and D activities for *product* innovations. If a firm is the first in the world to produce a new product, it may enjoy an export position based on monopoly supply up to the point of imitation abroad. Even then it may still be able to keep an export lead by technical improvements and the introduction of new models, through intensive and efficient R and D programmes. Such successful innovations would find their reflection in exceptionally high shares of the world market for particular new products or product groups. Cost reductions by process innovations may also enable a country to offset the disadvantage of high labour costs.

Posner[6] has postulated such a 'technological gap' explanation in theoretical terms and economic historians had explained the German lead in the nineteenth century chemical and optical instruments industries very much on these lines. Our studies at the National Institute of Economic and Social Research and at the Science Policy Research Unit[7] attempted to relate world export performance in the plastics, electronics and chemical process industries to the flow of firms' inventions and innovations and to R and D expenditures and provided strong empirical supporting evidence for Posner's theory. The results indicated the importance of 'lead time' in innovative success, of the threshold levels of expenditure which this implied, and some of the cumulative advantages of large-scale R and D in particular industries.

Grossfield's calculations on the potato harvester confirmed the sensitivity of the 'benefits' from R and D to the length of lead time in competitive markets. Development lead times could thus be an important indicator of relative efficiency in R and D output. Such calculations are also widely used in the Soviet Union,[8] where it is accepted that measurement of time lags is an important indicator of efficiency in the whole R and D system.

Hufbauer[9] made a major contribution to the theory of international trade, elaborating Posner's 'technological gap' concept, by relating innovations in synthetic materials to country export performance. Vernon[10] and Hirsch[11] further elaborated these concepts, relating the technological gap theory to U.S.A. performance in world trade and the concept of the 'product cycle'. Hufbauer's method was based on identification of major product innovations and measurement of 'imitation lags' to first production for each country for each new product. These lags were weighted by the relative importance of each material in the world economy, to give an 'aggregate imitation lag'. Thus all the principal countries could be ranked in order of their innovative and imitative success in this industry, and this in turn could be related to their export performance.

Another indirect method of measuring innovation achievements is to use the assessment provided by the international market for licenses and technical know-how. It is reasonable to assume that such payments will flow mainly to the most successful innovating firms, industries and countries. The inclusion of 'know-how' transactions in the statistics means that they do not refer only to that part of R and D output which is patented. Their main deficiency is that they do not reflect those transactions which are conducted on a barter basis or in secrecy. There are also difficulties in connection with the transactions between parent and affiliated companies, which may take a great variety of different forms. Nevertheless, the regular statistics maintained by the Japanese Government since 1953 have demonstrated the value of these figures for policy purposes. More recently most of the leading industrial countries have begun to publish them. A recent paper for UNCTAD[12] attempted to use these published figures to estimate world flows and to assess the transfer of technology to the developing countries through this market.

However, this discussion of indirect measures of innovation output emphasizes once more the difficulty of developing any standardized approach which can be applied across the whole spectrum of R and D activities. One ingenious and original attempt has been made to develop just such a method. Maestre[13] has suggested that an input—output matrix relating a country's industry to its R and D system could be constructed by a novel method of measuring research productivity. This method would rank the 'utility' of various types of research for each industry and would also take into account the upstream and downstream flows of information within the research system by a separate matrix for the transactions within the R and D system. Its successful application would depend, however, not only on some measurement of these difficult intermediate and 'feedback' flows, but also on a large number of peer judgements for every industry about the 'research productivity' relevant to that industry. Thus, in the end, the method comes back to dependence on the type of subjective evaluation of 'quality' and 'importance' of research output, which bedevils so many output measurement techniques.

Even by this method there is no real escape from the laborious and difficult work of case studies and systems analysis, industry by industry and even project by project. Such detailed analysis may ultimately yield the kind of data which could be applied in the way Maestre suggests. But as he recognizes, this is a long way off, and it may never be possible. However, the detailed studies of input and output at the micro-level, as well as attempts to generalize at the industry-level, or country-level, may very well yield important guide-lines for policy, crude though the output measures may remain. For example, Ben-David's secondary analysis of Jewkes' data on inventions and some of the OECD and NIESR studies[14] suggest the value of an approach which relates measures of inventive or research output and input to measures of *innovative* output. In the military field 'Project Hindsight' studied a large number of 'technological events' or sub-innovations and related them to the introduction of new weapons systems in terms of cost and time.[15] In the civil industrial field 'Project TRACE' studied five major industrial innovations, showing in detail how the results of fundamental research over the previous 50 years made these innovations possible, and the way in which the innovating organization brought these results together. This type of comparison may throw up contrasts and unexplained discrepancies between firms or industries, for example, differences in lead times or in 'coupling' of social organizations, which may in turn suggest better methods of management. By an altogether different route, sociologists have come up with interesting hypotheses which could explain some inter-firm and inter-organization differences in research and innovative performance.[16]

Most, if not all, of those economists who have been concerned with research and innovation have concluded that sociology has at least as much to contribute as economics to the understanding of these complex processes. The economist can measure some of the inputs into R and D. Taking his courage in both hands he can attempt to measure some of the outputs and some of the ways in which research and innovation affect economic performance, but the interpretation of these data requires sociological information and insight.

On the basis of numerous interviews within electronics firms, Burns and Stalker[17] elaborated a theory of two 'types' of management. The first type — 'mechanistic' — is appropriate to a firm operating under stable conditions and is characterized by a strong specialized hierarchy with vertical lines of communication familiar from organization charts. The second type — 'organic' — has a far less formal structure and is characterized by constant redefinition of roles and strong lateral communications networks. In their view the first type cannot adapt itself to rapid technical change.

Many of their findings on weaknesses in innovation systems have since been confirmed by further studies in industry in the U.S.A. as well as in Britain. Examples are: the attempted application of methods appropriate to the defence market to the quite different circumstances of the civil market; the relative isolation of some Government R and D laboratories; the lack of any constructive dialogue between sales and R and D departments; and other breakdowns in the formal and informal communication networks. The degree of consensus between sociologists and economists in the interpretation of these phenomena is encouraging.

## Coupling Systems in Industrial Innovation

A striking example of the importance of effective coupling systems for successful industrial innovations is the introduction of new processes in the chemical industry. Technical innovations in this industry and the closely related oil, gas and mineral processing industries arise from three main sources: the process firms themselves, the manufacturers of components for process plant (vessels, pumps, mixers, filters, valves, seals, etc.) and the contractors who design, engineer and construct large process plants. Some innovations represent only minor improvements to existing processes, for example, a more efficient or cheaper seal or filter. Others represent major modifications to a process, for example, the introduction of centrifugal compressors in large ammonia plants to replace reciprocating compressors. Such major changes involve a new process design and considerable development expenditure and risks. Still more radical innovations involve the introduction of new products and completely new processes to manufacture them, including new types of catalysis and other chemical reactions. Examples are the introduction of nylon or PVC.

Most of the major process innovations came originally from the chemical industry. This applies both to those innovations which represent the first process for manufacturing a new chemical product and to those which represent new ways of manufacturing established products. But in the second category, chemical engineering contractors and component-makers have made an increasingly important contribution, often in association with oil or chemical firms. Even if the initiative for a new process comes mainly from a chemical firm, it will usually involve new design and development work for components.

Consequently, intimate coupling between process firms, contractors and component-makers is a critical element in successful innovation and the world market performance of contractor firms has demonstrated this. American contractors have a very high share of the world export market for new plants. They have been especially successful in modifying and improving designs to meet the requirements of larger scale of output, especially for the 'building-block' basic chemicals and for refineries. For example, important process design innovations have been made by several American contractors for large-scale ethylene and ammonia plants, enabling them to dominate the world market for large new plants in this field. Thus process innovation and scale of operations are not independent factors but are intimately linked.

The contractor (whether captive or independent) who builds the first plant embodying a new process already has a head start over his rivals. With each successive repeat plant he extends his know-how and reduces his costs. If the contractor has himself made or contributed to the original process innovation, his position is even stronger, as his understanding will be deeper and he will be able to arrange for feedback of information from operators licensing his process.

There are many cases of successful technical collaboration between U.S.A. oil and chemical firms and the contractors who serve them, such as the Sohio-Badger cooperation on acrylonitrile. But good coupling is important not only with contractors, but also at the other end of the system — with the organizations generating fundamental research output. Access to recent fundamental research results was of critical importance in nearly half of the process innovations which we studied. This sometimes took the form of working closely with outstanding consultants (Natta, Ziegler),[18] sometimes of recruiting outstanding scientists from academic life (Carothers,[18] Twigg), or immigrant scientists (Tropsch, Ipatieff),[19] sometimes of academic scientists themselves exploiting innovations (De Nora), and sometimes simply of careful study of world scientific and technical journals. The last method is probably more important than is commonly realised, as the assimilation of new scientific and technical knowledge by engineers and scientists is not always consciously recognised as such. Both this and the training of scientists and technologists at universities have effects which are not easily measured. The Illinois 'TRACE' project is the most systematic attempt to relate basic research to innovation and has demonstrated the critical importance of assimilating both recent and older results of fundamental research.

The technique of operations research has been used by G. A. Lakhtin and I. Malecki to analyse problems of optimizing output in research organizations. G. A. Lakhtin has suggested that the information service within a research organization is a critical factor.[20] Continuing variety and experiment in the methods of assessing efficiency of innovation seems both inevitable and desirable. One attempt which we are making at the University of Sussex — Project SAPPHO — involves detailed case studies of a large number of industrial innovations.

There are many descriptions of industrial innovations and many myths, but little attempt has been made to compare systematically the projects which succeeded with those which failed. Studies of successful projects alone, although of great interest, do not enable the manager or the researcher to isolate those factors, or combinations of factors, which are critical for successful innovation in industry. Scrutiny of a bibliography of several hundred studies of industrial innovation shows no such systematic attempt.

This research project, therefore, aims to measure a large number of characteristics of both successful and unsuccessful (or less successful) attempts at industrial innovation. These will be subjected to mathematical analysis to discern the profile of success and failure respectively. This approach demands that for each attempted innovation a 'pair' of cases should be selected, one of which was a success story and the other a failure, or relative failure. The criterion of 'success' which is appropriate for each pair may vary slightly according to circumstances, but is normally a commercial one, such as market penetration.

About 30 'pairs' have been selected in the chemical and scientific instrument industries, and firms are being invited to cooperate in preparing detailed case studies for each pair. A careful study of the scientific and technical literature is made in every case, but much of the information necessary can only be obtained by detailed discussion with those who took part in the development work in each firm.

In reconstructing the story of an innovation a check-list is used, but as a mnemonic not a questionnaire. The check-list was prepared with the help and advice of some of the respondent firms. It covers the history of the innovation; a description of the organization and its R and D department, if any; changes in the environment during the innovation period; some characteristics of key people; production and marketing problems connected with the innovation; and a set of 'hindsight' questions. Particular attention is paid to 'coupling' within the firm and between the firm and other organizations. The project is being carried out with a grant from the Science Research Council and is being conducted by a small team led by Mr. R. C. Curnow and Mr. A. B. Robertson.

## Conclusions

It is difficult enough in the case of economically oriented R and D to measure and relate cost to benefits. Even in cases where good statistics are freely available, there are often judgements to be made about research output or innovative output, which are essentially non-economic in character. For example, in the case of a completely new product or service, its introduction may involve considerations of taste, quality of life and values which cannot be easily expressed in economic terms. In the last resort the assessment of 'benefits' of all kinds depends on values. Man does not live by bread alone and economic growth is desirable not as an end in itself but as a means to other ends. Consequently it is quite legitimate to assert the primacy of non-economic values in relation to innovation.

Bernal defined society's investment in research as 'all inquiries directed to changing the future state of civilization'.[21] The kind of civilization we want should determine the output of innovations and the way in which we rate their benefits. Consequently the direction of investment in new science and technology must always be the subject of political and ethical debate and choice. The change in quality of civilization for the next generation is the final measure of the 'output' of innovations.

Within an agreed system of values, choice of project and efficiency of the innovative process are likely to be significantly improved by a much deeper understanding of the coupling process throughout the R and D system.

### References

1. W. R. Baker and W. H. Pound, 'R and D Project Selection: Where we Stand', *I.E.E.E. Transactions on Engineering Management*, 1964
2. Z. Griliches, 'Research Costs and Social Returns: Hybrid Corn and Related Innovations', *Journal of Political Economy*, October 1958
3. K. Grossfield and J. B. Heath, 'The Benefit and Cost of Government Support for R and D: a Case Study', *Economic Journal*, September 1966, pages 537–549
4. E. Mansfield, *Industrial Research and Technological Innovation*, W. W. Norton, New York, 1968
5. E. Mansfield, *The Economics of Technological Change*, W. W. Norton, New York, 1968
6. M. Posner, 'International Trade and Technical Change', *Oxford Economic Papers*, October 1961

7.   C. Freeman, 'The Plastics Industry: a Comparative Study of Research and Innovation', *National Institute Economic Review*, No. 26, November 1963; C. Freeman, 'Research and Development in Electronic Capital Goods', *N.I.E.R.*, No. 34, November 1965; C. Freeman, 'Chemical Process Plant: Innovation and the World Market', *N.I.E.R.*, No. 45, August 1968

8.   *Puti Povysenija Effektivnosti Nauchnogo Truda*, Novosibirsk, 1966, Vol. 2

9.   G. Hufbauer, *Synthetic Materials in World Trade*, Duckworth, 1966

10.   R. Vernon, 'International Investment and International Trade in the Product Cycle', *Quarterly Journal of Economics*, May 1966

11.   S. Hirsch, 'The United States Electronics Industry in International Trade', *National Institute Economic Review*, November 1965, No. 34

12.   C. H. G. Oldham, C. Freeman and E. Turkcan, *The Transfer of Technology to Developing Countries, with Special Reference to Licensing and Know-how Agreements*, UNCTAD, November 1967

13.   C. Maestre, 'Vers une Mesure des Echanges Intersectoriels entre la Recherche et l'Industrie', *Le Progrès Scientifique*, No. 102, November 1966

14.   J. Ben-David, *Fundamental Research*, OECD, 1968; OECD, *Gaps in Technology*, 1969; C. Freeman, *op. cit.* (14)

15.   C. W. Sherwin and R. S. Isenson, *First Interim Report on Project HINDSIGHT*, ODDR, Clearinghouse for Scientific and Technological Information, AD 642400, 1967

16.   T. Burns and G. M. Stalker, *Management of Innovation*, Travistock, 1961; G. Gordon, 'The Problem of Assessing Scientific Accomplishment: a Potential Solution', *I.E.E.E. Transactions*, December 1963

17.   Burns and Stalker, *op. cit.*

18.   H. W. B. Reed, 'A Revolution in Polymers', *New Scientist*, 14 November 1963; 'Nylon', *Fortune*, July 1940

19.   M. P. Venema, *The Unique Corporate Life of Universal Oil Products Company*, The Newcomen Society, New York, 1961

20.   G. A. Lakhtin, 'Operational Research in Research Management', *Minerva*, Summer 1968; G. A. Lakhtin, 'Nauchno-issledovatel'skaya Deyatel'nost i Materialovoe Prozvodstvo', *Ekonomicheskie Nauki*, January 1966; I. Malecki, *Popytka Otsenki Parametra Effektivnosti Nauchnyhh Issledovanie* (Polish-Soviet Symposium), Academy of Sciences, Moscow, 1967

21.   J. D. Bernal, *The Social Function of Science*, Routledge, 1939

# Discussion

Mr. Wolff suggested that there was a third type of innovation, an addition to core and peripheral innovation, which did not lead to a new product but which increased productivity or reduced the price of a present product. 'It is a form of innovation which goes on within a company, is not visible in its products, but which could have significant implications for the labour force, thus relate to the debate on the kind of society to which we wish innovation to lead us.'

Dr. Goldman expanded on the importance of 'invasion' – the fact that many important innovations were made in one firm, or industry, yet developed and utilized in another. Today, he said, firms in America were recognizing increasingly that there had to be some system through which an organization could best utilize an innovation which did not benefit themselves directly. 'New ventures groups' were a means by which such developments were progressed. He described how the Ford Motor Company developed a rapid paint polymerizing process. The overall economic benefit of this invention for the manufacture of automobiles was practically nil. However, what was a peripheral and, as it happened, hardly worthwhile innovation for the motor industry was a core invention for the wood industry. In joint venture with Ford, the wood industry was now test marketing the product. But, the reason why any mileage at all was obtained from this development was because within the Ford organization there was a new ventures group, which was able to appraise the development in its own right and arrange appropriate progressing.

Dr. Knoppers agreed with this philosophy, and pointed out that a company's inability to work in every field forced innovative management to such a course. In his view, a limit must be set at some point to a company's activities. He illustrated this by reference to an anthelmintic product developed by Merck which, it was discovered, had important fungicidal properties. Merck had to decide whether to develop the product for ultimate use as a plant fungicide, or to pass it on for that development to another company. They chose the latter on the judgement that it was not really their market.

Dr. Gellman turned to the problem of 'how to get management's attention focused on innovation and keep it there'. He introduced the concept of the 'ricochet technique', which drew management's attention to the fact that another company was exploiting with great profit one of its own innovations, thus raising the question, 'If they can do it, why can't we?'. This was one of the most effective ways to keep management re-thinking 'the corporate mission'.

In closing the session the Chairman, Dr. Charpie, made the observation that as well as the two classes of innovation which had been discussed, core and peripheral, it might be interesting to consider the possibility that there were two sorts of company, 'those that are better at improving their products and reducing their costs, and those that are better at going outside and starting something completely new'.

# Chapter 19

# A Trade Unionist's View of Innovation

*Lord Delacourt-Smith*

Technical innovation and economic growth are recognized to be closely related creatures; perhaps even Siamese twins. Today, in Britain, we have a widespread acceptance that we need both, uneasily accompanied by an equally widespread disposition to ask whether we are not in danger of being asked to pay too high a price for their residence here. So we tend in practice to show ourselves dangerously in two minds. An examination of the terms on which technical innovation, especially in the context of industrial relations, can be made more rapid may do something to help clarification.

Such an examination can perhaps best start from the point that innovation results from decisions made primarily by the management of industrial concerns, either nationalized or privately owned. On managements rests the initiative in making decisions; frequently the response of the workers, both their formal response through their trade union machinery and their response as individuals, is influential. Generally, it presents itself as a negative, rather than a positive, influence.

Decisions on innovation arise for those who have to make or react to them not in the abstract, but as particular acts of innovation: the introduction of a new process, the complete re-equipping of a plant, or the closing of a plant so that resources may be concentrated elsewhere. Inevitably the decision to innovate means a change, large or small, immediate or gradual, in its effects.

A decision on whether to innovate or not presents the employers on the one hand and workers on the other with different but parallel questions to answer. The management may formulate their questions more precisely and reach their decisions more consciously; but if the innovation is on any scale the importance of the questions for the workers is no less real.

### Innovation and the Employers

The employers ask, 'Is the scientific and technological information available to undertake the act of innovation? Is the capital available to pay for it? Is the change worth making?'.

To the employers it will be the financial question which will always carry the day. Social considerations as such weigh very little (save in the case of the board of a nationalized industry who may have to conform with a ministerial directive or have regard to strongly expressed parliamentary opinion). For the board of a privately owned industrial concern the social considerations are reflected in the necessity to comply with laws on planning, public health and the other social disciplines which legislation imposes upon industry; and are reflected, too, in the fiscal system, which by the differential rates on distributed and undistributed profits, by provisions for regional employment premiums, selective employment tax, etc., provides rewards and penalties to encourage industry to observe social considerations. But for the company the decisions will be based on the long-term health of the balance sheet. This is a characteristic of the private ownership of industry, and it seems to a layman a clear implication of the rapid change in the structure of industry by mergers and takeovers, that there is now an even more powerful requirement and stimulus than ever for boards of directors to make the best financial use of the assets and opportunities at their disposal. This is not to say, of course, that decisions are always wise, or that there is always the thrust towards maximization of profits in practice which exists in theory.

This point, however, is not appropriate for development here; it is made merely to point out the contrast with the workers whose attitude towards an act of innovation presents itself for decision in a very different way. In the case of the board of management the impact upon the way their lives are lived by a technical innovation is likely to be very small. For the workers the effects on the way their lives are lived are bound to be much more important, and may indeed be profound.

## Innovation and the Workers

The questions which the workers will ask about a proposed innovation will also be asked to some extent by the management. 'Are the skills required available, or is the training available to produce them? Are the necessary workers available, and if fewer workers are going to be needed can the surplus be absorbed? Is the change worth making financially?' The workers, however, will formulate these questions differently, and often with a much keener sense of anxiety.

For them technical innovation may change the whole nature of a work process; it may, for example, place a greater premium on youth or better education, or may render the work more suitable for women than for men; it may dehumanize the work by comparison with the processes which have previously been used; it may mean that they will be called upon to work a shift system, or at weekends, or to follow some other irregular work pattern;

it may mean that to continue to perform the work even in a new way the worker must be prepared to move his home and family somewhere else; it may mean that some workers have got to get out of the concern in question, and perhaps out of the industry, because the new process does not require them.

It is easy to have in one's mind's eye a stereotype of 'a worker', or to picture a stream of workers coming through the factory gates. But workers are individuals; and generalizing is always risky. They are young and old, men and women, skilled and unskilled, ambitious and easy-going, able-bodied and disabled, those who like their jobs to be a challenge and a source of pride and those who are only concerned to get through it as quickly as possible. There are no two workers quite alike, and if we have got our priorities right we want them to extend the range of their diversity rather than increase their uniformity. If a number are engaged upon one particular work process, the fact that all can find it acceptable and can reach an acceptable standard implies some kind of common denominator among them; but if that work process is to be revolutionized as a result of technical innovation there is no guarantee that the individuals engaged upon it will all react in the same way.

Moreover, when we come to any need to make a collective decision there is frequently in evidence — implied if not always expressed — the workers' tradition of grievance against society. They believe that, in general, the scales have been and are weighted against the poor and in favour of the rich; this belief reinforces the tendency to look sceptically at any innovation. It is, of course, not an insuperable obstacle to constructive industrial relations based on mutual respect, but nobody can work seriously in industry without knowing that this tradition is there and that there is historically and socially a good deal of justification for it. It is the source of the distinction between 'us' and 'them'.

This sense of class solidarity is embodied for practical purposes in trade unions. A part of the commonsense which workers have accumulated from experience is that despite their diversity and individuality they must try through the machinery of their unions to arrive at common policies. (Of course, some of the diversity between workers is embodied in the variety and diversity of trade union organizations.) Any trade union representative, however, whether operating at the national, regional, district or work place level, must be aware of the human response, the human variety, and when any substantial innovation is proposed the human anxieties which will arise.

Thus, the reaction to technical innovation on the part of the workers and the trade unions which represent them has a complex background to which past history and present individual anxieties both make a contribution. It is important, too, especially when examining this from the point of view of trade union policy, to recognize two separable aspects of the reaction. One is the general attitude of workers to innovation; the other the reaction in the case of a specific proposal for change. Naturally these two interact. The approach in the case of a particular proposal to innovate will develop against the background of workers' general attitude of mind towards innovation and of the policies which the trade union movement has developed on the subject; and that tradition of policy itself will be influenced over the years by the skill or clumsiness with which individual acts of innovation are initiated and completed and by the consequences they are believed to have.

I have emphasized, perhaps rather laboriously, the two distinct points of view of management and workers towards the initiation of an act of innovation, because much frustration and misunderstanding arises from the failure to recognize such fundamental divergences of approach. Alan Fox in his study 'Industrial Sociology and Industrial Relations' (Royal Commission on Trade Unions and Employers' Associations. Research Paper No. 3) addresses himself to the 'frame of reference' through which management and public view the problems of industrial relations. He argues that although many employers, and much of the public, think of industry in unitary terms (i.e. essentially as a team, with one source of authority and one focus of loyalty), the realities of industry really suggest a plural society, with many related but separate groups, interests and objectives which have to be kept in balance.

### Innovation and Living Standards

Against this background, we return to the question of what the reactions will be in a particular case. The first major issue bound to arise in workers' minds is, 'How does the proposed innovation bear on the standard of life reflected in the pay packet?'. Innovation is certainly one of the major factors which over a period makes for higher material living standards for the community: indeed, it might be said to be in the long term the governing factor in their rise.

Naturally, this is a very important point; since it is by the influence of trade unions upon the wage packet that their effectiveness is mainly judged. Moreover, for some 20 years in the U.K., and in other industrialized countries, we have been going through a 'revolution of rising expectations' among workers, just as real as the revolution of a similar sort which Adlai Stevenson discerned in the developing nations. Workers hear constantly of the advance of science and technology; they see constantly on television (and not only in the advertisements) new possibilities of living and spending money; they have ceased to believe that there is necessarily one way of life for the wealthy and another for them. They expect their real wages and their real standard of living to go up year by year.

Does this then lead them generally speaking to extend a positive welcome to technical innovation and to press for its introduction? Certainly not in my experience. Most workers would not say that they were pressing for higher wages to raise their real living standards, or asking for their share of new wealth created by science. They would be much more likely to say they needed higher wages to keep up with rising prices. Many workers constantly and genuinely express the belief that their wages are going up more slowly than prices, even if official figures suggest the reverse. Anyone who has been associated closely with a particular body of workers over, say, the past 15 years will know how, in fact, the standards which they take for granted in housing, in furnishing, in clothing and footwear, in holiday provision, and so forth, have risen during that time. Prices which have remained stable, or even gone down, are not much noticed; since workers tend to demand better quality and styling, and therefore find themselves under the necessity of paying higher prices even when the general price list for a set of articles has remained fairly stable.

There is nothing to complain about in this situation. It is a good thing that standards should be rising, and there are many groups of workers, notably women, where standards have still a very long way to go. Workers, however, do not take the initiative in pressing for innovation, or see it in principle as a contribution to improving living standards.

This is a situation which gradually may change. The Prices and Incomes policy, if it has had no other effect, has brought much more prominently into the discussion of wage claims the factors of productivity and the consideration of final price of the manufactured product, or the service being provided. This is a substantial step forward in industrial understanding, and is permeating the active rank and file who set the tone of the trade union movement and provide so large a part of its effective leadership. Even here, though, productivity is not seen as consisting mainly of technical innovation. It is seen in terms of working harder, merging jobs, taking on new responsibilities or extended skills, reducing overtime, cutting out unnecessary work and workers. These are the staples of productivity bargains.

Where technical innovation is a factor of importance, employers seem to suggest it is something for which they alone are responsible, for which they pay, and in respect of which the workers are entitled to no direct share. Alternatively, it is argued that the benefits of innovation ought not to go specially to workers in those plants where it is most rapid, but should benefit all workers through lower prices. Just as with the broader issues of productivity bargaining itself, there can be endless arguments on the theoretical justification for these points of view. However, this represents a very shortsighted policy. For workers to see that technical innovation plays a direct part in raising living standards, as they are now beginning to see productivity does, can be a material factor in getting a much warmer welcome for innovation among those who are going to feel so much of its effects.

Indeed, the thrust of workers for higher living standards could be a powerful force for technical innovation and higher productivity if these were recognized as the soundest bases for wage advances. It is not too much to expect that in some areas of the economy technical innovation may be recognized in this way, and trade unions therefore may take a larger share of the initiative in pressing it.

The standard of living is moreover a wider concept than that of higher real wages. It embraces the need for better educational and health standards and for an improved social security system. These can hardly be a part of the judgment brought directly to bear by workers in weighing up the pros and cons of a specific act of innovation; but a recognition that achieving such social improvements will be facilitated by growing national wealth, to which technical innovation can contribute, will influence the general attitude of the trade union movement to technical change.

## Innovation and Security of Employment

Closely allied with concern for a rising standard of living is concern for security of employment. The two cannot be separated, and for many years the British trade union movement made it quite clear that the maintenance of full employment was its highest priority in economic policy. It was to this aim above all others that it wished Governments to have regard. Since the end of the 1950s the phrase 'full employment' has been replaced by 'a high and stable level of employment', and full employment as a prime objective has given place to economic growth. In the more recent pronouncements of policy by the TUC, strong emphasis has been put upon the need to find ways of reconciling a high rate of economic growth with an improvement in the balance of payments position; nevertheless, the maintenance of a high and stable level of employment continues a matter of great concern to trade unions.

By the standards of pre-war years, of course, the level of employment has been high; but technical progress still tends to be seen by many workers as a threat to high employment levels rather than as an indispensable way of maintaining them. How indispensable technical innovation has been is shown by taking account of the degree to which even over the past 10 years in such staple employments as textiles, coal mining, rail transport and shipbuilding, the decline of the industry combined with the necessity to raise output per man has led to a sharp decline in the labour force. Employment in those spheres fell in that period by more than half a million men — some 25 per cent. On the other hand, industries in which technical innovation is important and fertile have provided substantial numbers of new jobs during the same period; a relatively small group of these which in 1960 employed less than a million men have expanded by nearly one third to employ nearly 300,000 more.

In rendering acceptable any programme of technical innovation the maintenance of a high and stable level of employment throughout the economy is of the greatest importance; but it is no good imagining that such a principle or slogan satisfies the anxieties of those who do feel technical change, either in general or in a specific case, to be threatening their jobs. 'Full employment' or 'a high and stable level' does not mean to the individual worker that if he loses his current job there is another one somewhere to which he can go. He is concerned not with a job, but with one that is likely to involve him in no loss of pay or status, not to make materially greater demands upon him and not to involve him in an unacceptable removal of his home. A skilled worker who has lost his job on, say, the North East coast because his skill is no longer needed, is not resettled by telling him that he can get a job at £10 or £12 a week less in his own locality as an unskilled worker, or that if he wants to maintain his earnings he can move down to Birmingham or Coventry.

It is the bleak future facing those who have been encouraged to concentrate upon one skill, and who see the danger of the unique position of that skill being eroded by changes in techniques or materials, that is at the root of the most difficult demarcation problems. The degree of full employment necessary to create a climate conducive to more rapid technical innovation must be based upon a much more positive manpower planning programme. Too often, the reallocation of manpower seems to consist of shaking skilled men out of one industry and giving them no more than a general assurance that there are many other industries in the locality that want their skills. It ought to be possible to provide, on the basis of the forecasts of industrial development available, some much more positive indication of where the new jobs will arise, in which industries they will be, and what skills they will demand.

This is made the easier by the development of the various industrial training boards, and the tendency they appear to be showing to seek to put skilled training on a more comprehensive and flexible basis. The use of the Government training centres has also an important part to play. Gradually, the conception will have to grow for skilled workers and technicians, no less than for University graduates, that education is a process which will continue throughout life, and that any one in the course of a working life will have to be prepared for two or three periods of retraining to fit his skills and accomplishments to the current requirements of the economy.

The maintenance of a high level of employment cannot be ensured except by Government action. One aspect of this action is the sort of improved provision for earnings – related unemployment benefit and for redundancy pay which the U.K. is now beginning to make. But the deliberate maintenance of economic growth and the improvement of manpower planning are the indispensable background for such a policy.

### Innovation and the Conditions of Daily Work

The consideration of innovation, however, does not bear only upon the number of jobs and their location and their remuneration; it bears, too, on their character and the conditions associated with them. This is a matter in which different industries and different parts of the country have different traditions. The introduction of a shift system for a body of workers who have always been accustomed to working a normal day introduces very substantial domestic upheavals. My impression is that workers will go on expecting relatively more and more substantial compensation for a pattern of work which involves night and weekend work; and more and more will tend to secure by shorter hours, at any rate in part, compensation for the attendances outside the normal work day.

In a number of fields marked by technical innovation coverage for every hour of every day is necessary; the unwillingness of workers easily to disrupt their domestic lives has to be overcome in negotiation. Similarly, an increased demand for leisure may manifest itself in workers taking days off when they want to, believing the extra amenity is worth the pay that is thereby forfeited. In fact, if we try to study the complex subject of what hours are actually worked in different industries we find two contrary tendencies at work.* One is the tendency for some men, either because they have limited family responsibilities or because of increasing age, to put a higher value on leisure than on pay and to prefer therefore the leisure when they have earned in a week enough for their needs. In industries which put a substantial emphasis upon relating an individual's pay to his output, it is hardly surprising that he should expect to be able to make the choice of forfeiting pay if he feels the leisure is worth more. The example of this that has been more commented on is the so-called absenteeism in the coal mines; but there tends now to be growing comment upon the extra days taken without pay in extension of Christmas and other public holidays. The contrary tendency is probably most marked among men who have growing family responsibilities or who particularly want large incomes for some other reason and so welcome as much overtime as they can get.

Consideration of these two counteracting tendencies suggests that there is at present a good deal of scope for workers to vary the number of hours which they work over a period in accordance with their personal needs.

* The fullest treatment of this subject is to be found in E. G. Whybrow, *Overtime Working in Britain* (Royal Commission on Trade Unions and Employers' Association Research Paper 9).

Perhaps we ought to recognize this much more formally than we do, envisaging in some cases fairly flexible hours of work, provided the individual worker operates within some agreed pattern and his attendances made by arrangement can be relied upon. If, on the other hand, a concern wants strict adherence to standard working conditions, it will have to consider how far this can be combined with a pay system which relates itself so strongly as some do to individual effort and output. Continuity of production, which means a good deal more than absence of minor disputes, seems to be coming to the fore in negotiations.

### Innovation and Job Satisfaction

The final aspect of this is the satisfaction which the individual worker gets in his work while he is performing it. This change in the character of the work may be the most important long term effect of an act of innovation, persisting after the short term disturbances and stresses have been resolved. What will be the permanent character of the new job? Will it leave small scope for skill and responsibility? Will it have involved loss by the individual of control over the work process, the pace of work, the quality of the product, the methods employed? Will the satisfaction of the individual have been enhanced or diminished?

A variety of considerations will determine the worker's attitude: the physical conditions in which the work is performed; the degree of attention and respect for workers which the concern shows by the standard of canteen, washing, toilet and other facilities; the degree to which the group of men or women working together forms a pleasant social unit; and, of course, the satisfaction which can be secured from the work itself. Another set of considerations, perhaps even more important, will turn on the character and quality of supervision, and the recognition of achievement by the individual in work.

Research done on this subject of satisfaction achieved in work has had only patchy application in industry in the U.K. Some firms have applied the results of research; others have accepted in principle that their workers ought to be treated like human beings, and have found to their surprise that this is usually good business, too. In particular, there has been astonishingly little application of the results of research upon the effect of work — such as assembly line work, where the individual operative performs a monotonous and repetitive process which can, in itself, give him little human satisfaction. Neither trade unions nor employers generally seem to discern in this process itself a possible source of discontent. Very few people have commented, for example, on the influence which this form of operation, carried on in circumstances of considerable noise and strain, has had in the car industry, where it is so prevalent. Again, it is said very frequently that women

positively prefer a monotonous, repetitive job, although it is usually assumed
that this will be combined with a situation in which they can talk easily and
freely to each other, which may not always be the case.

While something has been done by the operation of job enhancement to
recognize the importance of the work process upon the individual worker's
self respect, there is a profound and urgent need for far more systematic
attention to the effects of the different aspects of working environment on
the worker, especially in circumstances of high productivity.

The planning of new work processes, since they often involve such heavy
capital investment, needs to be done carefully and in advance with full regard
to the demands which the methods will make on the workers. Once the initial
layout has been planned and the investment undertaken modifications cannot
easily be made. Those who think in terms of computers and computer control
are not necessarily those best able to envisage the kind of jobs which their
planning will create, and the early involvement of the trade unions in such
planning is becoming increasingly necessary.

### Joint Consultation

All this suggests that workers, even if they come to extend a positive
sympathy to the principle of innovation in industry, are likely to wish to see
the innovation at a regulated rate with full consideration of the human and
social effects which it will have. The more adequate the arrangements for
resolving difficulties in the human and social sphere, the higher the sustained
rate of innovation which will be acceptable.

The machinery for determining the rate is the joint consultative machinery
constituted by employers and trade unions. So an examination of innovation
in industry cannot be complete without an examination of the adequacy of
this machinery and its component parts.

The complete inadequacy of this machinery over much of industry was
emphasized most authoritatively by the Donovan Commission.[1] They
regarded it as essential to their study of British industrial relations, and their
diagnosis of its weaknesses, the contrast between the formal machinery and
the informal, between what was supposed to happen and what did happen.
They drew a picture, in general terms, showed elaborate joint machinery
covering industry on a nationwide basis, but laying down, in fact, only a very
limited number of minimum conditions – a basic, national minimum rate of
pay, for example, and a broad procedure for dealing with grievances. In
contrast to this, there was in the work place a great amount of bargaining,
usually by shop stewards, which produced lieu rates, bonuses and other
payments, which made up a very substantial part of the pay packet and which
varied considerably from one firm to another. In addition, negotiation at the
local level produced a variety of agreements and understandings on discipline,

redundancy, arrangements of working hours, holidays, and work operations. It is the task of the new Commission for Industrial Relations to try to assist industries to devise, according to their several circumstances, joint machinery which integrates the national and the local elements.

For our present purpose, however, the most important thing is the need to widen substantially the scope of such machinery, and to embrace in discussion at the national and local levels all the background factors which determine the decisions which companies make. There is need to consult much more fully and genuinely with workers, so that they may be made aware of the range of commercial and technical choices and decisions with which the concerns are faced, and may be given a much greater degree of effective participation in the forming of those decisions.

This is particularly relevant when any technical innovation is proposed, because of the substantial social consequences for the workers which it may well have. As with any major change, the trade union movement has for years been emphasising the indispensability of honest, full, and early consultation, in which the intentions of the management are set out clearly and are the subject of constructive discussion between the two sides.

Neither the employers, individually or in their collective bodies, nor the trade unions can claim to be perfect instruments for the handling of these matters. There is a need on the trade union side not only for a regrouping of unions, but also for much better research, publicity and educational facilities. However, we must remember that trade unions are democratic organizations and nobody who exercises authority in them, at whatever level, can move very far, or for very long, outside the framework of ideas accepted by those he represents.

On the employers' side, there is need again for greater expertise and imagination, as well as for the improvement of their specialized arrangements for handling personnel questions and industrial relations. Even now in many industries industrial relations does not get a big enough share of the attention of top management, until there is a crisis.

What is required, in effect, is a revolution in the whole concept of relationships between workers and managements, both in privately and state owned industry. The content of that revolution is not yet clearly defined by the trade unions — 'industrial democracy', 'workers' participation', 'greater joint consultation'; but industrial relations will not run more smoothly, and innovation will not be as speedy as it might be, until effective steps have been taken to bring about the sort of changes which those phrases seek to express. The Royal Commission on Trade Unions and Employers' Associations was unanimous in believing that this was a subject of great importance, but could not agree upon what changes might have the desired effect. The Government White Paper 'In Place of Strife' rather suggests that the Government has a similar attitude to that of the Royal Commission.

Perhaps in the scope of this present paper I may confine myself to three points. The first is that trade union organization should be much more widespread than it is. Various factors, not least the proposals of 'In Place of Strife', are likely to lead to greater trade unionism in the areas of employment where it has hitherto been held back by tradition, or by the small scale of the units in the industry, or by employers' intransigence.

The second is that there is need for healthy joint machinery, providing opportunity for considering not merely such subjects as wages, conditions, safety, and welfare, but the whole range of matters affecting the concern, and indeed the industry. To establish rapidly such a new scale of joint consultation will require conscious effort by both sides.

The third need is to end the concept that the shareholders alone are entitled to express a view on the composition of the board of directors of the enterprise. Whether the workers in a concern should have the right to nominate some of the directors; whether, if they have such a right, they would (or should) appoint trade union officials or shop floor workers to these positions are questions which I do not seek now to develop. What, however, is clear is that the process of perpetual co-option by which the boards of privately owned concerns appear to be recruited has weaknesses which some degree of influence by the workers might help to mitigate.

In particular, there are three respects in which such influence might be hoped to exercise some useful effect. First, used in conjunction with the wider degree of consultation already advocated, it might reduce the secrecy in which many major business decisions are shrouded. At present, a large private company with a substantial share of the nation's resources can make major decisions with a degree of privacy which is denied to publicly owned industries: denied even to the Government itself, which has to operate in far more delicate areas under a good deal of scrutiny. The condition of some of our major industries suggests that decisions reached in conditions of secrecy have not always necessarily been wise.

Second, the examination of the qualifications of individuals who are appointed to boards of directors would afford a guarantee of the unlikelihood of nepotism or personal influence playing a part in such appointments.

Third, such a practice could be a factor helping to widen the rather limited circles from which the higher ranges of management tend to be drawn. Those who set the tone in managerial circles tend to be drawn from too restricted a social class, and a more genuinely democratic flow through industry of able people, irrespective of their social orgins, or the point at which they entered industry, would be advantageous.

These considerations are not foreign to the question of speedier innovation. Social division impedes this country, because it creates a sourness and lack of communication in industrial relations; also because it distorts the recruitment to higher managerial and commercial positions it wastes human potential. The roots of social division must be tackled in the schools; but if we are to progress more rapidly, industry must take steps as it can to mitigate the consequences which social division has been having.

## Summary

What then can be said in summary about the human and industrial relations aspects of the pace of technical innovation.

First, that to technical innovation management and workers come with completely divergent viewpoints. It may well be that for management — to quote Galbraith — 'one would encounter less dispute on the whole by questioning the sanctity of the family or religion than the absolute merit of technical progress'; but for the worker the situation is very different. Unless the inevitable differences in approach are recognised and understood, conflict and misunderstanding are inevitable.

Second, that the support of workers for technical innovation can be won only by the careful creation of a climate of better industrial relations, based both on a great imaginative understanding of their view point and on the machinery for enabling matters which concern them to be discussed and settled by agreement.

Third, that any imaginative understanding of the workers' view point must include an acceptance that workers expect to see a rising standard of living, the maintenance of security of employment and the enlargement of human dignity — in the senses in which I have sought to explain these concepts.

Fourth, that the creation of adequate machinery for resolving by agreement the differences of view between employers and workers implies reorganization of trade unions and employers' associations. It means, too, the recasting of the procedures which are supposed to be the means of resolving difficulties in some of our greatest industries, but which have often got completely out of date and out of touch with the realities. It means an enlargement of group consultation and workers' participation to a degree that amounts to a revolution.

Fifth, that the problems of technical innovation in industry cannot be solved solely within industry. They must be seen against the background of social and political programme and achievements. The rising standard of living which an innovating society can accelerate must express itself in better education, housing and social security as well as in larger wage packets; security of employment cannot be ensured within one firm, and must be sought by governmental policies which embrace the deliberate maintenance of a high and stable level of employment with the facilities for manpower planning and retraining which that implies; the human dignity of the work in industry cannot be separated from the value placed upon him as a citizen.

There is a residue of scepticism among workers about the value of innovation; in our precarious national economic condition this is a dangerous scepticism, but it will not be overcome by telling the public in general, and trade unionists in particular, that 'in the long run' they will benefit greatly. For trade unionists are Keynesians in the sense, if in no other, of believing that in the long run we are all dead.

In a society with such democratic institutions as ours, which are at least effective in slowing down change if not in stimulating it, the claims of technical innovation can best be pressed by those who not merely see in it the generalised basis for a better life, but have pondered the words of R. H. Tawney (in *The Acquisitive Society*): 'Men will always confuse means with ends if they are without any clear conception that it is the ends, not the means, that matter — if they allow their minds to slip from the fact that it is the social purpose of industry which gives it meaning and makes it worth while to carry it on at all.'

### Reference

1.  *Report of the Royal Commission on Trade Unions and Employers Associations 1965–68* (Chairman the Rt. Hon. Lord Donovan). Cmnd. 3623. June 1968

# Chapter 20

# Strategy for a Post-Industrial Society

*Stephen Bodington*

Does it make sense to talk of a 'post-industrial society'? Even if it does, is it so far out of range as to be irrelevant to our present discussion? My answer to the first question is, yes, and to the second, no. Let me first, briefly, deal with the second question since the first, which does not permit a simple answer, will pervade much of what I have to say throughout this paper. On the second, I would say briefly that the fact that Britain seems to be dropping pretty fast down the league table of the industrial economies does not preclude the possibility of jumping forward again quite suddenly to some more advanced form of economy. With the Industrial Revolution, Britain surged forward to become the most advanced economy amongst the community of nations, and was in turn rapidly overhauled by American and German technology and industrial organisation at the end of the 19th century.

It is of interest — though I would not accept his view of the future — to review briefly the characteristics which Servan-Schreiber[1] takes as defining 'post-industrial society'. In formulating his ideas he draws heavily on Bell[2] and a Report on the year 2000 by Herman Kahn. He envisages a society in which industrial production is about 50 times as great as that of the pre-industrial period, and in which the emphasis in economic activity has shifted from agriculture and industry to services and research. Scientific and technical development would be largely in the hands of public bodies. The public sector and social investment will predominate over the laws of the market. Cybernetic control (presumably he has in mind computer modelling as a means of coordinating economic complexes) will be exercised over industrial organizations. Education will be the dynamo of progress, and itself will be a principal area for technological innovation.

In my view, it is not only difficult but fruitless to speculate about detailed characteristics of societies of the future. The possibility of change, and its nature, will depend very largely on what forms of social and political behaviour, what new types of social structure and relationships emerge. It is, however, I think, sound and necessary to recognize that we are living on the brink of a scientific revolution, and that the technological changes that it brings must cause far-reaching transformations in the nature of social life, man's aims and needs. The essential point about the scientific revolution is that to an increasing extent it will 'make nature work for us'. Automation is but one aspect of this: that is, the control of large industrial complexes by automatically operated systems, hence massive output of goods with small productive labour forces.

But there are many other ways in which science will make nature work for us, such as the development of new materials, new forms of energy, and new patterns of animate life. Some regard our technological revolution as being essentially an 'information revolution'. This approach may well be a sound one, since the feed-back of information about the operations of large economic complexes could enable us to control their workings and improve the output-input relationship, much as today engineering research improves the efficiency of an individual machine. Moreover, the potential that the computer offers for collecting, storing, analysing and communicating information has far-reaching social and political implications. Whether these powers are well or badly used, we have, by our actions, to determine for ourselves; but they hold out, amongst other things, the possibility of creating a fully informed democratic community.

On the brink of so many, and such far-reaching, possibilities of technological change, when the new potentials of scientific knowledge are so varied, hence the direction of social change uncertain and unpredictable, it would be foolish not to pause to ask questions about the kind of society that we might create, and the kind of society we want to create. In short, the qualitative questions about economic development and change are inescapable.

As a means of exploring the deficiencies of a purely quantitative approach, it may be useful to examine the economic concept of productivity. Can we not keep our feet on terra firma and set ourselves the straightforward, proximate objective of using science and encouraging innovation so as to increase productivity? No one can dispute that we could do with more of the material goods by which life is sustained and enriched. If one man can produce, say, 50 per cent. more of these without, or after allowing for, additional resources, then who can doubt that there has been a clear-cut quantitatively measurable gain? However, what seems clear and simple at the level of micro-economics is far less clear at the level of macro-economics. If economics were a game like the decathlon of collecting points for achievements to be measured according to the rules of the game, we could be in no doubt about what an increase in productivity meant. But the economic life of a large community is not such a game. There are acute fears on the part of those employed in industry that increased productivity at the micro-economic level may lead to serious dislocation and unused resources at the macro-economic level. As things are at present, these fears cannot be dismissed as unfounded. We have not yet developed adequate tools for evaluating the overall consequences of technological change, nor have we found the means of using all available resources at full stretch.

The solutions to these two problems, I think, are interrelated. We have tended to assume that we have already an adequate mechanism for deciding whether resources are well used and have treated this as an axiomatic starting point in terms of which all other problems are defined. The economic axiom from which, in practice, the definition of all our problems starts is that the effectiveness or otherwise of our production will, in the last analysis, be measured by ability to sell in the world market. For example, Cotterell[3] in an address that he made to the British Association in September 1966, said, 'The world has closely observed our economic problem and, by altering the value which it places on the pound sterling as an international currency, has expressed its views on it in a manner which no one could ignore. Thus, what is fundamentally a long-term economic problem has appeared superficially in the form of a series of short term financial crises. . . . We are a manufacturing country and most of our visible exports, about £4,500 millions a year, are manufactured goods. The principal means, then, by which we can hope to achieve economic growth without inflation and achieve a balance of payments through a higher ratio of exports to imports are higher productivity and useful technical innovation in manufacturing industry'. That this is the right approach, even on the assumption that the structure of economic relations is not going to be upset by the sweep of technological change, is disputable.

Gordon Tether, a regular contributor to the London *Financial Times*, has been a lone voice, though one of high expertise and experience in international finance, telling us for a decade or more that we have a cart-before-horse approach to the balance-of-payment problems; he has long urged giving first place to expansion (supported if need be by import or exchange controls). I am anxious to argue from a somewhat different standpoint, namely, that we should be looking towards the more far-reaching structural changes, social and economic, that can be expected to flow from the sweeping momentum of scientific advance. But for the immediate present, to make even the first start in tackling our problems, we have no choice but to rid ourselves of our balance-of-payment and financial fetishes. Anyone who has experienced financial squeeze knows that its effect is to nip points of growth and innovation in the bud and to protect the 'dead wood'.

would be wrong to underestimate the difficulty of finding an adequate alternative to reliance on market forces. Preoccupation with balance-of-payment and financial stability derives from a philosophy that looks to the market in the last resort to decide what is and what is not worth producing.

Crudely put, human beings vote for, or measure, degrees of satisfaction with products by buying, or not buying them. However, all our Keynesian wisdom and 30 years of experience have not yet taught us how to handle this market system satisfactorily. I think it is time we looked boldly for the alternative. Supposing we first looked at resources, asked ourselves what people, what equipment were available to meet the social and economic needs of our community. Such an approach clearly bristles with difficulties, but it has, at least, the virtue of showing a green light to initiative. Many might feel that this is more like showing a green light to chaos. How can one 'use resources' without knowing what to use them for? Moreover, no economic resources are insulated from the economic system as a whole. To use resource (A) we must involve also resources (B), (C), (D), etc. Immediately, we are confronted with the necessity of reimposing constraints when the whole exercise was an attempt to escape from constraint.

The 'discovery' of available resources is a far from easy undertaking in a practical sense. At root, it means finding out what people can do, and what supporting resources and activities are necessary to use their potential. It implies, also, identifying social purposes and needs towards which to direct this potential. By definition, almost, the job is to set in motion processes which the market has failed to set going. It involves locating not only patent unemployment, but also misemployment and disguised unemployment. It involves spotting what amount of pump-priming education and specialist help is needed, how far 'learning on the job' may be possible. It involves understanding the technicalities of alternative productive activities. And, possibly most difficult of all, it involves avoiding wasteful, pointless activities. The discovery of resource-potentials, therefore, calls (along lines referred to more fully below) for research and survey work on a generous scale by teams which include, in addition to various expertises, men and women familiar through work with particular localities and industries.

All the same, it is not Utopian to believe that we are living in times when our command over natural resources is considerable, and that we only have to give ourselves a chance of applying the new powers, methods and techniques of science to loosen the material constraints that have hitherto so tightly constricted us when we look at the performance of society as a whole. On the rare occasions when a few people are given a free hand to dip freely into available resources in pursuit of strictly limited purposes, most remarkable things, that have never happened before, begin to happen. For example, man lets slip his gravitational moorings to the Earth, sails round the Moon, and back again to the familiar pull of the Earth's surface. What economic pre-conditions could allow a people extensively to have a go experimentally at new ways of doing things whenever a reasonably feasible project had been worked out? Obviously Tom, Dick and Harry's technical or social adventures could not command supporting resources such as are made available for a space programme. Would anything less be worthwhile? Indeed, would greater freedom to explore and experiment with only the most restricted supporting resources be worthwhile at all? My contention is that it would, and that it is in the nature of the scientific revolution to enhance the importance of (a) people, (b) training and education, and (c) information in the mounting of new initiatives. Costly and intricate capital equipment, although essential for certain types of projects and for others a great advantage, may in other areas, temporarily at least, be a factor that can at the outset be dispensed with to a considerable extent.

Rejection of an economic strategy in which *ultimate* priorities are determined by world market condtions is not the same thing as saying that market mechanisms have no part to play. The stumbling block for Britain is that the corner stone of its economic strategy is to meet the competition of the world market, to give the pound sufficient strength to hold its own in the market place of world finance, to achieve a balance-of-payment surplus. Priorities in economic strategy are determined by conditions in the world market. The alternative is some measure of insulation from world conditions (though the necessary measure could be much milder than those commonly employed in times of war) and the allocation of resources to meet, as a first priority, certain broad social objectives. In order to bring into play resources that contribute directly or indirectly towards these objectives, some credits would have to be made available and these would certainly carry a certain danger of inflation. This danger is real, but it is the lesser danger. The greater danger is under-use of potential, and stifling of initiatives and what is new.

When it is argued authoritatively that there is no evidence to show that expenditure on scientific research accelerates economic growth, we might perhaps remind ourselves that development of engine power does not *ipso facto* mean moving fast. If one is to move, the power must be suitably transmitted and applied. To pause to argue whether science in this modern world is a necessary condition for economic advancement would be an insult to intelligence. But, necessary conditions are not the same things as sufficient conditions: we might perhaps say that this conference is convened in the hope of advancing the search for the sufficient conditions. These must, in my view, include the whole economic climate in which science is applied to industry, and this, in turn, implies broad considerations of economic strategy.

The mechanics of creating the right sort of economic climate is too broad and too deep a subject to investigate in this paper, and can only be referred to in a very cursory manner. The problem is how to make ultimate priorities planned social objectives and, at the same time, to have a flexibility and freedom for initiative far higher than that which at present is provided by a market governed economic strategy. Once precautions have been taken against certain dangerous forms of speculation to which an inflation-prone economy might give rise (for example, speculation in property and land), it would be possible, in my opinion, to use market relationships within a framework of planned objectives to effect the distribution and exchange of products for most purposes. It must suffice to say that the facilities for data collection and analysis, economic modelling and other facilities offered by the impetuous advance of electronic technology, the computer and the other developments properly summarized as the 'information revolution' make it possible, at what we might call the tactical as opposed to the strategic level, to leave market mechanisms to operate freely, whilst a watch is kept on the progress of the economy as a whole so as to forestall the consequences of serious imbalances, bottlenecks, etc.

How could we begin to move towards a new socio-economic strategy? The economic objective can be defined only in the very broadest terms, namely, to begin to construct the sort of economic system that advances in science and technology make possible: that is, one in which there is a rapid extension of automated production, and in which the flow and analysis of information is so ample that the deployment of resources is effectively directed towards the achievement of well-defined social priorities. To move in this general direction, we must have the courage of our convictions and choose purposeful policies that back the right growth points. In my view, there are four essential strands to such policies: (1) recognition that from the standpoint of the economy the revolutionary technical changes are to be sought in the electronics industry and, particularly, in the computer; (2) the key to progress will lie much more in the application of scientific knowledge to practical situations than in investments in capital equipment in the material form; (3), following directly from (2), technological advance in education and the widening of facilities for continuing education on a massive scale will be an indispensable part of the society of the future; and (4) the democratization of decision taking, involvement and control 'at the grass roots', and a democratic information system is the only possible basis for a stable society. (Electronic and computer techniques make higher degrees of centralization conceivable technically, but the social consequences of a power elite in a society requiring less and less productive labour from the mass of the people would be extremely explosive.)

Some comments on the above. The commonly held assumptions that technological advance carries with it a high degree of centralization, massive instruments of production, and a very long gestation period between investment decisions and production (Galbraith's view, for example) are not accepted. They are plausible, because they extrapolate from the industrial society that we know. If there is anything in the idea of a 'post-industrial society' it is something qualitatively different from the industrial society in which we live, and extrapolation may have little validity. The phenomenon of centralization in contemporary society may well be economic-political rather than technological. In the Soviet Union there is an extreme centralization of political power, and in the United States of economic power. Mass production of standard products is typically appropriate to the pre-computer age. Computer-controlled production can be programmed to produce varying products in varying quantities. It is even conceivable that some consumer goods will be produced on demand to the specification of the consumer. The study of systems that computer modelling will make possible will hopefully enable us to devise systems that will leave a high degree of freedom to the comparatively small component groups of people out of which large organisations and society as a whole is built up. Some speak of our contemporary revolution as an 'information revolution'; such a description, at least, points to an essential feature of our technological revolution. Power elites who try to use the new information technologies as a source of power over the mass of the people will not stand much of a chance against societies of people in which there is an increasingly wide diffusion of scientific understanding. The potential of modern science and technology to advance decentralization in certain fields and in certain senses is not likely to be neglected.

I speak of decentralization 'in certain senses' since there is no denying that decentralization, in the sense of devolution of decision making, must go hand in hand with increasing social unification in another sense. Decentralization in the sense of isolated communities is a thing of the past. Today, we are part of a world economy in which our system of communications makes any one part of the world aware on the instant of what is happening in any other. As never before, we are members of one world. So the decentralization of which we are speaking is that of individuals or groups of individuals acting separately and freely but always in harmony with, and in awareness of, relationships to a wider world.

Also, there must be centralization and a considerable amount of standardization in the provision of basic services and utilities. Centralization of power and water supplies, even of computing capacity, may well be essential and feasible without encroaching on the principle of decentralized decision making. There are certain basic needs of developed communities that will be met best in this way.

I have spoken above of the computer as being of central importance to the socio-economic changes that might carry us beyond the industrial society in which we live. What is so special about the computer is that it results in quite profound changes in the relationship of people involved in the production processes. Perhaps 200 years ago there were many who regarded the machine as just a powerful tool, as today many regard the computer as 'just a powerful calculating machine'. That the machine was not just another tool was evidenced by the world-wide social upheavals that followed its introduction. The machine was, from the economic standpoint, so important because it replaced the individual skills of the craftsman's hand and led to quite new methods of organizing the production process. The computer provides a means of performing automatically any routine that can be clearly specified. Indeed, to speak of a routine in this connection becomes somewhat tautological since a routine now comes to be defined as any sequence of instructions that can be set down unambiguously. So, the function of the labour force in production now is not merely being changed in character, but to a very considerable extent eliminated altogether. The salient feature of the 'scientific revolution' is that a mounting body of scientific knowledge enables us to 'get nature to work for us', but for a very long period of time the intermediary between man and nature will be programmes of work controlled by instructions fed into a computer. The scientific revolution is something far richer and wider than the electronic slaves marshalled in computer complexes, but it is the computer that will eliminate, in the course of time, the industrial armies of productive workers that typify the socio-economic structure of contemporary Britain.

I have been trying to imagine, to guess at possible forms of economic change and growth. To try to battle our way up the league table of industrial economies fighting for a bigger share of the export market does not, in my view, offer us a promising prospect. To set out on a new tack is a risky gamble. But it is an even worse gamble not to re-set our sights. Innovation means introducing something new, and technical innovation cannot be separated from socio-economic innovation. If we are seeking in science a magic which will enable us to pursue traditional patterns of economic behaviour with a sort of heightened tempo and level of performance, I think we are looking in vain. But if we are to move into new territories, we certainly will make many mistakes. On the other hand, a half-hearted adherence to a set of contradictory policies, a bit here and a bit there, is a sure recipe for total failure. The kind of economic strategy that is to be sought is, therefore, one of which the economic cost is not too high, but that liberates initiative and can be pursued with a will. The precondition for such a strategy is a generally expansionist financial policy, safeguarded by direct action internally against the most socially harmful forms of speculation, and externally by a readiness to resort to exchange and import controls to safeguard the balance of payments and the value of the currency. The objective of growth will necessarily include an enlargement of the product, but also advance to new socio-economic forms of activity.

The main elements of the technological strategy that I would favour might be summarized as follows:

1. Very heavy public investment in the production of computers and electronic peripherals (where large economies of scale may be expected).
2. Concentrate top mathematical brainpower on analysis and modelling of interrelations of organizations as a whole.
3. Computer utilities on a vast scale to centralize the technical headaches of programming, operating and choosing the right hardware.
4. Publicly accessible data banks and information services.
5. Plenty of research and survey work to identify problems, to draw up socio-economic plans 'from the grass roots upwards', and to bring to bear on the plans and problems the right sort of scientific/technological expertise.

In relation to a gross domestic product of, say, £30,000 million, a public investment of the order of £1,500 million annually should be able adequately to initiate such a programme. That is, we direct towards our strategy of the future no more than some 5 per cent. of the GNP: a bold strategy by some standards certainly, but one which involves public expenditure of a magnitude comparable with that for which more traditional policies have called. Even if mistaken, because over-optimistic or not soundly related to the actual tempo of social change, a strategy such as that that I am here suggesting pursued with vigour, determination and confidence must certainly have a most valuable social and technological 'spin off', and in this sense can be regarded as a heads I win, tails you lose bet.

The five strands of policy outlined above are interconnected. For example, the proposed heavy investment in computers and electronic peripherals must be seen as linked with the development of computer utilities. The electronic peripherals that are needed will depend upon the uses to which computers are being put, on needs identified by research surveys, on the kinds of models to which theoretical work leads. The structuring of data banks will relate to the models and modelling to the availability of data.

The reasons for making a really heavy investment in computers and apparatus associated with their use are as follows. The most rapid way to develop nation-wide facility in using and exploiting the potential of the computer, and indeed to shape ideas about the direction in which computer developments should be steered, would be to make computing power available to anyone capable of using it to advantage. To encourage such use computing facilities should be made available at costs only slightly above actual running costs. That is, the major part of the capital costs of making computing power available should be borne by public funds. At present, a very heavy slice of the high costs of computers goes on design and planning of the computers themselves, and of the components going into the computer. Production trends in the field of microminiaturization, large scale integration, and so on, are leading already to sharply falling cost for the hardware that goes into the computer. If the scale of requirement is sufficiently large, the heavy design and planning costs will be spread over a large number of units and the unit cost of computer power can be brought down considerably. Similar arguments can be applied to computer graphics, light pens, CRT display, terminals and other facilities for using computing power that have still to be invented. Should not our research also address itself to new types of computer? What, for example, would be gained from computers with Content Addressable Memories?

The direct object of heavy support from public funds for computer research, computer production and computer utilities would be to extend and diffuse use of computers and to raise technical standards at all levels from design through to use on the job. But there would be an indirect benefit of this policy that might go far towards paying for its cost, namely the strength given to exports because they would be underpinned by a vastly increased scale of production, research and experience.

As standard user needs come to be defined and scale production becomes possible, devices, today produced one-off at exorbitant cost for top-priority demand only, should be producible at costs comparable with those of radios, adding machines and other intricate products for which mass requirements have been determined.

At a meeting of the Institute of Mathematics and Its Applications in November, 1968 at City University, London, Mr. Dobson, of the British Aircraft Corporation, commented that very little powerful thought has been given to the mathematics of the interrelationships of organizations considered as whole systems. He added that the pay-off for such work might be expected to be much greater than for any of the applications of mathematics to industry so far made. This is undoubtedly so. One need only consider how fruitful the results often are when a careful mathematical analysis is made of the efficiency of a single mechanism. Systems modelling provides the possibility for studying the efficiency of organizations considered as wholes. Tremendous economies may be expected to result from the more effective use of resources that a deeper understanding of large scale systems is likely to make possible. Even partial modelling of limited aspects of a system, such as have been made already (e.g. inventory control), have already produced economically important results. A very considerable pay-off should result from a really powerful concentration of mathematical talents on the modelling of large scale social and economic organizations. To get good results, some changes in the institutional framework within which mathematical research is undertaken might be necessary. The type of mathematics that will be best suited to the modelling of social systems has still to be explored and discovered, and it might be necessary to tap a wide variety of streams of mathematical work to open the advance of mathematics into these new territories. However, in the opinion of some experts the pooling of mathematical departments at present dispersed between a number of Universities and Colleges to form one or two large, many-sided institutions, would have considerable advantages on other grounds, also.

It is very important that there should be strong links between those who are engaged in the mathematical work and those who have the practical problems in the arena of social and economic planning. It should be made very easy for planners in economic and social spheres of activity to obtain first rate mathematical/cybernetic/computer-modelling advice and help inexpensively. Public funds put into this area would be likely to pay off well in their overall benefits to the economy, even though any particular user, on any particular project, could never be certain about what benefits would result from seeking such help. Mathematical research in this area, fed with plenty of problems from practical life, could, at the same time, perform an educational function of great value orienting mathematical work to areas of social need.

Mathematical research work on its own would be far from adequate to identify the needs of the economy and society at large. It could do no more than provide tools to help.

Priority as high as that accorded to computers and associated electronics should be given, also, to (a) any techniques or research that would improve the quality of education, and (b) to any research of practical importance in relation to problems arising in the social field and in the economy. The needs of education should be interpreted widely, that is not only education of children and youths prior to taking up a job, but also education during work or training for change of occupation. However, the key to change may well lie in the secondary school. A good deal goes wrong with the orientation of education at this stage. Time, effort, and money should be generously spent on making it exciting and constructive and aimed at the future.

The idea that education is a gift by society to the individual is a very one-sided and mistaken idea. The best and strongest and happiest societies of the future will be those that have the fullest and most intelligently conceived provisions for acquiring knowledge, general and specialized. Investment in education should be looked at in the same light as, and alongside of – indeed, at a higher priority than – gross fixed investment which, in 1968, at 1958 prices, amounted to £6,000 million out of a GNP of £27,000 million.

The determination of what scientific research is of practical significance in the socio-economic fields is not an easy matter. However, it would probably be easier to judge research from this standpoint if scientific advisory services were made cheaply and generally available to economic and social administrations and planning teams. Nor does such an approach mean cutting out 'pure' research. The history of science has shown that it is very often the 'purest' research that turns out in the long run to have the most far-reaching practical impact. Clearly, it would be bad policy to turn social needs for science against pure research. But in addition to maintaining a place for pure research in general, it would probably become apparent from the needs of science applied to practical socio-economic problems what areas of pure research are likely, however indirectly, to contribute to the solution of society's problems.

On the problems of data banks and information services, nothing very much more need be said. One can envisage eventually a situation in which the mass of information that we at present collect laboriously, over and over again in various forms to record, file and lose in various places, will be collected once and for all 'at birth' in computer readable form, to be rapidly retrieved and analysed in such ways as we may wish. How long it may take to reach this ideal, what social and technical difficulties we will bump into, it is hard to say, but already there are elementary forms of data banking which could be developed at no great expense giving us experience, improving our ability to understand problems and reach administrative decisions and to communicate information widely throughout the community, so that social choices could be made on the basis of ample sound information. We might envisage every locality having an information centre to which people could turn and get detailed information, expert answers to any questions that they had, much as today anyone can walk into a library and get help from the contents of the library and the librarian through the agency of the available stock there of written words.

I have left to the last the most important aspect of all, namely research and survey work. An economic policy that makes its starting point the effective deployment of all useful resources needs, from the beginning, to find some answer to two basic questions: (1) What resources are available, and (2) To serve what social purposes could they be deployed? The means of answering these questions is, in itself, an educative and socially fruitful operation, namely the setting up of planning, research and survey teams comprising ordinary people, and experts, such as architect planners, engineers, economists, sociologists, etc., *insofar as available*.

At the outset, there certainly would be a shortage of experts, but with the involvement of a few experienced people on a part-time basis teams could become a training ground in which to gain experience. I do not share the feeling of some that the major bottleneck to technical and social progress is shortage of skilled and trained people. Readiness to spend more money and time, allowing people of promise to learn and test their skills by having a go at practically useful projects in suitably controlled work teams, could rapidly enlarge the potential. Moreover, we are failing, through lack of funds and organizational flexibility, to use the qualified people we have. This is most apparent in the case of married women, who cannot work ordinary factory and office hours but can, with imaginative organization, put in 20 or so hours' work a week. These include many mathematicians, scientists, economists, computer programmers, etc., with good qualifications and experience. Since many of the problems to be tackled are, in fact, new, the absence of ready-made experts in many fields is not so serious a drawback as at first sight it would appear.

Survey teams, building from small localities and production units well known to some at least of the participants in the teams, would need to spend considerable time linking their findings with those of others. There would be a network of activities concerned partly with studies directed inward on the areas allocated to them and partly with the external linkages and relationships.

Undoubtedly, there would be a good deal of confusion in such an ambitious programme of work at the outset, but whatever the shortcomings it seems likely that such activities would generate understanding and posing of problems that would be of social and economic value. It should be a particular function of such work to identify areas on which technical innovation and the help of scientific expertise would be most likely to help. Nothing would be more likely to stimulate the use of scientific knowledge for socio-economic ends than the bombardment of scientific centres with a number of practical problems to which solutions were being sought.

Many feel that the success of untried policies such as are here suggested would be very problematical. I believe that even if the main aims inspiring this strategy proved hard or impossible to obtain, nonetheless an attempt along these lines would have many valuable by-products. An investment of £1,500 million — as suggested above — is large, but not of an unheard of magnitude even by the standards of financial constraint to which we are used. The *Financial Times* reported (April 3, 1969) that expenditure on industrial espionage is believed to come to £350 million annually. The cost of Concorde is put at £600 million which, after all, is an attempt, only on a very limited front, to make a break into the future.

### References

1.  Jean-Jacques Servan-Schreiber (1967), *Le Défi Américain* pp.|43 – 45
2.  Daniel Bell, *The Reforming of General Education*
3.  Dr. A. H. Cotterell, F.R.S. (1966), 'Science and Economic Growth', *New Scientist*, 8th September 1966

## Discussion

Mr. Wolff drew attention to the conflict between the role of the trades unions, which were essentially to preserve interests, and the process of innovation, which involves change in work-content and relationships. 'Is it not degrading', he asked, 'to hold a job which involves no more than drawing chalk marks round the shoes of a television performer, because the union has been militant enough to insist upon a team of eight people, instead of the three people it requires?' This stemmed, he suggested, from the maintenance of the view that it was important to preserve full-time work. The economy was now capable of producing enough goods and services for everyone, without the need for everyone 'to strain themselves to the last ounce'. The real innovation required was to break the rigid relationship between being able to acquire the necessities of life and having to work. The question of putting more investment and labour into non-productive work of a social nature, looking after our children or our old people, was obviously an important replacement for work taken over by machines, but might not in itself suffice to give satisfaction to all those made redundant by technological innovation.

Lord Delacourt-Smith replied that the fundamental innovation that that would require was that resources should be owned by the community as a whole.

Professor Burke referred to the question of labour mobility. He pointed out that in the U.S.A. and Canada labour mobility was not seen as such a problem as in Britain, whilst in Sweden it was encouraged by a generous and effective scale of incentives and provisions. What should happen in Britain, he asked, to the displaced worker whose skills were no longer required, and who might be able to take up a new skill attaining his full potential but only in a new geographical location? And Dr. Fryers requested that Lord Delacourt-Smith link this in his answer with the place of the crafts in unionism today.

Lord Delacourt-Smith said that the influence of craft was decreasing. Unions which had originally begun as craft were organized now, in effect, on a wider basis than originally, for instance, the Amalgamated Engineers.

He defined the British unions' approach to the question of mobility as the attempt to take the work to the worker, and thus avoid the situation in which an increasing proportion of population and productive capacity was concentrated geographically. To encourage a greater degree of mobility would lead to the denuding of the remoter parts of the country of both population and industry.

Professor Oshima reported that geographical mobility was occurring on an increasing scale in Japan, but even so was very small still compared with western countries. Mobility inside companies however was very high. The organization of industry was democratic, and any new employee with ability could become company president. Many companies had expanded very fast and this had meant that relatively young people had gained large responsibilities. Observers for western countries, he said, had frequently come away with the opinion that the Japanese economy was relatively static as regards labour mobility. In fact, within the organization mobility was extremely high, and this was true even in civil-service employment.

# International Aspects

# Chapter 21

# International Interchange of Innovative Initiative

*Alan G. Mencher*

The application of technology to economic and social advantage is increasingly recognized as one of the most important and inescapable challenges in the remainder of this century. This Conference is an acknowledgement of that fact. Yet, as the Aladdin's lamp of the post World War II search for economic, and more recently for social improvement, technology has been more of a candle to indicate the contour of the terrain than a laser beam to evaporate the obstructions littering the path ahead.

In a 1968 report, the Subcommittee on Science and Technology of the U.S. Senate's Select Committee on Small Business said: 'Despite many years of wide publicity on the wonders of science, and despite considerable directed effort in technology transfer, relatively few firms, in a handful of industries, are actually consumers of technology'. During its hearings the subcommittee learned that the process of channelling new technology into new products is not osmotic. It discovered that technology must be adapted to an application, not adopted by it; and that existing technology must be actively sought out for application. It noted the convincing evidence that technological advance is many times more effective than capital investment in promoting the productivity of the working force. Agricultural technology, reducing the United States farm population in a century from 80 per cent. to 8 per cent. of the population, and medical progress, increasing the average lifespan from about 40 to about 70, are classical but not isolated examples. In addition, there are the countless ways in which technology improves the quality of products without changing production costs. Such qualitative improvements cannot be taken into account in the usual measurements.

In Europe, there is also a growing awareness of the urgent need to cultivate technological innovation. A danger is perceived of a gradual provincialization of technically advanced industries despite the availability of advanced technology. Projecting to 1981, one study[1] predicts that as much as one quarter of British industry may be American owned. As long as the export performance and productivity of American companies abroad exceeds that of corresponding indigenous companies, this trend is unlikely to be reversed even though it has negative connotations with respect to national sovereignty and to the formation of government policy.

This danger is only a manifestation of what might be called the principle of technological insufficiency, namely that no firm and no nation produces all the technology it uses. An NSF study of 560 innovations by private companies revealed that half of the innovations derived from information originating from outside the innovating company. It has been estimated that Britain by itself originates only 10 per cent. of the technology it uses. The U.S.A. is notorious at successfully exploiting the ideas of others, and Japan is perhaps more so. *Fortune* magazine reported that the Nippon Electric Company (one of the 200 largest companies of the world outside the U.S.A. and growing at a rate of 23 per cent. per year) spends 2 per cent. of its sales on royalties to use technology developed elsewhere, largely in the U.S.A. It is inferred that 40 per cent. of the technology used by Nippon Electric is imported and adapted.

Exploitation of the ideas, inventions, technologies and techniques of other people and other nations is a reasonable, legitimate, desirable and perhaps necessary objective. The following discussion reviews and evaluates some of the mechanisms by which technology and innovation transfer across national borders and suggests means to advance their international interchange.

First, however, a brief diversion is necessary to summarize the commonly used terminology. When people speak of 'innovation' or 'technological innovation', they usually mean the *process* by which an idea, discovery or invention is translated to the market place which, in fact, furnishes the ultimate judgement. According to this definition, those products, processes, materials and techniques which survive this process are innovations. The others, no matter how new, different, or ingenious, are non-runners. As has been made abundantly clear by the U.S. Department of Commerce report 'Technological Innovation: Its Environment and Management', the process of innovation is largely non-technological, but dominantly involves environmental factors deriving from management, banking, university, and governmental and other attitudes, and which are reflected in business motivation and behaviour.

'Technological transfer' is a more restricted term. 'Vertical transfer' is concerned with the *path* along which discovery, idea or invention leads into an operational system, product or service within the confines of one industrial or technological sector. 'Horizontal transfer' describes the translation of technology from any point on the vertical transfer path into other sectors. However, the term 'technological transfer' does not seem to be used to cover those many and important links of the total innovative chain which connect the prototype or finished operational system with the market place.

'Diffusion of technology' or 'diffusion of innovation' may refer to horizontal transfer, the translation of any link of the innovative chain to different technological or industrial sectors as mentioned above, with resultant propagation through wider ranges of the economy, or it may refer to geographical propagation to different nations and cultures.

In this context, we define the term 'innovative initiative', as used in the title of this paper, to refer to the development of procedures or arrangements directed towards implementing the process of innovation; towards transferring technology, vertically or horizontally; and towards diffusing it by economic or technical sector or geographically.

Systematic cultivation of innovative initiative by governments has been largely confined to Japan, where it has been a major matter of national policy, and to Britain and the U.S.A., both of which have national programmes of technology transfer. In terms of ultimate objectives of applying technology to economic growth, success of the British and American programmes has been very limited, at least in the sense of measurable results. This is particularly disappointing in view of the 15-year history of the U.K. programme and of the huge sums spent on R and D by the U.S. Government.

There has been no explicit effort among the nations of Europe to build any industrial or economic policy upon the availability of foreign technology (although the converse has been true). British overtures to EEC countries have been interpreted as an offer of technology as a trade-off to 'enter Europe', but, in general, international interchange of innovative initiative has been at best an inadvertent and ineffective by-product of inter-governmental arrangements designed for other purposes. It seems to be frozen into national orientations. This need not be the case.

Consider, for example, some propositions about technological innovation formulated by Professor James Bright of the Harvard Business School. Among these are the pertinent observations that since radical innovations often originate outside the traditional supplier—user sources, firms and governments should search more assiduously for technological opportunity off the beaten path; that major applications of a new technology are often not those for which it was first intended; that the interaction of technologies often results in successful innovation; and that the full process of innovation takes from 10 to 25 years, which imposes the exercise of management decisions based on a value system different from that applying to most business problems.

It is not altogether naive to recast these propositions into geographic terms. They might then read: 'Since radical innovations are often exploited outside the country of origin, foreign sources should be more assiduously examined; major applications of new technology often do not occur in the nation for which they were first designed; the interaction of foreign with indigenous technologies often results in successful innovation; and the 10 to 25 year time span of the full innovation process may impose management decisions based on foreign methods'. Many, if not all, of these transposed propositions are already true to some degree. The comments which follow are directed toward their extension and intensification.

If past experience is any guide, the usual form of technical and scientific agreement between governments is unlikely to constitute an effective mode for the international interchange of innovative initiative. To a great extent, the reasons for this lie in the almost inevitable failure of such agreements to formulate any but the most general common objectives. This is because technical and political considerations are not easily separated, even on the national level where decision making is less complex. There is a legion of examples to demonstrate this point. They occur in the space, nuclear energy, communications, and aviation sectors, and apply to individual projects as well as to broad programmes. In most cases where technological factors dominate an area of prospective multilateral collaboration, an agreement between governments is never reached at all. CERN is an exception which proves the rule.

Perhaps, when cooperative programmes are developed internationally on urban, environmental, and transportation problems there will emerge more direct channels for the international interchange of innovative initiative. Although politically loaded on the national level, these matters are less so on the international plane. Such programmes could lead to deeper understanding in Europe of the full meaning of the systems approach, an essential tool for innovative exploration in these areas. Although the techniques are well known and meticulously applied in government ministries, especially military, the fact that there is very little indigenous capability of the think-tank variety in European industry imposes a constraint in the exercise of systems thinking. This constraint results partly because, as put by the Rand Corporation, 'It is very hard for those who have had operating responsibilities in government to view without bias the selection of alternatives which may call into question their own prior accomplishments and choices'.

Moves to compensate this deficiency do not, of course, have to await the formation of cooperative programmes in the social technologies. Discussions have already taken place among private representatives of several interested nations to explore the possibilities of an International Institute to study common problems of industrialized societies. Another as yet unexplored idea for government initiative in Europe is to develop a collective systems analysis capability in the form of a network spreading over the participating nations. Each member would establish a national unit having one or more areas of speciality. The aggregate would contain expertise in depth in the gamut of disciplines relevant to the pertinent range of problems. They would share common computer facilities. Each would act as a consultant to the others in the performance of any project which would be attacked on a community basis with provision for training each other's personnel in the various specialities. Since this scheme does not involve a single centre, it avoids the usual objection that all but one of the participants lose the cream of their talent to a centre located abroad. It would also eliminate dispute about the location of such a centre with the concomitant economic benefits which are alleged.

Another area where governments can become involved in promoting international interchange of innovative initiative is, of course, that of management education, particularly the business schools. Possibility for government action results from the fact of its direct control outside the U.S.A. and its indirect control within the U.S.A. of all and much, respectively, of the funds for operations and programmes of institutions of higher learning. Unfortunately, business schools outside of the U.S.A. are generally not yet equipped to undertake strong research programmes involving theses leading to advanced degrees. Nonetheless, they might well be interested in collaboration on research relating to the process of innovation. For example, as part of a study on interpersonal communications in R and D laboratories by staff members at MIT's Sloan School of Business Administration, information was required on communications channels between different divisions of a company. Investigation revealed insufficient inter-divisional communications among American companies to constitute a significant sample so that it was necessary to carry out that part of the study in Japan.

Patterns of an unsuspected nature have emerged from such studies. Their results might motivate analogous undertakings in and between other national environments to learn more about the infrastructure through which innovation propagates. For example, from the Sloan School studies it was learned that the frequency with which information channels are used by engineers in American industry correlates most strongly with their accessibility and most weakly with their technical quality; that the average engineer, unlike his scientist colleague, is not capable of understanding the journals of his own profession, so that the literature, including trade magazines, is not an outstanding source of technical ideas (fortunately, his performance has little relation to use of the literature); that the architecture (the physical configuration of offices and facilities) is far more important in influencing the extent of oral communications than are either the formal or the informal organizational structures; and that there exists in every R and D laboratory, independently of the formal organizational structure, a complex, internal, self-contained sub-network consisting of key performers who serve the function of restructuring information from the outside world and from the literature and channelling it into the organization in a form the others can understand.

It is acknowledged increasingly that direct visual, person-to-person contact is the most effective mode of technology transfer, surpassing by far the complex computerized information systems. Means for promoting such contact could form the subject of useful studies. One such mechanism is the mobility of scientific manpower. In the international context, mobility has a derogatory connotation reflected in its characterization as a brain drain. As such it is already the subject of intensive study, particularly with regard to the flow from developing countries. Within the borders of a given nation, however, increased mobility may be desirable. It might be examined usefully in the context of national environments other than the U.S.A. where it is already highly developed. The mobile engineer brings to his new position the residue of his experience, usually with a competitor. In addition, the process serves to float talent to the top, because salary increases and promotions to those in demand are frequent causes for job changes.

In Europe, the well-known obstacles to the mobility of the technological work force relate, in some cases, to failure of employers fully to compensate for dislocation expenses; and, in others, to an understandable reluctance on the part of the employee to forfeit his non-transferable pension. In addition, sociological factors can play a dominating role in societies where acceptance by the new community is a slow and painful process. Professor Bright has pointed out that families of the professional military man provide an interesting example of harmonious adaptation to the requirement for mobility. They are moved at no expense, usually to facilities and social environments identical with the one they left. They know, accept, and even welcome the idea of moving, and newcomers to a community are treated with great hospitality. A search for other examples of mobile groups could usefully lead to a better understanding of the factors which promote and which inhibit mobility. In Europe, this could result in a higher degree of mixing of technical work forces both within and between nations. The advantages of the great diversity of the educational and training systems of different countries might then be exploited more profitably.

Industrial objectives are both more limited and more universal than national objectives. The profit motive encourages the expansion of markets, the development of new products and the cultivation of efficiency through new managerial techniques. The need to implement technology as a tool to further these objectives is generally understood at the top managerial level of most major enterprises. In concert with government, industry has, therefore, an important role to play in the international interchange of innovative initiatives.

There are some interesting ways in which this occurs. The transfer of managerial techniques through the intermediary of the computer manufacturers is by now well known. Computer users in Europe demanded of their European suppliers the same management consultant services as provided by the American competition which, under pressure of the highly competitive U.S.A. domestic market, had included as part of their marketing programme advice to clients on special management applications to which their machines could be applied.

Another example is provided by Professor James Brian Quinn, of Dartmouth's Amos Tuck School of Business Administration, who cites an interesting case in agriculture where British farmers became curious at the practices of some of their neighbours under contract to American frozen-food companies. These included new planting, harvesting and other techniques departing from conventional practice, and performed according to a strict schedule. When advantages to these procedures became apparent, they were adopted by many other farmers. Quinn points out that know-how is also transferred by courses to train technicians concerned with maintenance and follow-up service of a product. In the case of one American company operating in Scandinavia, the facilities for training were equivalent to those of an additional technical college.

At least two leading U.S.A. aerospace companies included foreign firms (in England, France, Germany and Japan) in their bids for a contract to develop the worldwide INTELSAT communications satellite system. This entailed transfer to foreign aerospace industries of American technological know-how, and was done despite an increase in cost of about 10 per cent.

The preceding examples illustrate some of the mechanisms by which innovation is transferred by industrial channels, usually in connection with direct sales foreign ownership of subsidiaries, the dominant modes by which such exchanges take place. However, the flow is not always directed towards the host country. The American subsidiary of the French company, Air Liquide, is said to have acquired from its American environment a vigorous, competitive, innovative approach allegedly in sharp contrast to the more conservative, less venturesome attitudes of the parent company, which cannot help but be affected eventually by this example. This is a further indication of the importance of the environment and of the contagion of the innovative climate.

We might infer from the discussion thus far that large companies are the sole transfer agents of innovative initiative. This would be a contradiction in itself. Size has been singled out by Europeans as a major cause of the so-called technology gap, but despite the advantages it provides with respect to financial resources, size is a deterrent to bringing new ideas to the market place. In recognititon of this fact, such giants as General Electric (U.S.A.) and Westinghouse are dividing themselves internally into separate entities in an effort to promote the entrepreneurial mood essential to innovation. Other large firms are experimenting in other ways, and 28 of them have set up New Venture Divisions in the past year to locate new opportunities.

The small, rapidly growing technological company plays an important role in fostering the innovative environment, particularly by its built-in flexibility to respond quickly to rapid change, and by the example it sets of the contagious phenomenon of entrepreneurship. It also plays a role in the transfer of technology, literally by transporting it out of larger laboratories or companies where for a variety of reasons it is often not viable. This phenomenon has been studied in considerable detail by Professor Edward B. Roberts, at MIT's Sloan School. There are reasons to think that Europe should accord higher priority to helping more vigorously to create a climate favourable to the formation of the small technological company.

One of the more persuasive of these reasons is illustrated by the case of the semiconductor industry as described in the OECD study on 'Gaps in Technology Between Member Countries'.[2] Here a pattern was outlined in which the large American companies such as Westinghouse, GE and others took up licences from the Bell Telephone Laboratories for first-generation components. Their fortunes in this sector subsequently declined, allegedly because of complacency and a failure to develop and market new products with sufficient energy. This left an opportunity for the smaller but aggressive and sophisticated newcomers, such as Texas Instruments, Fairchilds and Motorola, to move in with later-generation products. In Europe, on the other hand, the established large firms started out licensing from Bell, and continued with the manufacture of integrated circuitry without local competition from a European equivalent of the new aggressive American companies. As a result, the latter moved into Europe, filling an innovative gap and gaining considerable economic advantage.

Appropriate organizational structure can also stimulate the international interchange of innovation. One example of a mechanism for spanning the multiple gulfs of incommensurate institutions between nations is persuasively argued by Christopher Layton in *European Advanced Technology*.[3] He cites the bi-national case of the Agfa-Gevaert model which got around legal and tax barriers by a merger that linked, rather than combined, a German and a Belgian firm in such a way that each of the parent companies, Agfa A.G. and Gevaert Photo-Production NV, holds 50 per cent. of the shares of both the Gevaert-Agfa company at Antwerp and the Agfa-Gevaert company at Lovertusen. As a result, important economies of scale have been achieved, particularly in research and marketing. The important point is the establishment of a base of power and ownership in more than one nation.

Layton proposes several examples of other such possible combinations, including Fiat-B.M.C. and Bayer-Rhone Poulenc, which might be promoted by what he refers to as a 'European Industrial Marriage Bureau', a new European institution along the lines of Britain's Industrial Reorganization Corporation, which would foster 50—50 type mergers of two large companies from different countries with separate (but identical) boards and integrated activities guided by joint committees on production, research, administration, sales and planning. A weakness of this imaginative suggestion might be that it depends on the creation of an intergovernmental institution to foster cross-national industry ties, which are likely to be forged only if such an institution exists. The formation of such an institution, in turn, would depend on the likelihood of developing such ties. However, a sober business view might be extremely pessimistic of this likelihood in view of the many institutional obstacles. There is needed a mechanism to cut the cycle.

There is much to commend the strengthening of the European competitive situation *vis-à-vis* the U.S.A., and innovative initiative is symbiotic with a competitive environment. Modes for the interchange of innovative initiative within and across national boundaries might be usefully explored in common by competitor nations with diverse economies and differing policies for technology. A good start would be the cataloguing of case histories of successful transfer similar to those mentioned in the course of this paper. Such an enterprise could be a modest beginning to more ambitious schemes such as the industrial reorganization corporation suggested by Layton. However, innovation occurs in response to perceived or anticipated need. Until the need is seen to be sufficiently urgent, the result is likely to be inertia rather than initiative.

### References

1.  John H. Dunning, *The Role of American Investment in the British Economy,* PEP, London, February, 1969
2.  *Gaps in Technology Between Member Countries, Report on the Electronic Components Sector,* OECD, Paris (CMS (68) 5)
3.  *European Advanced Technology — A Programme for Integration,* A PEP report, Allen and Unwin, London, 1969

# Discussion

The general feeling of the Symposium was that it was a major problem to generate effective communications between different departments in a business, different disciplines in a university, or different staff levels in the civil service. No matter what artifices were used – and a common meeting room was a suggestion – it was difficult to break down the barriers which the differences imposed.

Mr. Pavitt suggested that management education, as it was conventionally practised, did not help to solve this fundamental problem. In teaching students methods of prediction, control, and formal organization, it ignored questions of how management should manage so as best to foster innovation. Dr. Charpie agreed with this: solutions, he said, could not always be found from conventional sources. Innovative success was not something that could be taught; it was the outcome of an ability of certain individuals. Mobilizing these abilities, therefore, was a major management responsibility. The same thing, he added, was true of generating effective communications. Good communicators were also rare, and the management problem was 'to seek out those people who had a record of success. I don't think that it is sensible to try and enforce a pattern of conventional solution on a problem when what you are looking for are departures'.

Dr. Gellman pointed out that time was an important additional factor. A large company that 'suddenly gets the religion of innovation' and has early failures might not recognize such failure as part of the process and would return to conventional, closed systems of management. Some currently successful innovative firms, he suggested, had started out in this way, but had been fortunate to realise one or two early successes.

Dr. Knoppers accepted, with Dr. Charpie, the importance of spotting the people who had innovative flair. On communication, he said that one of the first tasks of the research director within a firm should be to stimulate exchange between disciplines, to utilize to the full the informal and formal organizations so as to establish a stimulating flow of communication within the firm.

Dr. Pannenborg described how his firm organized R and D to obtain good communications. A first requirement was set by the fact that today much basic research originated outside industry, and industrial research must be sure to make maximum use of it. Half of his company's research organization, therefore, was grouped according to scientific disciplines. Its members carried out basic research and were essentially outward-looking, that is, they formed the bridge between the company and external research work. They mingled on equal terms with their fellows in university and other outside laboratories. The other half was inward-looking, organized according to product groups. It linked within the firm with the development and functional departments. The task for the director of research was to promote communication of the one half with the other.

Dr. Goldman took this example as illustrative of, to use Mr. Freeman's term, 'coupling' between the firm and outside research work. An organizational form which allowed this kind of communicative coupling typified all successful research organizations. And, he continued, there was only one fully effective way to obtain this, the actual movement of people from one job to another. Only in this way would they learn to understand each other. The essential ingredient of what Dr. Gellman called the high 'innovation quotient' (high I.Q.) industries was, he suggested, top management which had had experience on the R and D side of the company, so that by the time they reached responsibility for company operations as a whole they had an understanding of the R and D process and could communicate with its executives.

So far the discussion had tended, said Dr. Archer, to concentrate too much on the couples that related science to industry, and too little on the couples which related industry to society. The role of marketing, which Dr. Gellman had discussed yesterday, was concerned with that couple which associated cost and value; it could be argued that the object of operations, whether of a company or national economy, was to create this disparity between cost and value. 'We have heard a lot about creating the conditions within which innovation can occur and be recognised, but we have not heard enough to satisfy me that anything adequate is being done to collect and tabulate data about the way in which value and cost are related; the way in which risk and yield are related; and the way in which R and D and certainty are related.'

Chapter 22

# Patents and Economic Growth

*Kenneth Johnston, Q.C.*

Although this paper has been conveniently assigned to the session on 'International Aspects', the patent system may, of course, influence nationally the extent to which technological change takes place and is developed commercially. Indeed, in so far as this symposium is concerned, whether there exist any factors peculiar to the U.K. that may hamper our economic growth, it is essential to examine how the patent system operates nationally as well as internationally.

The justification of the patent system has always been, and is, that it will be an effective inducement to invention if, in return for the public disclosure of an invention, the inventor is given a temporary monopoly to enable him without competition to exploit his invention commercially. The patent system is, therefore, fundamentally concerned with innovation, by which is meant technical change that is put into practice.

The questions that will be discussed are:

(a) Does the patent system encourage innovation? *Operation of the Patent System.*

(b) If yes, does the system nevertheless have features of law or practice that handicap the fulfilment of its purpose? *Barriers in the Patent System.*

(c) Are there any features of the U.K. patent system that handicap innovation by comparison with other countries? *U.K. Patent System and other Systems.*

(d) *Patents as International Barriers.*

### (a) Operation of the Patent System

We might answer this question by pointing to the increasing use of the patent system, the number of applications in the U.K., for example, having risen from about 40,000 in 1957 to about 58,000 in 1966, and by saying that this would not occur if industry did not favour the patent system and value its advantages. But any system has its own inertia, and a high proportion of patents are taken out by the patent departments of industry, which are no more likely than other institutions to vote their own decease. Obviously, there can be no means of knowing to what extent the research that has led to the discoveries protected by patents would have taken place had there been no patent system. There will always be innovation, as is shown by its existence in fields, such as the service industries, where innovation can rarely be patented. All we can do is to examine how in fact the system works and judge its merits from our experience.

Although each patent grants a legal monopoly, in fact very often no effective monopoly is obtained. Many patents are of doubtful validity, because to obtain a grant in the U.K. only novelty has to be shown if there is no opposition; only the barest possibility of invention, if there is opposition. There is the further factor that improvements are made as a series of small steps by different firms, with the result that no one firm can get a strong hold on another — there is always a counter-monopoly on the other side. This naturally promotes cross-licensing, either by agreement or by tacit understanding. Large companies tend to have their own patent departments, which operate on a budget, and these departments may be very active in obtaining patents, although the company may not be at all active in using them to enforce monopolies. The patents for such a company are largely defensive, in that their function is to provide a possible counter-weapon against any other company claiming that its patents are being infringed. The patents become just one of the instruments of competition; the monopoly they give is not used to stop competition but to protect the company from interference. The larger the company the more likely it appears to be that its patents will be regarded in this way, and it is not unreasonable to suppose that in fields where patents are so regarded the position might be very little different if there were no patent system; the research would still go on, although less of it would be published, and new manufacture would proceed with fewer possible barriers. This is a point of view that does exist, and one does wonder how far large concerns with patent departments really assess against cost the value of the patents obtained.

It is often difficult, however, to assess which inventions are going to be successful, and this discourages those concerned from taking the responsibility of deciding not to obtain, or to abandon, patent protection. The patent system would work much better if it was used less.

Although, as it has been so far described, the patent system does not operate in the way it is supposed to and might be said to be unnecessary, it is also true that patents can be essential for enabling inventions to be developed commercially, since only if there is a monopoly is there inducement to do so. Patent protection is often necessary to enable inventions in a new field of manufacture to be used, since money will not be risked otherwise. It is necessary, also, for inventions where the cost of R and D is high and that of manufacture low; this is so for many pharmaceutical inventions, for example.

## (b) Barriers in the Patent System

There is no doubt that the main criticism of the patent system is directed against the time taken for obtaining patents. So long as a patent application is pending, rights are uncertain, and this fact must constitute at least a potential barrier to innovation. Delay in obtaining patent protection may not be to the disadvantage of the patentee, since, especially where the merit of the invention is doubtful, it will suit the patentee to delay publication of the specification and definition of the rights for as long as possible, but other manufacturers are thereby handicapped in their development. Delay may also hinder the development of an invention by the patentee, who may not be able to obtain finance or wish to commit himself to extensive manufacture until a patent is obtained.

The time required to obtain protection is a major problem, mainly caused by the ever-increasing number of patent applications, the growth in the documents to be examined to test the novelty of inventions, and the competition from industry itself for suitably-trained staff. The Working Group Report No. 1 from the European Industrial Research Management Association (EIRMA) states that, for example, there were in September, 1967, 300,000 pending applications in Germany, which brought the average delay before completion of examination to over six years. This kind of situation is described in the Report as intolerable. Extensive delay is also reported in other countries where patent applications are examined before grant. In Japan, it has been recently reported, it takes three years for an application to be published. In the U.K. there is the advantage of a time limit of four years for the examination and acceptance of a complete specification, but the provision for opposition after acceptance may in practice extend the time for grant by several more years.

These delays have resulted in a move towards the publication of specifications at a fixed period after application – 18 months. This step, adopted in Holland in 1964 and in Germany in 1968 and now proposed for Japan, does remove the disadvantage of long secrecy, and enables industry to make its own judgement of what protection is likely to be obtained, although at its own expense. But, no advance in final definition of monopoly rights is obtained, although it is hoped that, since a patentability search and examination is only carried out at the request of the applicant or a third party, there may be less of this work to do, with consequent less delay in obtaining final rights.

The above remedy is only a palliative, and the only remedy for delay, it is suggested, must be to institute an international search system. This would not only avoid duplication, in that one search would be substituted for the several searches in different countries, but it would also enable the work to be shared out between a number of searching authorities and thereby speed up the process. Such a scheme has been prepared by the United International Bureau for the Protection of Intellectual Property, and is entitled the Plan for a Patent Cooperation Treaty, 1968 Draft. Time does not permit a detailed explanation of this plan, but, broadly stated, it envisages in respect of the contracting states the institution of international applications which will be subject to an international search. The searching authorities would be the International Patent Institute and some of the national patent offices. Unofficially, it is expected that the German, Japanese, United States and Soviet patent offices would share this work, and it is sad to record that the U.K. patent office does not feel it would be able to be a searching authority. There would still be national patents for which the national patent offices would conduct the examination for patentability on the basis of the international search report. There would, however, be an optional international patentability examination by one of the preliminary examining authorities, of which the U.K. patent office might be one. The report on the preliminary patentability examination would be used by the national patent offices, but would not be binding on them. Nevertheless, the introduction of international examination of patentability, if satisfactorily carried out, would further avoid some present duplication.

An advantage of the plan is that it might be adopted by some of the non-examining countries. In such countries patents are quickly granted, but, there being no examination into novelty, the rights are uncertain, since this system is incompatible with clear and novel claims to monopoly. Specifications tend to be framed in general terms and rights can only be determined, either by industry or (if there is a dispute) by the courts, by a difficult comparison between the specification and such prior art as has been discovered.

Under this scheme it is hoped that it may be possible to have the search completed in 16 months, and the preliminary patentability examination within 20 months. The further timetable of an application would depend on the national patent offices, but, if the scheme is effectively operated, a substantial advance in obtaining patent protection should be obtained. In any event, the plan provides for publication within 18 months. We must confess doubt whether this timetable would really be achieved.

It is contended sometimes that inventions would be more quickly and reasonably developed if all patents were made the subject of licences of right by others. Anybody would be entitled to a licence on payment of royalty, agreed or settled by arbitration or decided by the patent office. This may seem attractive as a means of ensuring the development of inventions, but in many cases it would have an effect the opposite of that intended. It is in practice difficult to recoup by licensing alone heavy expenditure on research, development or new capital equipment, and manufacturing profits protected by a monopoly are generally essential. Many important inventions have come from new or small concerns, and the proposal would make it difficult for these to establish themselves, since, once an invention looked like being successful, large companies could in effect take over a large part of the market. Moreover, U.K. patent law already provides for the grant of compulsory licences for inventions which are not commercially worked, either at all or not to an extent that is reasonably practicable. This has been so in effect since 1883. There has not been much direct use of this provision, but there is no doubt that its presence has tended to hasten working, or at least to encourage licensing. An application for a licence cannot be made before three years after the grant of a patent, and the present delays in grant, therefore, must diminish the effect of the provision.

### (c) The United Kindom Patent System and Other Systems

It has already been pointed out that the delays in obtaining patents in the U.K. are no greater than elsewhere, possibly less. It would be of advantage if protection could be obtained more quickly here, but it would be most difficult to achieve this, because world-wide publication against novelty will in due course be introduced to comply with the Strasbourg Convention, and presumably the patent office search will have to be wider and will, therefore, take longer.

The author cannot think of any amendment to U.K. patent law which would remove some barrier to innovation that exists here and not elsewhere. Our patent system may limp along, but no more than other systems. Patents have their problems – but they are not peculiar to us.

### (d) Patents as International Barriers

Patents do not have extra-territorial effect, except that some of the smaller and less industrialized members of the Commonwealth still give effect to U.K. patents by ordinance. Consequently, a product that might be in infringement of patents cannot safely be marketed internationally until it has been cleared as non-infringing in all countries concerned, and a patentee cannot enforce his rights internationally except by bringing proceedings in each country where infringement occurs. The economic disadvantages of this could be avoided if there were truly international patents which would have effect in all countries. We are far from that, but a beginning was made with the draft Convention on European Patent Law prepared by representatives of the Six Countries of the European Economic Community, published in 1962. This scheme, broadly described, provided for European patents to be issued by a

European Patent Office and to have effect in all contracting states of the convention. The national courts were to enforce the patents and to decide the issue of infringement for this purpose, but the issue of validity of the patents was to be reserved to the European Patent Office with appeal to a European Patent Court. National patents were still to exist, but it was not to be permitted for an invention to be protected by a European patent and also by a national patent.

Much skilled and detailed work went into this draft convention, but it is not surprising that so revolutionary a scheme ran into difficulties.

There seem to have been two main difficulties. One was the question whether use of the system was to be open to applications from nationals from countries other than the contracting states. The other was the provision that working of a patent would be sufficient if it took place in any one or more of the contracting states, provided it was to an extent to meet the needs of all the states — a provision with obviously significant economic implications. The project was shelved soon after the publication of the Draft Convention, but there has recently been a revival of interest, and it is now expected to be reconsidered in a modified two tier form. According to this, the patents to be granted by the European Patent Office would have extra-territorial force within the European Community, presumably in much the same way as in the Draft. They would also have the force of national patents in such other countries as might subscribe to the convention. There is much to be done before anything of this kind is finally agreed, and the extent to which individual states may insist on local manufacture is likely to be much disputed; the aim is most desirable, and if we become impatient with its slow progress, we can comfort ourselves with the question put by somebody in its earlier stages, 'By the way, over how long did the Council of Trent sit?'.

**Summary**

The patent system is fundamentally concerned with economic growth because it is intended to encourage inventions and their development by the inducement of temporary monopolies. In practice, many patents give no effective monopoly, partly because of doubtful validity and partly because invention proceeds by small steps by different firms and no one firm can get a hold on others. The result is much express and tacit cross-licensing.

Patents are often largely defensive only, i.e. they ward off attacks by others and are not used to assert monopolies. To this extent the patent system may not fulfil its purpose, but there are fields where patent protection is essential for innovation and its use, e.g. in new industries and where research and development costs are high and manufacturing costs low.

The major defect in the operation of the patent system is delay in obtaining protection and this may hinder development. Some countries have introduced compulsory publication to avoid long secrecy, but the real need is for a system of a single international search to replace national searches. The Draft Plan for Patent Cooperation Treaty of 1968 provides for international applications subject to an international search, the result of which would be sent to all countries where protection is sought, each country still granting its own national patents but using the international search. There would also be an optional international patentability examination, which would act as a guide for the grant of national patents. This system would avoid much duplication and, if effectively carried out, would much hasten the grant of patents with defined rights. It would be especially valuable if it were adopted by some of the non-examining countries.

The U.K. patent system presents no more barriers to use of innovation than do others. That patents are not extra-territorial must form some barrier to international trade. This could be avoided by international patents having validity in many countries. The draft European Patent Convention of 1962 was a first step towards this desirable end and, although it was shelved soon after publication, there are signs of a revival of interest and it is expected to be reconsidered in a form by which the European patents give extra-territorial rights within the European Community and national rights in other subscribing states.

# Discussion

Dr. Knoppers took up the reference to the place of patents in the pharmaceutical industry. A weakening of the patent system, he agreed, could severely damage or even destroy the whole structure of the industry in its innovative function. On the relationship between pricing and patents, he said that the pharmaceutical firm's approach to pricing necessarily involved consideration of 'what the market would bear', but that this term was often wrongly interpreted. The approach to pricing was, he explained, more correctly described as an attempt to assess the real worth of the new product. In this assessment, social and medical considerations were of equal importance to economic factors. A life-saving drug which needed to be given continuously must be priced very differently from one which effected a cure in a few days.

Dr. Knoppers was asked whether innovation in the American pharmaceutical industry had been curtailed by the political controversy which had surrounded it since the Kefauver Inquiry. He suggested that the Kefauver hearings had been a response to the growth of the industry. Some of the intensification of the Food and Drug Administration procedures which had followed was perhaps in principle necessary. But he felt that the present relationship of the FDA with the industry did restrict the innovative effort, and he contrasted the FDA with its British equivalent which, he said, was more efficient in making available new drugs to patients.

Dr. Wilson offered some comments on patenting in Canada. In the recent past there had been more companies in Canada taking out patents in order to improve their bargaining capacity. They were using them as the keystone of a package of information which they hoped to sell. But he warned that to talk of a patenting system in industry as a whole was misleading, because 'you can get pockets of industry that had no time for them'. Small electronics companies, for instance, did not find patenting worth their while. Many small Canadian-owned companies objected to the U.S.A. patent system. The date of invention for foreign-originating patents was taken in the U.S.A. as the date of submission to the U.S.A. patent office, and this constituted a severe drawback.

Dr. Pannenborg agreed with previous speakers that of the total body of patents taken out only a minute proportion were of any real significance. On the other hand, the fact that such a multiplicity of patents was taken out had one important justification. He had already explained the importance for industrial firms of ensuring that their basic-research workers were able to maintain their scientific status in relation to university-based scientists. This could only be done through publication, and no firm would agree to publication unless the results being discussed could be protected. This condition the patent system fulfilled. It was important both to the quality of industrial research and to the whole process of innovation, 'because the publication is a much more effective means of disseminating new knowledge than the patent'.

Sir Gordon Sutherland asked whether the Russians were now more interested in international collaboration on patent systems. Mr. Johnston confirmed that this was so. The value of the patent system as a means of publication was increasingly appreciated by them.

Mr. Wolff questioned the value of patents as a means of preserving sole right. Would it not be in the greater interests of some firms, he asked, to attempt to keep their processes secret to the minimum necessary number of their own employees rather than to patent them? And if they did so, was there any legal redress against misuse of the information? Mr. Johnston replied that a number of firms did do this, sometimes supporting it with a patent, 'but leaving the secret out of the patent'. He pointed out that there were some fields in which it was easier than others to preserve a secret. He agreed that the risk of a secret process was the treacherous employee. Such a person was wrong in his actions: he was legally bound to preserve the firm's secrets, but the remedy available was often of limited value.

Dr. Gellman questioned whether the Goodrich-Latex case had had an impact on the conditions of employment imposed by high-technology companies, especially on people coming from firms in similar areas. Dr. Charpie suggested that this very much depended upon the type of technology. He mentioned the electronics industry as an example where a high rate of technological obsolescence reduced the importance of such protection. But in industries where very intensive investment led to a basic discovery which would be useful for perhaps 30 years, the ability to maintain secrecy and control over employees was of great importance.

Mr. Duckworth supported the point that the importance of protection varied from industry to industry and said that from his discussion of these problems with a wide range of industrialists, he would generalize that patents were discussed at top board level for certain industries much more than one might imagine, for example in pharmaceuticals, but were not so important in others, for example in motor cars. Since even the Russians were coming to the conclusion that they needed a patent system, he concluded that one could at least say of patents that while the system was not very good it was impossible to think of anything better.

Dr. Muttelsee asked whether there was any legal requirement for a company to reward an employee/inventor in respect of patented work. Mr. Johnston replied that there was no legal necessity, because the English system decreed that the patent itself belonged to the inventor. However, most firms in which this problem arose did have forms of agreement with employee/inventors to cover this situation. Dr. Gellman pointed out that employees were directly rewarded in America. 'Our company', he said, 'has just increased payment for a patent from one dollar to two dollars.'

# Discussion
General Discussion of Matters Arising During the Morning's Proceedings

Dr. Peccei was grateful to Lord Delacourt-Smith for his introduction of the human element into the Symposium's discussion of innovation. 'The human aspect of innovation is something that we have to pay much more attention to.' These problems, he said, were baffling. He thought that his own firm was more forward-looking than some in management—worker relations, but even so he felt that management had to revise their attitudes 'many times a year' in order not to depart from the requirements and expectations of the work-people. Manpower budgeting and planning, in principle, could help to solve these problems, but he wondered if these could be implemented realistically when it was not possible to manpower-plan the economy as a whole. Lord Delacourt-Smith did not view the situation so pessimistically. He thought it was possible to do a certain amount of intelligent forecasting as a minimum. Where the U.K. had not done enough was, he felt, in forecasting 'which industries are likely to expand and what their manpower requirements are going to be'. Complete precision was impossible, but broad ideas could and should be arrived at.

Mr. Goldsmith referred to the importance of 'luck' which the Symposium had earlier discussed. He agreed that it was an important element in many technological advancements. But the element of chance, he felt, was not entirely random. Chance favoured what Pasteur had called 'the prepared mind'. 'Luck must be interpreted as being an expression of the "prepared mind".' One must therefore seek those who, as a result of education or other circumstances, had this prepared mind and could see what was original and new.

He went on to consider the 'importance of being aimless', of non-mission research. He quoted results of an analysis by the Illinois Institute of Technology Research Institute of the key research events which led up to five major technological developments. These events were categorized as non-mission, applied, or development. For all five innovations, non-mission research provided the origin. Of all the key events, 70 per cent. were non-mission science and three-quarters of them occurred in university.

Such findings had important implications for the debate about funds to be devoted to basic research. But he was also interested to ask Dr. Pannenborg what implications they had for the research organization which he had earlier described. This was the question, said Dr. Pannenborg, of how to choose the subject areas in basic science for an industrial research department to engage in, operating in the way he had described. The frequently used expression 'diversification' should in industrial research imply work aimed ultimately at new product lines, and the entry into additional sectors of basic science. One of the guiding criteria for the choice in the latter category was the observable rate of progress in the various disciplines of external science. For example, today, physics was moving much more slowly than 20 or 40 years ago, while molecular biology had a very fast pace. This observation had led his firm to enter the field of molecular biology. A second important approach was to invert the old saying and to 'start before you consider', that was, build up some expertise in an unknown field in order that the company could obtain some insight as a base for decision, whether to expand in that field or not.

Dr. Goldman accepted Lord Delacourt-Smith's point that in looking at long-term objectives one must not lose sight of the short-term human dislocative effects. He agreed that to the man who has to eat dinner tomorrow the fact that things improve in 10 years' time was meaningless. But, he asked, in how many cases had an industry been ruined because unions had looked only to short-term objectives? Dr. Goldman also suggested that in its proposals for union/management relations advancement, the U.K. was 10 years behind the U.S.A. For instance, the automobile workers in the U.S.A. had demanded worker participation on boards of directors, but as soon as companies had made steps in this direction the unions had backed down because, he suggested, this would have destroyed the whole basis of collective bargaining — 'they could not bargain with themselves'.

On the first point, Lord Delacourt-Smith agreed that the sort of friction which had existed on occasions had restricted progress. This was, he said, why he had requested greater consideration of ways of obtaining a deeper understanding and ways of jointly solving the immediate problems. On the question of worker participation, he pointed out that he was not suggesting putting trades union representatives, *qua* trades union representatives, on to boards of directors. In his view, what was needed was a fundamental upgrading of joint consultation, which should include management—union discussion of who should be on the board. This was not at all the same thing as trade union representation on the board, but rather trade union influence on the constitution of the board.

# The Next Steps

# Chapter 23

# The Right Climate for Innovation

*G. R. Fryers*

Innovation includes invention as well as the process of getting users to profit by inventions.[1]

Climate is the environment of living things and the title 'The Right Climate for Innovation' therefore implies that the innovating process has life. Whilst inventions are material, the process of innovation is a complex social function with many of the transient, dynamic and reactive qualities of living things. It calls for the collective enthusiasm of a group of people at the hub, sufficient to generate the impetus needed to spread concentric waves of action through society. 'Dampening' of enthusiasm for change in society not only hinders the propagation of innovation, but as the central group are themselves very much members of the society, their initial enthusiasm will also be affected. The climate is, therefore, much more complex than just the way society rewards inventors.

Recently, I heard the details of a new contract that a bright young employee of a large British company was asked to sign. It was so restrictive and all-embracing in the company's claims to the inventions of its staff as to be likely to produce a non-cooperative reaction. In fact that is why I heard about it, the man wanted to know his rights. It is hard to imagine the insensitivity of such a management to the need to generate enthusiasm, excitement and job satisfaction whilst their task is to get value from their investment. The legalistic or restrictive approach at company or national level cannot get that something extra out of people which innovation calls for.

In effect, if we don't enthuse people we are saying that man and enterprise ought to innovate as a duty, and that the more successfully they can do it the larger share of the burden of society they must carry. Is this the climate for innovation?

How far our declining share of world trade in manufactured goods indicates a relative failure in commercial innovation will not be discussed here, but it will be assumed that the increased share of world trade we need

*245*

will require more or better innovation. The extra cost of selling goods or services in other countries can be met either by selling exports at a discount so that they compete on level terms with local products, or by exporting products which can be sold locally at a premium price compared with the nearest equivalent native product. Only the second process allows of both a high rate of export and a high domestic standard of living, and finding new 'premium exports' will depend on innovation.

At one time we did lead the world with men like Stephenson, Brunel and Babbage, but Professor Duncan Burn showed that we began to lose the lead in the mid-nineteenth century.[2] This cannot have been due to change in genes (the time was too short), and must have been due to deficiencies in the climate for innovation. We must still be a nation with plenty of inventors, yet we have insufficient innovation. The swashbuckling, gambling extravagance, the patronage of novelty for its own sake, changed during the nineteenth century to a belief in stability, solidity and permanence in all that was done. The Victorian era produced the monolith of the insurance company and bank headquarters, in contrast with the pavilion at Brighton. First satisfaction, then complacency, have probably played a part in our loss of initiative.

How far is our relative failure due to lack of material encouragement to enterprising innovation? How far to a lack of a national sense of excitement and pride in successful commercial innovation? How far is it due to society setting up specific inhibitions and despising change? Zuckerman has pointed out that 'too many resources were being put into research and development and not enough into the consequent follow-up in production and marketing'.[3] In assessing these possibilities we must remember that taxes and other processes not only have logical, but also psychological, effects. Tax from this point of view is as high as it feels. Arthur Seldon in a monograph on Taxation and Welfare[4] has shown how much higher than reality people in Britain believe their taxes to be, especially in the lower income groups. One of the key issues which emerges is that whenever the encouragement of innovation is discussed the policy of weakening the strong in order to help the weak, whilst laudable, has dangers and could harm, over the course of time, the very people it is intended to help. For if innovation lags, the economy will suffer and sufficient funds will just not be available however they are redistributed.

I suggest that the emerging issue – the right climate for innovation – is one that cannot be satisfactorily resolved purely by a compromise between the disparate needs of enterprise and the welfare state. If that is so, then it is important to try to determine the principle involved, the consequences of their being compromised or neglected, and then try to see at least a method by which a workable solution may be found. In this paper, that is what I will try to do. Whilst I will give some hypothetical examples of possible solutions,

I would like to make it clear that they are merely advanced to help explain the method proposed. In fact, it is a central theme of this paper that these solutions cannot just be dreamt up or produced by committees: they must be worked out by many people applying appropriate methods and working in a suitable climate. I suggest that the right climate for material innovation will be best created by applying the innovation process to the problems of society.

First, then, to try and demonstrate the conflicting forces within society which influence the climate for innovation. Innovation has not been mechanized, it is a human function, and the qualities necessary are not shared by all people in equal amount. It is difficult, if not impossible, to define and measure innovative capacity satisfactorily, and for this reason the assertion of its unequal distribution amongst people is hard to prove. Equally, it is hard to base selection of potential innovators on the same inadequate theoretical grounds. If we must select on practical grounds (i.e. by observation of the quality and quantity of innovative output) then suitable opportunities to show ability must exist. Additionally, there must be real opportunities to display the ability early enough in life to permit recognition before age erodes the facility, and often enough to allow for selection at successive stages. Each stage must be a comparative evaluation amongst ever more highly selected confreres. Without detailing all the connecting threads, I will assume that you will accept that these conditions are best met by having a large number of highly competitive, small industrial units. And that it is very hard to meet these conditions in very large organizations, and even harder if there is not a sufficient measure of competition.

I hope I have said enough to allow me to state my first conflicting principle. That something not too far removed from a laissez-faire climate would be best for selection of innovators and the encouragement of innovation. Of course, in particular fields very large enterprises are essential but they will operate still better if they can draw many of their innovators from dynamic small enterprises operating in different fields where smaller resources suffice to back young men. I would expect to get almost universal opposition to a proposal to recreate a laissez-faire society. None of us is prepared to pay the price in human terms of 'the devil taking the hindmost': it would not necessarily be their fault that they were behind.

Therefore, the second of the conflicting principles is the desire for progress towards an egalitarian society. The two principles are not only in conflict on selection of innovators, but also when society tries to do something about its unfortunates, society must do it by drawing much of the necessary resources from the strongest, including the most innovative. This selective handicapping of resources of the successful would be reasonable if it happened throughout the world to an equal degree, but it does not. In consequence, our innovators may well be handicapped by comparison with those in some other countries, and this could be dangerous.

As has been discussed elsewhere, the future of international trade for the advanced nations will be predominantly in products with new technological content. No country can have a monopoly of such advances nor can it cut itself off from using the best produced elsewhere. The pattern, therefore, will tend to be that the international market will be increasingly in those products at the top of the world league of innovation, and that only those very near to the top will be traded in at a useful profit level, i.e. both our exporting success and our ability to minimize imports will depend on our success in the unrestrainedly competitive world market for the commercial exploitation of innovation. Dare we handicap our innovators in proportion to their domestic success and, if we do, can we at the same time expect to get anywhere in world markets? The answer can only be 'no'. We could attempt, of course, to get other countries to operate equivalent handicaps. They may even do it without our encouragement, but we cannot rely on this happening throughout the world, nor can we act in the meantime on the assumption that it will.

I would like to propose that a compromise between the needs of innovation and egalitarianism will lead to failure on all fronts: our products will be generally just not good enough to succeed in world competition, and our welfare activities will be inadequate from lack of resources. If compromises will not work, laissez-faire is rejected, and egalitarianism will lead to equal shares for all of an ever diminishing cake. We must try, therefore, to find some third approach for selection, stimulation and welfare. This must not be a compromise, but a system that will allow sufficient competition, sufficient backing of successful innovators with resources, and sufficient help for those who have need of it. All this should be accompanied with an increase, not a reduction, in human dignity.

I suggest it is possible to see the outline of a system which might itself, through multiple social innovations, evolve the answers that society so desperately needs. This might be achieved by applying some of the lessons learnt in evolving new technologies to our social problems. In retrospect, it is possible to see how the industrial and technological revolutions occurred, and to interpret these observations in terms of the processes that have been operating in society and which were essential pre-conditions to the changes. One lesson we have learnt is that a committee one hundred years ago could not have mapped out modern technology and industry. It seems odd, therefore, that in the even more complex field of social change we have put our trust in the brilliant prediction of one saviour or committee after another without apparently wondering if this is really the right way to get the changes we want. Should the theories of Marx or Beveridge be given more credence or place in history than Leonardo's inventions? They are all fascinating and stimulating, but are more like virtuoso performances than major contributions to the composition of the society that will exist in the future.

What, then, are the processes involved in material innovation? Material innovations have been made under many circumstances, but a key unit has been the competitive company striving through innovations to grow in resources, people, profits and prestige. The successful have con.e to control more resources than the unsuccessful. When the process is efficient, this accretion of funds from the public and profits from the company's total revenue, i.e. the buyers of its products, an adequate flow of funds has come to mean providing what the customer wants. Because of the time lag between the conception of the idea and the availability for sale of the 'thing' the innovator must be good at anticipating the customer's desires. The history of competitive innovation indicates that many of the most valuable ideas arise outside the apparently appropriate existing industry, and therefore the condition of the competitive climate should make new ventures feasible.

Fulfilment of the market takes time, and the innovator must get most of his earnings and be on to his next innovation before his first is copied. Some products, such as airliners, are very hard to copy, others are easy, e.g. some medicines. The easier it is to copy, the greater the need for society to provide some methods by which an inventor can obtain a franchise giving protection from copying of his innovation, too early or too completely. Hence, the importance of patents, brand names and copyright in the history of material innovation. 'The customer' is also very important. In fact, if he is a single customer the risks of competitive innovations are generally too great to be borne, i.e. one competitor gets all and the other loses his shirt. The mortality amongst such business, over even a short period, would be such that only one would be left, i.e. either way the single customer is incompatible with the process of competitive innovation.

Could there be a parallel between the process in industrial/technical progress, and a process for obtaining essential social progress? I would like to suggest that there is a real similarity, and that with adaptation the successful processes used to innovate 'things' could be applied to obtaining social innovations. And further that through large numbers of social innovations we could evolve a society that succeeds in material innovations, and at the same time is a kinder, warmer place to live in.

To recapitulate, the main requirements for effective competitive innovations appear to be:

(1) Some form of franchise which is effective enough to ensure that the average results amongst competitive innovators are good enough to attract new entries.

(2) Multiple customers.

(3) As rapid an accretion of strength as possible for the successful innovators.

If we could fulfil these requirements in the social field we might, and I believe we would, unleash gradually a great power for progress, and through the innovations produced we could well answer many of the problems of reconciling competition with social conscience. At least, it is clear that within our present social climate a potential social innovator would not find the above three conditions to be operating. It follows, therefore, that the failure to solve our social problems does not arise from a failure of social innovation, but from failure to attempt to get the process working.

If the three conditions could be met, would competitive innovation produce the answers? One can never be sure. We have in Britain large numbers of highly creative people, many with ability which is going to waste. It is reasonable to conclude that our present social policy for innovation, largely committees and national legislation (i.e. non-competitive), cannot meet the needs without hampering the material innovation nor use the latent capabilities of our nation. Why not then try competitive innovation?

(i) Can the three conditions be met so as to create a climate for social innovation?

(ii) Will there be some rather ill-defined evil effect from allowing competition to try to serve people's social needs, as well as their desire for 'things'?

I am sure you will need to be satisfied on both these counts before you will give much attention to the rather obvious proposal to solve many of our remaining social problems by competitive innovation.

Could society grant an effective form of protection to social innovators? Even if it could be done, would it have harmful effects? Protection would give an opportunity for profit (it might be abused by innovators being overpriced or withheld from general availability). However, if protection is given only to new ideas, then society cannot suffer from excessive pricing or withholding of these ideas, at least in the time such an idea would have appeared if there had been no protection and no competitive innovations. On the other hand, any scheme for protection should require disclosure. Society should gain by the disclosures because these then form an earlier and better base for the next step in progress. There can be no general doubt that society has benefitted on balance in the material field. It is an act of faith to predict a similar balance of advantage in the social field. Without evidence of its effects, and that can only come later, any franchise scheme evolved should be treated as provisional only.

I suggest that copyright and patents between them provide some relevant background, but neither on its own would do. A description of a social innovation could have the same sort of protection from plagiarism by copyists as an author now gets, e.g. in regard to film adaptation. But, unlike copyright, where it is the pattern of words rather than the thought that is protected and, like patents, it is suggested that there should have to be a demonstration of utility. Protection would be on a time basis. Absolute rights or protection might be rather narrowly confined, but it could be surrounded by a grey area in which licensing would be compulsory. To stimulate early disclosure, the U.S.A. patent system of dating priority from first recording of results in laboratory notebooks might be adapted, so that the sooner the disclosure was made after the priority date, the greater would be the court's bias in favour of the innovator when considering interference and infringements, that is, earlier disclosure would be rewarded with wider protection.

The proof of utility would require an experiment in a society. This would be very difficult to arrange, unless there were to be many variants of social pattern and decentralized control, which brings me to the second of my conditions, namely, decentralized control of social service. Looked at on a world scale, social services are decentralized, and if the protection system were international some progress might be made, even though arrangements in Britain were monolithic. But the cumulative resistance to progress resulting from any monolithic structure is impressive, and must, I believe, in the end be accepted as overwhelming to the gallant attempts of those who are trying to be effective whilst caught up in the toils of the machine. It is paradoxical that one of the main reasons for centralization is the economy from rationalizing wherever there is evidence of duplication, yet this is also one of the greatest liabilities. Biological evolution has been by natural selection from amongst the contemporary variants of a species. If the range of variation was not sufficiently wide to include some that could survive under new conditions, then extinction of the species was the inevitable fate.

Society is ever changing. We cannot measure in absolute terms the efficiency of any welfare system, nor whether it is satisfactory in quality, for it is designed to satisfy human needs, and these are individual and cannot usually be quantified. Our best guide is the choice of the user when choice is available to him. Even if we can't measure, he can choose, and in so doing we can get a measure of acceptability, not once and for all, but for the time being. Waste is everywhere. It is made obvious by duplication, but it is very easy to have even greater hidden waste simply because lack of measurement prevents it being recognised. In the social field, without absolute standards we can only compare and contrast in the manner normal in biological experiments. Without contrast we have no 'control', we cannot avoid hidden waste, and we can only achieve the low order of satisfaction that the user gets from taking what he is given rather than exercising his preference.

If we are to have contrast, then the groups responsible must have comparable resources and goods, but should pursue their objectives by different means. For full comparability, competitive systems should all be national, but if this is not practicable then a regional division might be made to work provided each region had real autonomy over its use of resources, its ability to try new ideas and to buy new products or services. Regional autonomy obviously could be contrived in the health field, it could be strengthened in many fields where control is already at a local authority level, but may prove impractical; for instance, in treating those with criminal aberrations, in administering pensions and in providing the means to overcome poverty.

If the method works, and starts to solve social problems more effectively at lower cost, then it would become progressively easier to satisfy the third criterion — 'that the successful should get sufficient backing'. Left to themselves they tend to gain strength. It is only by handicapping the successful to help the weak that the strong are kept down, so that the lifting of inhibitions would do most of what is necessary.[1] Many of the inhibitory factors are quite small, but they are cumulative and, just as most taxes are said to be progressive or retrogressive, so they also tend to favour competitive innovators or copyists, but I have not the time to dwell on this very complex subject here.

Let me try and give an instance with somewhat 'science fiction' wishfulness of what competitive innovation might do in the hospital service. There would be some 20–40 autonomous regions receiving a subsidy per head from State taxes, but also progressively raising additional funds in other ways because the State figure would be relatively constant. Each board would set up a scheme of management and the State would establish a central auditing and comparison unit which would have access to all information and would publish its findings. A board might well accept the proposition of a company offering contract management for the running of one hospital (A) in a district where suitable safeguards could exist. For instance, that there was at least one other hospital (B) in the area and transference of too much medical/patient support to (B) would break the contract. Professional freedom to treat patients would be granted subject to the same penalty.

Funds would be available based on historic total costs for each sort of patient, corrected from time to time by any changes in an index of costs in other hospitals. Managing companies would tender on the basis of receiving a percentage of any savings, and would have freedom to use the remainder for improvements, to pay staff, or to improve conditions within the hospital. The managers, therefore, would control incentives, but not the basic terms of employment. If a company could be found to take on the job, then it would be in a position to become a social innovator provided also that protection were adequate. For example, it might see that a concept of domiciliary stabilization of many diabetics would be possible if they were supplied with testing reagents, and if the results were reported by a telephonic presentation to the hospital doctor. Perhaps this would involve the need to develop new techniques of assay and to employ new means of communication. They could prove the scheme, write it up and apply for a 'Copy Patent' (C.P.). Subsequently, for the life of the C.P., any other hospital would have to pay a fee per patient treated.

In other regimes and other hospitals, different schemes would be tried and a better diabetic scheme come forward quite quickly. So our first company would try to be first to market its scheme to all other potential users. It would discuss its merits with them, make special adaptations as needed, and would be a powerful force motivating change throughout the country, or possibly the world. Diabetics would be free to go to the other hospital if they preferred it, and those in fringe areas might even go to other regions so that disliked schemes, new or old, would soon be revealed either by patients' references or by the central auditing and comparison unit. Why shouldn't such a process lead to an unimaginable snowball of progress in the way that technological progress has increased in momentum?

Could such schemes apply to education, housing, unemployment and the other welfare services? I don't see why not nor do I see any disadvantage in opening the door to such progress by establishing the three necessary pre-conditions: (1) protection; (2) multiple buying points; and (3) building on success.

Will it be possible to devise ways of meeting social needs selectively whilst maintaining human dignity, that is, without the old-fashioned means test? If welfare is to continue as an overall provision, there will generally be a need to ration it and protect society from abuses. Formerly, this has meant hard rules and hard cases, whilst the individual with his special social problems now has to take it much as he finds it. Such a system would be rejected in the satisfaction of material needs where customer choice leads to the most satisfactory, but still far from perfect, results. If we had many ideas and, as a result, many social alternatives, they could be provided for by a variety of insurances and loan schemes. These could be subsidized by the whole public to cover the abnormal risks; for instance, the extra liabilities to an insurance scheme of a haemophiliac. Every individual would probably be compelled to take out a minimum of cover, but this minimum could still take different forms, and he would have the satisfaction of having chosen the one he wanted. For instance, schemes would be cheaper, but less pleasant, the more they provided protection against abuse. The choice would be personal, services and facilities would not need to be subject to central control, and the opportunities for multiple buying and for comparison to develop would exist. There would never be the need for the nation to put all its eggs in the theoretical basket devised by a policy commission review every decade or so. Instead, conditions would encourage natural evolution with extra growth of those services found by the consumer to be most desirable, and relatively rapid withering of those which were less used. Changes could be tested, proved or discarded, and incorporated and sold to buying public in rapid succession. Is not our social progress stuck because we want an overall system? There are many special needs, can we not find satisfactory answers for each?

If I have in outline made out a case for reconsidering our approach to welfare, then I am sure you would want to know how big the potential benefits could be. Apart from benefits already suggested, such as: giving the user choice, fitting the service more closely to the need, and encouraging new and better forms of human interdependance and interrelationships, you will want to know whether substantial resources could be released so as to provide funds to encourage and maintain the new concepts and reduce the burden of taxation. Let me give you an example by going back to the hospital environment and choosing a very clear cut disease entity — non-acute hernia. Morris, Ward and Handyside studied the effect of early discharge after hernia repair in Manfield Hospital.[5] The length of stay after operation varied from one day to five to six days for selected patients (i.e., those without adverse medical or social backgrounds). The study showed that early discharge was not detrimental to the postoperative progress of those patients concerned, nor was there any unforeseen increase in the workload of the general practitioners involved, thereby permitting increased bed turnover where theatre facilities, sufficient hospital staff and the cooperation of general practitioners were available. The daily cost per patient in hospitals treating this sort of hernia varied in 1967/1968 from £10 1s 8d for Basingstoke and District Hospital to £3 4s 4d for Retford and District Hospital.[6] There is, already, in this case enough evidence to suggest that costs for equally effective and less expensive treatments might easily halve the current cost per patient. The cost of the Hospital Service was £905 million for 1967. Even a 5 per cent. saving ploughed back largely into competitive innovation might well give impressive results.

The role of government in innovation must be different for those cases such as some defence fields, where the judgement has to be central and therefore the pattern of competitive innovation must change. The government's function generally should be to create the right climate, not to direct, to keep a close watch and by gradual and subtle variations and incentives ensure that all fields get a more or less appropriate level of effort. The more we are to create a society of change, both industrial and social, the more impossible it will be to centralize even the key decisions on the geometrically increasing number of new alternatives that must be made available to ever smaller groups of people. The parallel of the increasing segmentation of most markets for material things, even at the expense of not getting full production effectiveness, is probably relevant.

The theme of this paper is to suggest that to succeed in material innovation we must also succeed in social innovation, and to do both we must learn how to make a decentralized society work and develop into a better society to live in. To make a biological analogy, society must avoid becoming a dinosaur. It must maintain its ability to evolve. It may be surprising to many that our bodies are very decentralized collections of very individual living cells. For locomotion and defence we are centralized, but the vast bulk of activities are done by nearly autonomous cells responding to pressures in the climate around them. I suggest that multi-cellular organisms evolved by trial and error on a vast scale could show us the way to build a better multi-person living entity – society.

Pushing the analogy further, our bodies get rogue innovations – some cancers are probably of this sort and, on a social scale, thalidomide is a well known example. It is generally accepted that governments have a role in providing security for the populace against 'thalidomides'. The Dunlop Committee on Safety of Drugs provides an audit of an innovator's work. It collects evidence of early use to get the quickest warning possible of any adverse reaction, and it can publicise its fears where it wishes. All of this is done without diminishing the innovator's legal, financial and moral responsibility. A change to a central body to maintain public safety could only obtain the required security, at a high cost in lost progress. A compromise between the risks has to be found, and the Dunlop level seems about right. Perhaps it could be a prototype for other fields where innovation might carry with it concealed risks.

Turning to the question of overcoming the individual's inhibitions to change, and this is another ill-understood subject, it is presumably largely a matter of the 'climate', but we need much more research before we will know how to influence the national 'climate' towards acceptance of innovation. Just discussing the problem could help. Fortunately, the research which has been done suggests that innovations are better accepted when people feel they have participated in their evolution, however slightly.[7] The user orientation of modern competitive innovation arises from a recognition of the great importance of dealing with users as personally as possible.

The successful competitive innovators of products will therefore include successful innovators of communication and motivation techniques in their teams, and it is probably not too hopeful to assume that they will succeed in reducing the consequences of resistance to innovation though it will not be done without cost. Could we recover this cost by lifting some of the inhibitions that now surround innovators, so that we can achieve the economic benefits from more rapid innovation?

In conclusion, an innovating economy requires an innovating society. Such a society will be decentralized and competitive, but the people will be ever more highly interdependent. It will have to capitalize the differences between people, and encourage successful enterprise to achieve even greater heights, and at the same time be ingenious in providing selective help where it is needed. The many problems needing solution, if all the difficulties are to be resolved, call for the application of the proven process of innovation to society itself as well as to increasing its wealth.

### References

1. G. R. Fryers, 'Profits, Public Opinion and Innovation', *Science of Science Foundation Symposium*, May 1968
2. Professor Duncan Burn, American Engineering Competition, 1850-1870, *Ec. History*, January 1931
3. Sir Solly Zuckerman, *Report to the National Economic Development Council* on the report of the Central Advisory Council for Science and Technology, March 5th, 1969
4. A. Seldon, 'Taxation and Welfare', *I.E.A. Research Monograph 14*, 1967
5. D. Morris, A. W. M. Ward, A. J. Handyside, 'Early Discharge After Hernia Repair', *The Lancet*, 1968, March 30th, 681–685
6. Taken from the *Annual Hospital Costing Returns* to the Ministry of Health
7. Paul R. Lawrence, 'How to Deal With Resistance to Change', *Harvard Business Review*, Vol. 47, January/February, 1969, page 4

Chapter 24

# Logic and Variety in Innovation Processes

*F. E. Burke*

**Abstract**

Variety of economic results, and of time lags between discovery and adaption, are examined and categorized. The logical difficulties of evidence gathered from case histories, and inferences from information limits, are related to a need for more explicit disclosure of assumptions and models in future innovation research. A multi-participant, uncertainty limited conceptual model is suggested.

## Introduction

I would like to tease out a few threads from the enormous amount of discussion we have had. Hopefully, this will aid us in stepping forward, on to some new ground. I intend to take more notice than our group has done of the challenge of the Director of the Science of Science Foundation when he opened this Symposium, that we should remember the very wide spectrum of the innovative process. So I would like to end up with a little bit of anatomy of the processes of innovation.

I shall try to deal with some myths that are very prevalent. One, right in the title of this Symposium, is that innovation seems to be associated in our minds only with growth. I believe this is very dangerous. Growth, as an econometrically determinable result of technological innovation, is an uneasy aggregate. In Part I of this paper, I would like to disaggregate economic results, by one stage, as an example of the kind of variety in my title. In Part II, I shall use what I believe is common sense, but also logic, to warn about too free a use of case histories. We have to learn from history, as Professor Burn has suggested, and perhaps we should go even much further back in time. There is a mine of data. But most of us are used to science, and there a fact seems a fact, so we do not let the logic boys get in the way of progress. We have not got that far in our work, and we have still to consider what, logically, is really evidence.

In Part III, I shall resume tilting at myths, and return to variety, by re-examining the speed-up in the innovative process we have heard so much about.

Part IV examines the logical implications for our kind of research, or future research, of information limits. I shall probably sound very esoteric there, but I want to say that I have been driven to this chapter of my studies by hard engineering difficulties. I hope I can convey these to you.

In Part V, I shall tie these few threads together in a skeletal 'anatomy'. I hope it will set the scene in your mind for some next steps, largely by showing a little more clearly what we don't yet know. It is part of the basis on which my own work will be carried on, for a year or two at least.

## PART I

### Variety in Economic Results

Some of the most sustained, successful and largest volume innovations we have had are not related, in any direct or unconditional way, with economic growth. They have been connected with negative growth, or the release of employed labour, in a direct and simple manner, by increased productivity combined with inelastic demand. I shall give examples, such as agriculture, below. Thus there exists a variety of innovation, quite non-negligible, with a negative economic growth as its result if it occurs by itself.

Now the best way economists have measured technical change up to now is that pioneered by Robert Solow's celebrated 1957 paper,[1] following closely upon the study of Abramovits.[2] This school measures productivity — and assumes that, just somehow (because it happened more or less like this in the past), there will be no unemployment problems. I believe this is another myth, supported by a long series of accidents.

The Solow School taught us two very important things: that neither labour, nor even capital, have been as important to 'technical change' (that uneasy aggregate?) as we believed till 1957; and secondly, that in some way technology and management account for the majority of this change.

If we go back to 'pure' productivity change, and labour release, I think it is a more rapid and spectacular thing than we tend to visualize. Take the familiar average of 3 per cent. per person per year improvement in productivity by itself, and start at 96 per cent. employment with any given set of products, and begin the displacement process. Then in a decade, if I have my cumulative arithmetic right, we will be approaching the 60 per cent. employment line (worse than the great depression) and be going down fast. This is the result of the normal, competitive developmental productivity increase, other things being equal.

Other things, of course, are not equal (or we would not be here), and the variety of innovative processes of the Charpie report is close to the other extreme of economic results of technical innovation, and is labour absorbing — that is, for a while. I think that this labour absorbing variety has happened rather accidentally, and in a way I hoped we had come here to discuss how to render these accidents manageable. We have not, I think, gone very far. Hence, this excursion of 'variety', to help lead our next steps more explicitly in this direction. In section 1·1, my crude form of labour displacement balance (hopefully biased and towards growth), in 1·2, examples of labour release, in 1·3, of labour absorption.

Again, I leave illustrative examples, such as the automobile from 1900 to 1929, for later. Here, I will just add that when we look at decades of time, rather than the five- to ten-year spans we have been discussing most, then almost all important (i.e. fairly permanently needed) goods reach an elasticity of demand smaller than one. Thus if you reserve consideration, as I will, of the first 20 or 30 years till later, we will find labour releasing economic results for almost all goods. To paraphrase Dr. Gellman: as an economist devoted to competition, he would (as an innovator) like to be in a monopoly position, and as far away from competition as he can get! I enjoyed that remark. Innovators want to be on that part of the elasticity diagram where any small change in price will increase their revenue substantially, and we do not care whether in cash terms, or market penetration, or employment, providing we are consistent.

## 1·1. A Crude Conceptual Model of Balanced Labour Displacement

Figure 1 indicates how these two different effects of technical changes may result in essentially full employment, providing both kinds occur in reasonable and requisite balance. The upper diagram (modelled on the automobile industry since about 1900) indicates the thesis outlined in the next two sections concerning labour absorption and, after about 30 years, the resulting labour release. The lower portion of the figure contains two curves: the left hand one indicating the aggregate rate of labour release in illustrative terms only. In fact, about 1 per cent. p.a. net labour release, in the 'non-automobile' economy, has been plotted in Figure 1(b). The upper curve constitutes the addition of the labour percentage values of the upper figure at each time period indicated to the aggregate labour remaining after net labour release. The nation of balanced, or growth promoting, technological change then, is a combination of labour releasing, productivity increasing, competition maintaining, technical change, occurring at a rate at least compensated by an adequate number and amount of labour absorbing technical innovations, or its equivalent in other innovations, over long periods of time. Neither is practical without the other. Without adequate labour release, as England has shown to the world's sorrow, even the most ambitious technological innovations will merely cause inflationary pressures. Without labour absorbing technical innovation, even the most competition preserving productivity increase will do little more than gradually create employment problems on an almost unimaginable scale.

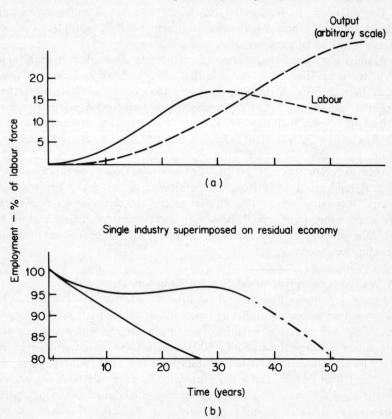

Figure 1. Labour displacement balance

## 1·2. Labour Releasing Technical Innovation

Food is a particularly clear instance of labour releasing technical change, for well over 200 years, with relatively low elasticity of quantities demanded in the long run, on a per capita basis: people cannot be much more than well fed. While excess eating is the predominant nutritious pathology of the North American middle class, there is enough poverty even here to say that, on average, demand for food has been proportional to population, within something like a factor of 2.

The proportion of the labour force needed to supply the population's requirement has dropped steadily from about 70 per cent. in 1700 (see Gregory King's 'Income of Families in England' 1688, approximately analysed to yield 70 per cent. food production, 25 per cent. trade, etc., 5 per cent. rulers, administrators and clergymen) to a present level of about 1 per cent. There is room for debate concerning the latter percentage within a factor of about 2: on this continent, 6 − 8 per cent. of the labour force, in fact, is employed on farms, although it has been shown that less than 1 per cent. is needed by economic criteria − the rest constituting structural and frictional under-employment. This value may be biased towards low estimates because of specialization: early farmers undertook functions of distribution, etc., not now counted as agricultural employment, and supplied their more comprehensive subsistence needs to a greater extent than now, even allowing for the enormous differences in real wealth in the periods compared.

After allowing for both types of corrections, a factor of about 20 times (even ± many per cent.) represents the massive increase in productivity in food production and its accompanying labour release. Clearly, the vastly greater quality of North American food supply in terms of protein content, vitamins, and variety is the main long term effect of elasticity of demand for food, but has not changed the pattern of labour release. In such a 'pure' case, then, we may find grounds to mistrust the popular argument (although repeated by economists of the stature of Brozen and Nelson in the U.S.A., for instance) that productivity increase will expand markets sufficiently to offset the labour release initially observed (of course, at one remove, the released labour is potential wealth, *if used*!).

To avoid the charge that this exceptional case has few parallels, and should not be given the importance it has had in this argument, further examples are added, more briefly still. In the early 19th century, textile production employed in the order of one-third of the British labour force. Currently, textiles and apparels employ about 3 per cent. of the U.S.A. labour force. The earlier figure may be inflated by a high export rate, but there is no doubt that there have been market expanding changes since: the U.S.A. population is, on average, surely more adequately dressed than the vast majority of nineteenth century Britons!

Again then, we find labour release resulting from improved productivity, to a much greater extent than is counter-balanced (in the same occupations) by increased demand of quality, variety and quantity. Other examples are legion: the production of filament lamp bulbs employed its greatest percentage labour force in the early 1920s, although the number of bulbs/person/year has increased (in the U.S.A.) about three-fold since that time. The peak percentage of labour employed in car manufacture in the U.S.A. occurred in 1929, so that labour release has taken place since then, although the sales/person/year of cars appear to have increased very substantially, particularly if quality is taken into account.

There is nothing surprising here for the business empiricist: the 'S' curves of penetration, saturation and eventual decay have long been regarded as the normal course of product history, or life cycle. Elements of the new perspective are:

(a) the use of the non-dimensional number of per cent. employment — concepts natural to an engineer. Over the long time periods here considered, it is believed that counting people may be less open to the strictures of O. Morgenstern's 'Accuracy of Economic Observations' [3] than money or product counting.

(b) the 'S' curve ends in product or dollar volume collapse or replacement, but some examples have been given to show that labour release will quite generally occur even while physical output of the product still rises, and certainly when it stabilizes.

## 1·3. Labour Absorbing Technical Innovations
### (i) The Boundary Problem

As in the previous section, a historical perspective may help clarify the thesis. Before 1850, there was no communication of the personal kind exemplified by the telephone. Today, telephone service is a very substantial employer of labour in every country in the west. The actual amount of labour absorbed in per cent., or a detailed time scale on which the absorption occurred, will not be evaluated here. It is more important to clarify within what region, or in other words within what system boundary, we can speak of labour absorption rather than labour release. There is little doubt that the use of the telephone, properly considered, has immensely increased that aggregate productivity of western society. There are two reasons why this productivity effect will be overlooked for the present purpose. Firstly, it is extraordinarily difficult to quantify the productivity enhancing effect of a service or good as revolutionary as the telephone was at the time of its appearance. Secondly, the effect is too dispersed, i.e. beset by too many 'externalities'. If a more stringent boundary is drawn around the telephone industry, comprising those manning telephone exchanges, producing telephone equipment, and installing and maintaining such equipment, then a quite meaningful set of empirical data can be obtained as inputs, and these can be related to product output. That this output, in the case of the telephone industry, is the number of telephone conversations connected, related to the distance over which such communication occurred, and compounded with the amount of information conveyed in each such contact, does not affect the principle that a product can be quantified and productivity studies undertaken. This example is used to show that there is an empirically verifiable meaning (to the notion of labour absorption by a technical innovation) only if a reasonably identifiable boundary is drawn around the industry, firm, or product line under consideration. The same boundary will serve, later, to observe transition to labour release.

*(ii) Examples*

There have been so many labour absorbing technical innovations that neither a listing, nor even a comprehensive set of illustrations will be given here; it would merely waste your time. The automobile, the aeroplane, modern domestic appliances, may give an idea of the kind of goods visualized in this connection. So do the cases in the Charpie report. Quite a different class of such innovations, although not of a technical kind, are the hugely expanded services of health and education, as well as the general provision of expanding welfare, typical of our society. The latter examples are mentioned here only to show that it is not claimed that technological contributions account for all labour absorbing innovations in our society.

These examples show that the concept here offered leaves the final authority for what is (or what is not) an innovation entirely in the hands of members of the public who choose, in comparison with whatever else is offered to them, whether to devote their resources to the innovative good provided for their use, or not. I shall try to show in Parts IV and V why I believe that this, rather than central control, is right in the long run.

# PART II

**Disclosure of Assumptions – A Logical Deficiency of Present Case Histories**

In the first part of the paper, I have given quite a few historical examples of technological innovation, although I tried to stick to countable effects; I shall be in enough controversy even then. But we need to study other, more uncertain factors. And here I would like to inject a logical warning. Clearly, in this field of innovation research we have to proceed historically and at the moment by case studies. But I have a slight yet serious misgiving that, in general, when we have completed a good case study then we are left with something like half an hour's reading to show for the work of one to a dozen of the most able kind of people who ever lived. The time compression of the case history compared with reality in this instance is then, if my arithmetic is correct, something between 1,000,000 and 10,000 to 1. It matters a great deal by what cookery recipe you undertake the selection of what is relevant, and consequently should be included in this case history; and what is irrelevant, and should therefore be excluded. But, if two people happen to use slightly different cookery recipes for this selection and rejection process, they will come to quite discordant and non-comparable conclusions. And this, I submit, is happening all the time.

Therefore, I make a strong plea that we should pay a great deal more attention to explicit hypotheses, assumptions, measures and finally models. If we do not explicitly disclose the cookery recipe by which we have culled our evidence, from the almost infinite variety of the total sample space of evidence, then we are not conveying information in a testable, or reproducible (i.e. scientific) manner. And with this short warning and plea for change in our next steps, which is just a door opener to the heavy dose of what I hope is logic, in Part IV, I shall go on to some of these questionable case histories to explore another facet of this variety.

## PART III

### The Variety of Time Spans in Technological Processes: are we Really Speeding up?

I am hesitant about the case histories I am going to discuss and relate because they do not meet the demands in my last Part. As an engineer, I shall go ahead anyway, hoping to add some cautions as I proceed.

We are very prone to say (or at least, to hear) that the process of technical innovation has speeded up a great deal in the last 150 to 200 years. We can be in considerable disagreement about the time lags, and not be surprised by this. But let us go back to 1850, or just before (and this is the smallest historical base that makes sense to me), and select just one piece of evidence that has been offered for the hypothesis of speed-up. We find it on p. 87 of 'Technology and Social Change', a report of important seminars held at Columbia University for more than four years. It is a diagram prepared by the Bell Laboratories, showing 10 case histories in the interval of 1820 to 1960. I am intrigued that they left out the innovation of the telephone! If we replot their data, as in Figure 2, we see quite a convincing speed-up, and given their sample space, it is certainly significant. A straight regression line is less convincing, as it would predict negative time lags of some magnitude, either now, or certainly by 1980.

If we add a further selection of cases, trying to 'match' where possible, and also add a few teasers to show there is no ill feeling, we can readily find another sample space to show an increase in time lags. I have listed the two sets of cases in Table 1.

Now, I do not believe any more than you do that we can 'prove' an increased time lag this way, but perhaps the discussion of information spaces in Part IV will remind you of this point. Nor do I believe the original diagram proved a speeding up either.

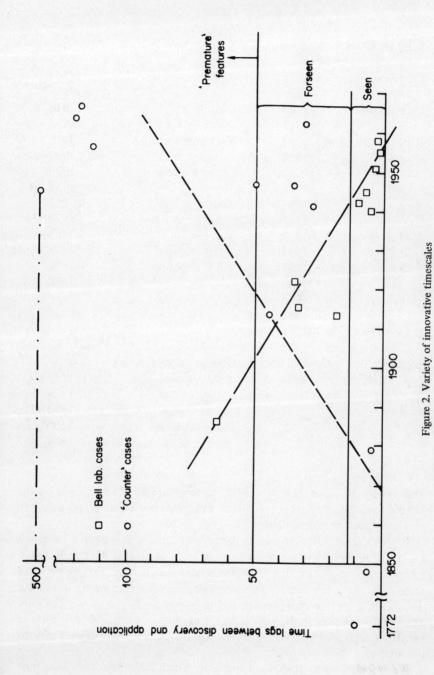

Figure 2. Variety of innovative timescales

Table I

| Bell Lab. Cases | | | | 'Counter' cases | | |
| --- | --- | --- | --- | --- | --- | --- |
| Electric motor | 1821 | | | Fuel cell | | 1840 |
| | 1886 | | | | | ?1962 |
| Vacuum tube | 1882 | | | Kodachrome | | 1910 |
| | 1915 | | | | | 1935 |
| Radio broadcasting | 1887 | | | Black and white T.V. | | 1910 |
| | 1922 | | | | | 1947 (?38) |
| | | | | Colour T.V. | | 1929 |
| | | | | | | 1962 (?) |
| X-ray tubes | 1895 | | | Laser | | 1955 |
| | 1913 | | | | | 1970+(?) |
| Nuclear reactor | 1932 | | | Watt's steam engine | | 1765 |
| | 1942 | | | | | 1775 |
| Radar | 1935 | | | Bell's telephone | | 1874 |
| | 1940 | | | | | 1878 |
| Transistor | 1948 | | | | | |
| | 1951 | | | | | |
| Solar battery | 1953 | | | | | |
| | 1955 | | | | | |
| Sterospecific | 1955 | | | Goodyears' vulcanizing | | 1848 |
| polymers | 1958 | | | process | | 1853 (?) |
| | | also | | Stirling engine | | 1824 |
| | | | | | | 1970+(?) |
| | | | | Rocket: before | | 1400 |
| | | | | | | 1944 |

This variety of innovation process is (to misquote Sir Ernest Gower on the British Civil Service) such a complex thing that facts can be produced to prove anything whatsoever about it.

It seems more useful to me, at the present time, to assume that we have a variety of innovative processes, with time spans associated with each. In our ignorance, let us assume that some things have not changed: that we have had some cases in the last century that were fast, and some that are fast now; let us discuss these as one variety, until this proves misleading. Also we had some cases that were slow in the last century, and some now; let us discuss these as another variety. Of course, the classes will merge, but the extremes may be instructive.

We will find some cases, then *and now*, which have impossibly long time scales, and we wish we could tell this variety by foresight rather than hindsight. I doubt if we will be very good at this for some time, unless we want to miss some of the greatest plums, in the second band, and I believe we cannot afford this if we want to balance effects, as in Part I.

In the right-hand margin of Figure 2 I have done my best to disclose my preferred 'measures' of these various cases. You will probably disagree, but this may take us a step further.

In the 'fast' band, I believe opportunities can be seen, or perceived (measure I) by three major classes of participants to an innovation: managers or sponsors looking for pay-off (and their economists), scientists and engineers concerned with feasibility, and users and their representatives prepared to declare themselves on acceptability (market people like Dr. Gellman and his psychologists). At the same time, each of these sets of participants would assign fairly low uncertainty (measure II) to such ventures.

In the second band, read: opportunities can be foreseen – uncertainty would be greater. In the third band, one of the uncertainties would turn out to be beyond reach: even while 'foreseen' (or there would not be pre-history), the information required for the uncertainty reduction would turn out to be beyond limitations, with available measures, theories or assumptions.

We can now see that the 'good' scientist must not bother about applications, or he would try to handle more information than his limits permit. But the same with the 'good' manager – the sponsor; and the 'good' marketer – like Dr. Gellman, or like Edwin Land.

To sum up: I think both slow and fast innovation processes are with us to stay; and I believe even labour absorption types are apt to be slower than labour releasing types: there is less uncertainty if you already have a product, and a market, and a plant, and you merely want to increase its productivity and volume.

## PART IV

### Information Limits, and the Logic of Exploring Pre-scientific Areas

Among the most important aspects of variety in technical innovation are the learning processes and their information needs. We recall that uncertainty (to the electrical engineer) is equal to the information needed to remove it.

The following passage points at the contention that assumptions are the most uncertain things we use, and imply the most information. Unless we acquire much information about assumptions, we tap in the dark. These are the slowest things in any field to establish; they may turn out to correspond to the slower kinds of innovation in the last part, because the human being cannot process more than about 10 bits of information per second. Can the computer help in these learning processes? Let us see.

Ashby[4] has been concerned with information capacities in connection with the physical simulation of intelligence, including memories. He did not want to assume what scientists take for granted: well defined facts, well ordered sets, etc. So he proceeded as follows:

Postulate an array of 400 lamps (say in a 20 x 20 square), where each lamp can be independently switched on or off. This is an example of a direct representation of a set of binary states. The number of patterns that can be generated by this array is, quite simply, $2^{400}$. More generally, for $n$ sources of binary states, the available number of patterns (or the state space) is $2^n$. Ashby now shows that even this fairly simple state space cannot be physically represented:

We have $$2^{400} \cong 10^{120}$$

because $$2^{10} = 1024 \cong 1000 = 10^3$$

But the number of atoms in the Einsteinian cosmology is about $$10^{79} \frac{atoms}{universe}$$

the age of the universe is (in seconds and the same cosmology) *less than* $10^{20}$ *secs*

the frequency of atomic transitions (smallest energy physical events, small integer multiples of Planck's energy quantum) is *less than* $10^{15} \frac{transitions}{sec/atom}$

*Total*, or multiple of the 3 factors: *less than* $10^{114} \frac{transitions}{universe}$

This shows that the above modest source of patterns cannot be represented physically, by a great margin, even using the whole universe as a computer, without restriction on how this 'memory' may be tapped for retrieval, and the time at which storage or use of information may occur. It is beyond the feasible limits on representable information spaces. So, on any problem of this size, we proceed by assumptions, whether as human minds, or by any conceivable computer. Of course, the computer helps, but mostly by helping to expose the assumptions, and to take over clerical work.

Two implications are now mentioned, to show that such limits are even more restrictive than may appear already, or that they place even more emphasis on order, theory, model or measure than the traditional Razor of Occam.

On the one hand, we may enquire how a map may be acquired (in terms of signals sent or received) by such random exploration as corresponds to *untrained* sacchadic eye movements (this corresponds to the notion: how much information is conveyed by such an instruction as 'conceive a square of 20 lines of 20, and number left to right in ascending order'). If the first switch to be encountered randomly is number '1', the chance of agreement with a fixed map is 1/400; if this is fixed and no longer revisited, the next point carries a chance of 1/399 and so forth: thus, the map agreement for 400 points (on the assumptions of unique visits and instant agreement) implies the information equivalent of $10^{87.6} \cong 400!$ messages! This implies that 70 binary sources, or a square array of maximally side 8, would exhaust physical representation, if *this* process of map exploration were needed.

On the other hand, we may not only be interested in patterns arising from binary states, but also the patterns of their properties. If each state in the pattern may have two properties independently (true or false, zero or non-zero on some measure, etc.), then the field of property-state patterns as events is of an extent $2^{2^n}$ rather than $2^n$. We will now estimate $n$ so that $2^{2^n}$ is as close to physical limits as is meaningful:

$$2^{2^n} \ll 2^{400}$$

We observe that $2^8 = 256, 2^9 = 512$, thus $2^{2^9}$ is clearly in violation, but $2^{2^8}$ is not, and $n = 8$ is the maximum number of binary state sources for which all first level hyper-patterns can be searched without *strong assumptions* of order, even if the physical limitation limits can be reached. The simplest evaluation of all greater information tasks depends on agreed assumptions, models, theories, etc.

To sum up: the patterns arising from astonishingly simple signal sources are beyond representation, and even more, beyond evaluation, without strong ordering.

Thus any physical 'memory', including the human brain, and any learning with time endurance, is likely to be both an exceedingly partial representation of our physical environment, and a very conventional one. Of course, as engineers and scientists, we are stuck with this. But we ought to know how much we assume, when we enter a field *without* well tested models, such as the science (??) of science.

More specifically, 20 x 20 matrices are among the simplest system descriptions for technical innovations. If all coefficients are meaningful, we would grope for a solution forever.

The only way we can avoid this in practice is to do what we would do in Ashby's example, and use a measure. You take a light meter with 400 divisions on it, then you can determine the light output from these patterns. You have only 400 pieces of information left about this particular array of patterns. You throw away the rest. That is the purpose of a measure. And because we cannot handle amounts of information that are as great as the original as human beings, or with computers, we have to have measures, etc., and we want to *reject* the bulk of the information that is involved in anything we do, and talk about. We must not attempt to trail reality behind us, because all we live in is measure space, or theory space, or model space. Now, again I want to emphasize this is engineering, at least to me. If you want to estimate a probability (this is the most widely used linear measure), you can't do engineering unless you have confidence limits. And modern statistics teaches that (as no tickee, no laundee) you cannot have a measure without defining the sample space on which to map it. Hence, the logical need for this chapter.

There are many implications of this. One of the most urgent ones, that Dr. Fryers has already given us, is that there is no point in thinking of the centralization of anything involving large degrees of uncertainty. If you have 20 variables in any problem, then however pretty a diagram Dr. Knoppers might draw, you can make it work for 20 variables only if you make assumptions about it, or you have models concerning it. And I submit we do not yet have 'good' assumptions, from the research point of view. But we must go on using what's best, with humility, in the meantime. This is the slow learning process in the face of uncertain assumptions, etc.

## PART V

### A Skeleton 'Anatomy' for Technical Innovation Processes

I shall try to take the four rather bare bones that have been presented so far, and connect them up. There are, of course, more bones needed to form a reasonable skeleton but they are beyond my scope for this occasion. In addition to the two dimensions of variety in Parts I and III, there are at least three more, and if all dimensions are independent, we would end up with hundreds of varieties of technical innovation. We would then be able to make precise statements of interest to practically nobody.

There are some very preliminary indications that there is considerable clustering of these types, and thus hope of some sense emerging. But that is for the future.

Even with the limited material here, I hope I can tangle with another pair of myths. We hear much, since Schumpeter's days at least, about the pre-eminent importance of entrepreneurs. The technical man seems too unimportant to the economist. At the same time, if you move in scientific circles, the 'practical' people are looked down upon, because they (poor things) always know where they are going and why: they haven't the mystique of high uncertainty, in which accidents are almost holy. (Let us remember Part IV. I think in new science, real accidents in the statistical sense would happen perhaps once in 1000 years, and science would be out of business. I think the 'accidents' are the rendering explicit of some marginal perceptions, that all others refuse to see. This reminds me of 'tacit knowing', but is not the same.)

I believe both of these myths are unrealistic, but understandable in the light of human information (i.e. uncertainty) limits. They merely represent, as Mr. Freeman so well put it, a sad state of uncoupling, which I have illustrated in Figure 3(a).

Each of the potential participants (I have drawn this for individuals) has his 'area of uncertainty', and if they are of equal rarity of ability, these areas are of about equal size. If they are quite uncoupled, interaction (i.e. information flow) is unlikely, as in tunneling. This was Freeman's point.

In Figure 3(b) I have drawn what may be optimal: a small information region shared pair wise, and perhaps even a common intersection which is smaller still.

You may ask, why not more overlap? Surely, everybody wants to communicate! Here I use Part IV on you: there are simply limits. If you had complete overlap, you would cover a lesser information space. You could also fire two of the participants. The only reason Edwin Land is not known to have done such firing, is that he never had equal participants in the first place.

Now I think the entrepreneur, though I call him sponsor, is very important. But I agree with Dr. Goldman and Dr. Pannenborg that someone had better understand science: and only in rare cases can we do without the Dr. Gellmans.

But if there is so little overlap of information, what should be in those intersections? I would go for mutually accepted measures. They will map on to different information spaces for each pair (or triple), so they have to be handled, learned, and nurtured with care. I think this 'team' of unlike participants is an important model for innovative processes, their organization, and management. Limited uncertainty, an extension of H. A. Simon's limited rationality, is, to me at least, the central measure when observing the variety of processes that we have. In each case, one or the other participant may face uncertainty up to, and beyond his limit: this could be extended to cover the question to which we returned so often. What kind of world do we really want to innovate? But this, surely, is even beyond my next step.

*Acknowledgements*

The research on which this paper is based, and the opportunity to attend this interesting Symposium, were generously supported by both the Killam Awards Programme of Canada Council, and the University of Waterloo.

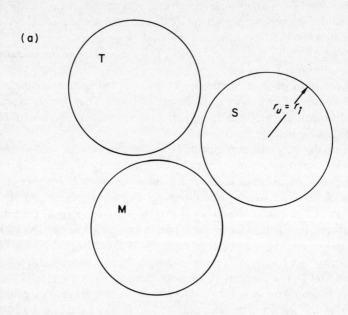

(a)

$r_j$ (tech.) $\cong$ $r_j$ (spon.) $\cong$ $r_j$ (mark.)

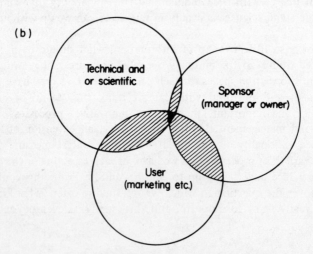

(b)

Figure 3. Information coupling and uncertainty

## References

1.  Robert Solow, 'Technical Change and the Aggregate Production Function', *Review Economics and Statistics*, 39, pp. 312–320, August 1957
2.  Moses Abramovitz, 'Resources and Output Trends in the U.S. Since 1870', *American Economic Review*, 41, No. 2, May 1956
3.  Oskar Morgenstern, *On the Accuracy of Economic Observations*, 2nd Edn., Princeton University Press, 1961
4.  W. Ross Ashby, in 'Computer and Information Sciences', *Proceedings* of 1963 Symposium at North Western University, Editors: J. T. Tou, and R. N. Wilcox Publ. Spartan 1964

## General Closing Discussion

The Symposium had not discussed, said Lord Bowden, the problems of introducing innovation into the academic world. Components of the university were 'virtually immortal'; some of them tended to ossify with time. This meant that innovation could only be introduced by a process of maintaining the ancient while adding the new.

This interaction between growth and decline not only occurred in the case of institutions. He pointed out that most agricultural innovation came not from farmers but from growth in the business of agricultural machinery, agricultural chemicals and agricultural education. It had led to a decline in agriculture as a source of employment.

This interrelation had interesting implications. If one plotted the growth, in terms of numbers employed, of any of a dozen industries or professions, for instance electrical engineering manufacture, it was seen to be exponential. Extrapolating the growth-paths indicated that these professions would arrive simultaneously at a point where each employed the total working population of the U.K. He suggested that our present economic problems, in part, could be attributed to the fact that conflict was already occurring between certain sectors of industry. Demands on resources of men and capital were beginning to conflict. Some countries had so far missed this problem by being able to draw on the resources of others. He referred back to his illustrations of West Germany and North America. But countries which had been unable to draw on external resources had often come to the end of their innovative career on reaching the point 'where there was no more to give in the system'.

This led to the possibility that the Chinese nation may yet return to its traditional position of world cultural and industrial leader. If — with its vast natural and human resources — it innovated at, say, the same rate as the Russians had done, its innovative process would make it the leading industrial power in the world in perhaps 50 years. 'I wonder how far we have been neglecting', asked Lord Bowden, 'in our concepts of innovation the basic limitations of the population and natural resources which we have.' Referring back to his earlier point, he questioned how far Britain's present problems also reflected the early start of its innovative process which had led to a commitment to a rigid structure which it was now very difficult to change. 'Just as it is extremely difficult to change the structure of a university by closing anything down, so it is difficult in England to change the industrial machine by stopping something.'

Dr. Goldman suggested that the basic quest of the Symposium had been to find 'what was done right in the right innovations and what was done wrong in the wrong innovations'. In answering this question it was fallacious to take a single-discipline view, to postulate any single coupling, for instance science with engineering, as of fundamental importance to innovation. All aspects of the process combined equally to yield the whole.

In his final comment, he referred to Dr. Fryers' emphasis on the 'champion'. One ingredient which had not been mentioned, yet was important to the champion, was, he said, the feeling of security, or confidence in his ability to find another job. Only under these conditions would he be disposed to take the innovative chance. Dr. Fryers commented that security was perhaps not quite the right word, with its overtones of pensions and benefits of this kind; what was really meant was a sort of self-confidence in one's ability to get ideas sold and moving. He suggested that the openness of top managers to innovation may well be correlated with age. It should, he said, be possible to carry out studies examining this relationship. Mr. Bodington warned that we should not be too obsessed with the problems of 'the champion'. This question of security related to everyone. Everyone should have the confidence to stand up and criticise the prevailing direction of management.

Dr. Gellman returned to the question of geographical mobility of labour. He suggested that the unions might be severely confusing the location of their interests by opposing greater geographical mobility. He pointed to the disastrous effects of immobility on certain groups of workers in the U.S.A. With the decline of the textile industry, in parts of New England enclaves of poverty had remained which had not entirely been mopped up by the influx of the newer electronics industry. He felt sure that the labour unions, by putting short-term welfare of members first, had directly contributed to this poverty. This came back to questions of security, which the Symposium had just been discussing. He agreed this was important, but it was possible for people to be over-secure. 'If you don't make us all run a bit' the process of innovation would lose much of its impetus.

Professor Burn, too, felt that unless mobility of labour could be improved, based upon a mobility of industry, we would not obtain great advances in technology. The only way in which we would overcome the difficulties of the past was by finding ways of making adaption. Calculations aimed at showing the social costs of higher mobility, for instance, as created by concentration of population — costs which were not borne by the firm whose actions gave rise to them — always greatly over-estimated the magnitudes involved, as they were only carried out to reach a pre-conceived conclusion. Dr. Fryers agreed; on the other side of the equation they tended to under-estimate the value which could be derived from having re-located the industry.

Dr. Archer viewed these attitudes to mobility as over-simplistic. Taken to its extreme, mobility of labour in England would mean the concentration of the entire population within 15 miles of Charing Cross. This would merely serve to intensify problems from which we were already beginning to suffer.

Concluding, Lord Delacourt-Smith said that it was very unlikely that there would ever be a situation, in either the U.S.A. or in Britain, in which workers would passively accept reduction in their wages or security. It was inevitable that workers would continue to form trade unions and that these unions would play an important part in industry. They would also exercise substantial influence on the climate for innovation. These were the premises of his position. From them stemmed his basic view, which was that it was, therefore, of cardinal importance that greater efforts be made to find ways to make innovation much more acceptable to workers.

# Chapter 25

# Summing Up:
# Social and Political Innovation

*Lord Jackson of Burnley*

I think you will appreciate that I have had some difficulty in knowing what to say at the conclusion of what to me has been an extremely interesting and profitable presentation and discussion of the varied aspects of technological innovation.

At the beginning, Maurice Goldsmith asked us to be specific rather than general, though he had in fact made this difficult for us by the very comprehensive nature of the programme. It would have been difficult enough, even if we had been dealing only with the situation in a single country, whereas — and I consider very beneficially — we have embraced several countries, which are different in several respects. These differences reflect the state of unbalance which characterizes the world community, and they would, of course, have emerged more specifically had we covered some of the developing countries, to which I shall want to refer later.

This unbalance arises in such respects as the scale and nature of fuel and mineral resources; the availability of water for power and irrigation purposes; climatic conditions; dependence on agriculture and degree of industrialization; income per capita and capital resources; educational development; and the traditions, types of institution, social practices, machinery of Government, etc., that have been inherited. In fact, the differences even between the countries represented here this weekend in these respects, and in their effects on the character and pace of technological development, have not come out as explicit as I had hoped and expected.

Nevertheless, we have heard of the success which has been achieved; of the organisational factors which have affected and governed this success; of the impediments which lie in the way of further and more rapid progress, and which need to be removed, in industry and Government; and in the relationships between the domains of education and employment.

But what I have found of greatest interest, and will prove for me to be the most lasting impression of the Symposium, has been our searching for a clear

277

concept of what we mean by technological innovation and what, in the already developed countries, we are really seeking to achieve by it.

The first thing that has come out more clearly than is often the case is that innovation is much more than the application of scientific principles to the solution of essentially technical problems. It covers the whole range of interrelated activities from R and D, through design, production, marketing and management to the achievement of competitive, saleable products or systems, aimed at satisfying, and sometimes creating, a need of the community.

The second point, which has also come out very explicitly, is that technological innovation has so far been related too restrictively to the satisfaction of the material needs of the community. We tend to assess its benefits in the quantitative terms of economic growth, rate of rise of GNP, standard of living, etc., and not yet in terms of its contribution to improving the standard of life. I was delighted, therefore, when Dr. King, Mr. Freeman and others emphasized that it does not suffice to think of technological innovation in purely material and quantifiable terms, and that we must regard technological innovation as only one aspect, though often an initiating one, of a much wider concept of sociological and political innovation. Indeed, I would suggest that one of the factors which has retarded innovation is not lack of scientific or technical knowledge, but the impeding effects of inherited characteristics of society. And different countries are in different states of difficulty in dealing with these effects.

To draw attention to this wider approach is not, of course, to deprecate the economic aspects of innovation, because it is only through the economic benefits that we shall be able to afford to do the things which most need doing. The problem is how to get a clearer insight into the kind of community which we hope to create with the aid of the immense potentialities of science and technology, and how to measure the contribution of technological innovation in these terms. I have an uncomfortable feeling that the contribution may prove to be negative, unless we proceed on a broader basis and seek more deliberately to anticipate and prepare for the sociological impact of further technological advance.

Something which has not been discussed very explicitly this weekend is the new kind of intellectual endeavour known as scientific and technological forecasting. This is the attempt to predict along a time scale the likely achievability of definable scientific and technological objectives. What I have found particularly interesting about these speculations is that the majority of them are likely to be achievable, or to lead in their pursuit to more promising achievable objectives. On the other hand, it is open to question how many of them are likely to be economically attractive. And even greater uncertainties lie in the time scale, and in whether some of these technological objectives will prove to have been worth achieving in humanitarian terms.

Some of the results, undoubtedly, will bring unadulterated benefits to the community: others will give considerable cause for anxiety. I am alarmed at the vigour with which we scientists and technologists pursue our objectives in purely scientific and technical terms, and, however great the consequential benefit in particular respects, I feel in all cases there should be a parallel and commensurate study of the social situations which they are likely to produce.

Is it not time that technologists insisted upon the reverse starting point for some, at least, of their activities – a formulation of some of the major social problems that already exist, or may soon arise, and an analysis of the contributions to their resolution which technology supported by science will need to make?

An outstanding example of what I have in mind is that of urban planning. There seems no escape from very large urban concentrations in the highly industrialised countries, and indeed in the developing ones as well. The questions they pose concern the physical forms of these areas; how they are to be developed and re-developed; how the 'obsolescence' cycle can be eliminated so that there are not large numbers living in slums or near slums; how expansion can be contrived without strangulation of transport and other forms of communication; how people are to be employed, and their social aspirations and leisure activities catered for; how the essential services are to be organised, the finances provided, and the communal affairs administered; and so on. It is difficult to think of a contemporary scientific or technological discipline which does not have a part to play in the unravelling of these problems. The field probably presents the best example in the world today where an inter-disciplinary effort by scientists and technologists, in partnership with representatives of other disciplines, is needed.

This leads me to say a few words about education, and to ask whether in this country, and indeed in Europe and the U.S.A., we are making a deliberate enough attempt to produce people who, while capable of solving increasingly complex technological problems, can also see these in terms of their interrelationship with other disciplines such as economics, sociology, psychology and politics. Are we sufficiently teaching science and technology in terms of this interdisciplinary complex, and thus presenting technological innovation as a part of sociological progress?

I am also concerned whether we are ensuring that those who do not wish to pursue careers in science and technology, yet who will live in a community on which science and technology are making an increasingly vigorous impact, understand the origins of change sufficiently to enable them to play their responsible part in the process of adaptation to the evolving situations which flow from technological innovation. In my view, we cannot continue to ignore the necessity for the community – and this includes Government – to understand more fully how they must adapt to change.

These educational objectives cannot nowadays be achieved within the period of formal education as this has so far been conceived. The attainment of a degree or diploma in the 20s must no longer be regarded as the end of the process of formal education, but must be seen merely as the preliminary phase of an educational process which must continue throughout a career. Men and women must be able to withdraw from employment to participate in further education and retraining to assist the adaptation process.

This touches on the question of mobility between the different domains of employment, to which frequent reference has been made. I am convinced that we shall not produce a sufficient number of people who can see technology and its role in the community comprehensively, and who can carry responsibility and exercise authority adequately in the wide sense that we have been discussing, unless we take more deliberate steps than we in the U.K. have so far done to give selected people a much broader range of experience. All too often we have locked highly able people in limited environments for life.

Finally, I want to re-emphasize that the strengthening of the technology and economy of the western world must not be regarded as an end in itself, even if we conceive this end as the improvement of our standard of life and not merely the improvement of our standard of living. There must be associated with the aim to benefit ourselves the determination to bring the standard of living of the developing countries of Africa, Asia and South America to closer comparability with what we ourselves already enjoy.

As compared with an annual growth-rate in income per capita for the highly developed countries of the West, which runs about four per cent., the increase in the developing countries is around two to two-and-a-half per cent. For some, the growth-rate of GNP has been of the same order as that of the developed countries: but population growth has been at such a rate as to reduce this to about two per cent. per capita. Unless we, in the highly developed countries, accept a much greater responsibility for tackling this situation, I do not think that we are going to get anywhere worth going to by increasing our growth-rates, our income per capita, and our GNP. The western countries' contribution to assisting the developing nations to adapt themselves to the impact of science and technology is about 0.75 per cent. of their aggregate GNP. This is quite inadequate. But even if it were adequate in quantity we should have to admit that we have not learned how to apply it in the most effective way.

I think it would have been wrong to close this Symposium without some recognition of this problem. It does not suffice for us to talk about technological innovation in our own terms, even if we interpret it in the widest possible sociological terms. We have got to regard as part of our responsibility the application of the fruits of our technology to resolving the discrepancies between ourselves and the developing countries. Let us hope that we in the western world may be found worthy, and able, to help the developing countries to greater wisdom, as well as to improved material wellbeing.

# Index of Names

Names of authors of chapters are followed by the corresponding ranges of page numbers, like 55–61, to distinguish them from those of persons cited in the text or of those who spoke in the discussions.

# Index of Names

# Index of Subjects

Subjects of whole chapters are followed by the corresponding ranges of page numbers, to distinguish them from topics touched upon incidentally at the stated page numbers.

## Index of Subjects